THE SCENT OF DAISIES

THE SCENT OF DAISIES

PTG MAN

M. WITHNAIL PRESS
SYDNEY, AUSTRALIA

Copyright © 2012 by **PTG Man**

All rights reserved. Without limiting the rights of the copyright reserved above, no part of this publication may be reproduced, stored in or introduced into a retrieval system, or transmitted, in any form or by any means without the prior written permission of the copyright owner.

The scanning, uploading, and distribution of this book via the Internet or via any other means without the permission of the publisher is illegal and punishable by law. This is a work of fiction. Names, characters, places and incidents are the products of the author's imagination or are used fictitiously. Any resemblance to actual events, or persons, living or dead, is entirely coincidental.

"This Is Just To Say" (poem), William Carlos Williams 1934

The Diary of Samuel Pepys: A Selection, Samuel Pepys, Robert Latham (Ed), Penguin Classics 1993

Cover photograph: Bangkok © Jack Kurtz

Daisy image: © 123RF antique-flowers-engraving 7153465

M. Withnail Press

The Scent of Daisies. -- 1st ed. 2016

ISBN 978-0-9874316-5-3 PRINT
ISBN 978-0-9874316-0-8 EBOOK

CONTENTS

Now (Part 1)	1
Sometime Before	3
Two Years Later	217
Now (Part 2)	241
Epilogue	269

> *Draw to the shore,*
> *draw to the land,*
> *where, in the arms*
> *of glowing love,*
> *let blissful warmth*
> *soothe your desires.*

R. Wagner, The Choir of Sirens, *Tannhäuser*

Now

(Part 1)

On the last day of his life, Emmanuel Soutard woke as he had for the past two and a half years—alone.

He focused on the fractured light that shone through a high set window—a little box of a window, from which a rutted beam projected a slice of striped shadows on one wall. The wedge of light would creep down to the linoleum as the morning sun lifted.

Rubbing the sleep from his eyes, he found the metal dome placed on the stool at the foot of his bed. Silver-colored plastic cutlery wrapped in a white cotton napkin and a small cup of apple juice nestled against the dome. He arched his neck and torso, limbs tingling, and slowly raised himself to the edge of the bed. His naked feet touched the cool linoleum and, with eyes closed, he rotated his head to each compass point—every movement deliberate, self-absorbed, slow.

Emmanuel moved to the chair and sat hunched over with the dome cradled on his lap. He lifted the cover to release a sweet nose of hollandaise sauce. Eggs Benedict; Ronnie's favorite. His plastic knife and fork buckled against the crusted bun, egg oozed. Everything in slow motion. He mixed the spinach, egg, ham and sauce, and brought the warm mixture to his mouth.

Then became numb. No taste or touch. No elation or sadness. Time slowed with the seeping yolk.

The sunbeam crept further down into the quiet.

Emmanuel put the pulps of his forefingers to his temples, massaged up and around, felt the pressure points tingle deep inside his skull. He listened to the flow that sucked through his nose and deeper down—the sound of shifting air a strange bedfellow on this morning alone. He sniffed further into the room detecting a whiff of antiseptic—freshly mopped though out of sight. Who did this protect? Surely not him? Or was this sickness something they could catch?

Mechanically, he finished the food, then lay down on the mattress, sweating on its plastic cover, and contemplated the day. He had no doubt visitors would come. The previous night, before sleep found him, he had imagined them coming—could feel the heat of their breath, of their flesh, for some at least. He rolled over on his bed facing the stark white wall, freshly painted, shiny clean. He had no right to hope, no right at all. Yet he closed his eyes to bring the first one on, a silent grin, who came tender to the touch. And so, as was his wish, a second one came, not as fast as the first, but with stealth, a tepid glare, though quickly transformed into a candied ray. These visions settled him, stroked his brow.

And carried him gently into the mouth of this wholly onerous day.

Sometime Before

ONE

The fat man squirmed. Sweat blistered from his forehead, drenched down under his arms—a soggy flab that rubbed into a crawling itch. He stirred further on the seat, squeezed then released the handle of his bag. Sucked his pelvis up into his mouth—holding it there—with blue breath held tight. And all the while, through the rear-view mirror, two almond eyes stared down at him.

"Faster . . . faster."

The taxi inched further into the traffic. Horns bellowed above Bangkok's late afternoon rush. Tuk-tuks and bikes jammed tightly into the horde, creeping forward into stolen space.

He straightened his back and lifted himself up in the seat, one hand pushing on his rear, and sucked his pelvis higher into his innards.

"Faster . . . faster."

The taxi hiccupped on.

A swift twisting to the man's guts doubled him over. One of his hands grabbed deep into his stomach, the other his shorts, squeezing butt cheeks together. As sweat poured.

"I got to get out now . . . got to."

The almond eyes turned to see the man rolling on his side. And moved the taxi to the curb.

The fat man left the car and moaned into the choking rabble, dragging his suitcase that scraped where one wheel was missing. Dragged himself against the pedestrian swarm, scanning for an entrance. Soon he found a mall, entered, down the stairs, and under. Scratched his case through the mass, ignoring their stares, sweating into the cool with his guts bubbling loud.

The man wandered this scraping trail into the labyrinth, his melon head swinging. At last he found the entrance. Now on his toes with his back arched high, muscles pinching his hole tightly closed, he pushed into the swinging door, his girth swatting away those in his way, and entered the foul cubicle—dancing high on his feet, a gargantuan ballerina—and grabbed the paper roll, unraveling its sheets, tearing long strands into the bowl stained with fetid crud while hopping a foxtrot on pointed toes.

When the inside of the bowl was covered with white, he sat. Deeply down. The flow loud amongst the still. His eyes now closed, relishing the loud. His sweat easing away.

When the noise had softened to a sigh, only the flush of urinals trickling into the hush, he stood, his shorts chained around his ankles, and looked into the bowl. Bent his swollen knees and put down his swollen arm. Into the toilet.

And grinned.

The two teenage girls sat on the warm asphalt, facing the pedestrian flow, their backs slumped against a street vendor's cart, their knees tucked up to support elbows, with palms carrying rested chins. Their worn, lemon-colored shirts still held the scent of peach soap.

The beautiful women glided by. Some were bunched, pairs or threes, with arms linked. Some strode alone, with more stoic masks attached, though most were yet adorned with the powder and paint of their trade. The lemon-shirt girls watched this human traffic, their eyes scanning without the need for head movement—like an umpire at a ping-pong game.

Lalana lifted her head, her ink-black ponytail swinging around, and twisted to face the street vendor behind her. "How's business, Mr. Intalak?"

"Slow." He ladled noodles into a bamboo basket.

"It's too early yet, Mr. Intalak."

"Then why are you here?"

Lalana shrugged. "How about us giving you some luck . . . by being your first customers?"

"You aren't my first customer. You're not even my tenth."

"First *night* customers, Mr. Intalak."

"It's not night yet." He continued to ladle the rice river noodles. Then, as if under Lalana's spell, red and blue neon lights ignited on the large overhead sign that straddled the pedestrian corridor.

"How lucky you are, Mr. Intalak!" She rose quickly from the asphalt; Durudee—the other lemon-shirt—slower to rise but sharing her eagerness.

Lalana inspected the cart, the basket of freshly cooked noodles accompanied by a small wok of recently fried meat; condiments of dried chili, sugar, vinegar, and ground peanut, all displayed in individual ceramic white-colored cups.

"Don't your families feed you girls?"

"We're growing, Mr. Intalak," Durudee said. "We need to eat more than an adult or our bones will fuse."

The man pulled at his long chin-hairs; feigned a considered expression. "And how do you propose to pay for this banquet?"

"Lalana can clean your shoes for you."

"I have sandals on."

"Leather?"

"Rubber."

The teens stole a quick glance at each other, though their heads remained hovering over the vendor's kitchen cart.

"When you wear your shoes next time," Lalana said, her gaze fixed on the offerings, "I'll give them a double polish, Mr. Intalak."

The man twisted a group of his long chin-hairs into a feeble plait, and sighed. "First night customers seem more lucky for the customer than the owner." He brought out two plastic bowls from under the cart. "Your usual, ladies?"

"Thanks, Mr. Intalak! You be sure to wear your best shoes tomorrow . . . as long as they're black or brown."

The man smiled and garnished the Sen Yai with the girls' favored seasonings. He looked beyond the human traffic to a grinning woman, who sat cross-legged at the open bar on the opposite side of the walkway. Both affirmed their eye contact with a beaming nod; warmed by their common bond of servitude in these sticky surrounds. He shifted his gaze to the passing crowd who gushed toward the mouth of the plaza—this visceral pump of heady nightlife—where all the juice of human subtlety had been squeezed out—like a wet dishcloth—and then discarded.

The girls resumed their slumped position on the ground, again resting their backs against the vendor's cart. They twirled their noodles into spirals with their plastic forks and eagerly devoured.

"Look at her, Lalana."

"At who?"

"That one over there. She is so beautiful."

Lalana shrugged and spooned more noodles into her mouth.

"How come we aren't allowed upstairs?"

"We're kids, remember," Lalana said.

"Just to look . . . and business might be better."

"For you perhaps, but who wants their shoes cleaned up there?"

The girls returned to their feast as more neon lights ignited around them, welcoming customers with their rainbow glow. On the opposite side of the walkway, the bar began to swell.

"I'm sure your mother could organize it. Just a quick look."

Lalana shrugged.

"What do you think it's like?" Durudee whispered.

"Terrible," Lalana said without raising her pitch—like her teacher giving the answer of a math question—and turned to her friend. "You want to work up there?"

The girl poked her dimpled friend playfully. "No silly. Never like them. I just want to take a look . . . for business."

"Well, I know mum wouldn't organize it, and I know your mother would kill you if she found out." Lalana mopped the chili sauce with a finger.

Both resumed their slumped position, resting their chins on cupped palms. A tall woman of carved beauty sauntered past, almost touching the girls' feet. Her presence lingered in a trailing perfumed bouquet.

Lalana looked up from her seated position, arcing her neck back towards the vendor. "Great noodles, Mr. Intalak!"

The man nodded.

"Why don't you sell your noodles to the girls upstairs, Mr. Intalak?"

The vendor smiled.

"What a great idea." Durudee twisted her frame to face the man. "We could take orders for you, and deliver the meals to them—door to door. We could make a fortune!"

"We?" He scattered slices of beef onto a wok, a haze from the charcoaled meat spitting into the air.

"You wouldn't take advantage of kids, would you, Mr. Intalak?"

Lalana quickly joined in the banter, a double assault. "Remember what the Buddha said. 'The master finds joy in giving, and happiness is his reward.'"

"Brilliant," Durudee whispered, though her gaze remained fixed on the vendor's eyes.

The man rested his ladle against the steaming wok, wiped his oil-soaked hands using a small, worn towel that dangled from the edge of the cart. He twisted his chin-hairs into a matted spiral, and nodded. "Okay, the master will hire you . . . at least until you've paid off the free meals I've given you over the last year. It shouldn't take too long, and happiness will be my reward."

The lemon-shirts faced each other, with eyes that mirrored their defeat.

"We'll get back to you on that, Mr. Intalak," Lalana said with as much eagerness as she could fake, then turned again to face the parading women. Without moving her head, she whispered to her companion, "I don't think he understood the Buddha's meaning."

Behind, the vendor tended his wok with a grin, scraping away curled beef from the central heat of the pan. Ahead, the bawled splutterings from the open bar spilled down onto the pedestrian corridor, occasionally distracting the gliding women who continued to hover high above the teens—who had now resumed their scanning, with chins in cupped palms, slumped against the vendor's cart like umpires at a ping-pong game.

Emmanuel lounged on his balcony at the Shangri-La Hotel. Below, the Chao Phraya River snaked past, the afternoon breeze raising a high cool from its swell. Nearby, the Oriental's rust-colored boats, passenger ferries, and long-boats—pink, aquamarine, and lime—moved like goldfish jostling for free water. He had spent hours gazing at its expanse, watching the mix of colors intensify with the descent of the late afternoon sun.

The hotel maid had just turned down the bed and left a small bowl of rambutan, mangosteen, and custard apple. Inside, the room's warmth mirrored the wet air outside—burnt orange blossom walls framed a large traditional painting on a timber panel, crowning the king-size bed from pillows to ceiling.

He closed his book and changed for drinks. A Hawaiian shirt seemed appropriate this evening; retained the upbeat mood. Usually he found himself avoiding mirrors; too many defects for his liking, but his tall, thin frame pleased him. Like many men having only entered their later twenties, he had yet to yield into a lazy paunch. He scooped coconut gel through his dark chocolate hair.

The elevator descended to the poolside entrance.

Splashes of green from shrubs and palms reflected from the pool's glazed water. An oasis. A few children waded at the pool's edge; some deck chairs were occupied by oiled bathers capturing the last of the sun's rays. Emmanuel entered Angelini's outside bar overlooking this vista and slumped on an unoccupied cream-clothed lounge. He ordered a bottle of wine and nested between two cushions. Diesel fumes from the river's life mixed with the scent of asparagus. Couples nearby, sipping pink and orange cocktails, giggled. A man sitting adjacent, cherry from too much sun, greeted him with a smile.

"Heaven, isn't it?" the cherry man said. He was neatly dressed with a white, long-sleeved silk shirt folded at the wrists. On his hand, a bulbous gold ring formed an extra knuckle.

Emmanuel nodded with a grin, his loitering eye contact inviting the conversation to linger.

"Ronnie James." The man raised his beer glass.

Emmanuel echoed the introduction.

"Here's to paradise." Ronnie emptied the remnants of his drink and slumped back onto the lounge, dragging his fingers through his short-clipped, snow-white hair. "How long you're here for?"

"Not sure. Just an extended holiday."

"Sounds great. No better place for it. No better place. You're Australian . . . yes?"

"Yeah."

"Then you'll make a good drinking companion."

They consumed two bottles of wine over as many hours. The golden glow of lights draped over palms and passing cruise boats replaced the frenetic late afternoon colors. Further into the night, a brilliant sapphire light glowed from the unoccupied pool ahead and flushed their cheeks in blue.

From their first words, Emmanuel liked Ronnie. His softly spoken English drawl relaxed him; never loud, even after a glut of alcohol.

"What do you do for work?" Emmanuel asked.

"Gems. Diamonds mainly," Ronnie said, his face a ruddy purple. "Sell and buy. You're a good listener. Let me guess. A teacher?"

"Nothing that interesting. Just a shoe salesman."

"What's your poison?" Ronnie asked.

"Poison?" Emmanuel raised his glass in question.

"Alcohol is fine. But me . . . I'm a bit of a sniffer." He flared his nasal orifices while softening to a whisper. "A big sniffer."

"I don't have much experience there, I'm afraid," Emmanuel said.

"Yeah, a bit of the coke-a-doodle-doo is my medicine. I might be able to get some if you're interested."

"Sounds fun . . . I guess."

"But the stuff here is poor. Nearly not worth it. I'm used to the best. Pure. Nice to have a break, though. I feel better for it." He paused. "I met some girls who might help us. Though I left them a few nights ago not on the best of terms." Ronnie took thin, silver-rimmed spectacles from his shirt pocket and opened his mobile phone. Wading through names, he nodded. "Worth a try, I think . . . lovely girls . . . elegant, with class." Soon he made contact, and, with words gently delivered, offered pleasantries that flowed like treacle. "Is your girlfriend with you tonight? Yes . . . Nimu . . . nice girl . . . though not as nice as you, my darling." He raised his eyebrows at Emmanuel. "You girls free tonight? Why don't you come on over and meet a friend of mine." Ronnie listened with an affect of uncertain grimacing. "We're set up sweet here. The Shangri-La Hotel." Again a long pause, Ronnie frowning between his delivery of softened words of submission. And all the while he looked out at the river—a goldfish bowl that calmed.

After a few minutes he ended the discourse with departing words in tender brogue, like talking to a sick aunt. Replaced his phone and spectacles.

"They want us to go over to the other side of town." His gaze fixed on the river scene. "This is a bloody palace compared to the bar they're suggesting. These girls . . ." He shook his head. "They just lie in bed all day with nothing to do, and wait to go out at night." He paused, returning his eyes to Emmanuel, and grinned. "Even with old fuckers like me."

Emmanuel studied the man. Though having entered his late fifties, Ronnie bore scant proof of that age. Even his white hair failed to age him.

"Ronnie," someone bellowed in a high pitch, an almost bird-like screech. "Ronnie!" Heads turned in unison to locate its source.

Emmanuel twisted around. A tiny rotund man, just over five-foot tall, gave an open-mouthed smile. With his girth almost exceeding his height, and an attire of black shorts, T-shirt, cap, and sneakers, his body resembled an eight ball. His bloated face was carved with every event on its surface, where age could not be easily discerned—late twenties to forty, perhaps. The man pulled out both earpieces from the iPod clipped to his waist, then rubbed at sandstone stubble of two days growth. Emmanuel waited with interest for the scene to play out.

"Jesus," Ronnie said. "You look like a bloody penguin."

"Oh, Ronnie." The penguin man scrunched his face to bring all his features to his nose, then failed an attempt to squeeze through two nearby lounges. Squinting, he scanned for an ample path, waddling past the stares of open-mouthed customers. His arms resumed their outstretched position, but more tentative.

With a grin, Ronnie accepted the invitation and hugged the man-child; and they sat, just fitting between the arms of the lounge. The fat man removed his black cap, revealing sandstone hair of a length that tried to hide that it was receding. Again he rubbed at his stubble and squawked, "Great to see you, Ronnie. Really great."

"You too, Arthur." He shot a sideways glance to Emmanuel and back. "How long have you been here? This place isn't your usual style."

"Not here, Ronnie. No, no. You know that."

"So you're visiting?" Ronnie asked, in a tone displaying indifference to the answer.

"Visiting. Yes, Ronnie, visiting."

"Who has the pleasure of your company this evening, Arthur?"

With the arrival of the new guest, the waiter returned, handing a menu to the man.

"Actually, it's me." Emmanuel shifted in his seat.

Emmanuel's gaze met the older man's. A somewhat uneasy pause followed.

"What a small world," Ronnie said.

"Wonderfully small." Emmanuel's unease melted away with a smile.

And Arthur, open-mouthed, grinned expectantly, rotating his gaze back and forth.

This was the time she liked best; that period where Dusk promised relief from the day's tiresome heat. The sun, though hidden from her sight, still managed to illuminate with a softened light that soothed. She curved her shoulders back, her trunk climbing higher against the wall, resting her head on the cushioning brick. Stretched out her stick legs and wiggled her stick toes.

The young deaf mute looked around—her head rolling on invisible surf—and studied the faces that floated past, all oblivious to this happy lull. The lights glimmered in the gray—and watched them hover and sparkle—laughed at the pretty lights, laughed a silent loud that turned the floating heads toward her—their faces smudged of detail—cheeks and nose and eyes that swirled and rolled.

Slowly the shining of the new-lit streetlights sharpened the swirling into real. She could now read the words painted on signage some fifty yards away, which pleased her, these good eyes of hers—blindness one fear that nobody of her kind could bear. She studied the faces. Looked for a hint she could latch on to, trap with her stare, pulling them down into her place. A teasing gaze, but gone, another, curt, then gone. Not that it mattered now, during this, her swimming time.

The neon lights blushed into the dim, glowed brighter as her head drifted and settled down. She had eaten well today—almost a feast—and laughed, a restrained laugh to avoid attention. Her head continued to clear, senses sharpened, but she had an antidote for that. And took her medicine from the tin can resting at her feet, the volatile syrup her regular chum.

Soon she hovered high, drifting against the bobbing heads, her fingers and toes a stone-numb tingle. Did they see her? They smiled as they swam past, always ignoring, faster now—she like a buoy, tied to the bottom of a rapidly moving stream of bobbing heads. The lights were pretty; painted their cheeks with rouge of blue, green and red.

See all the pretty faces . . . how I love the pretty faces.

As dinner arrived.

He knelt beside her, his face darker than the floating faces, and went to task. He took the container from the bag and placed it onto the worn cardboard square, peeled the plastic film off the container, and sniffed at the steam of chicken and soy. She watched him eat—slow mouthfuls spooned from one side of the shallow tray—savoring the flavors.

Can he see me, am I here?

Her shoulders hunched forward from the cushioned wall, her chin now resting against her chest, with spittle that dribbled down unhindered; and spat.

What a feast we are having today. What joy could be had when all things came right.

Soon she drifted back within the stream of bobbing heads. And swirling eyes.

Oh, how I love these pretty faces .

"Tell him, Ronnie. Tell him," Arthur screeched.

Mid-evening now. Port and cigars, Ronnie's Cubans, had long replaced their wine. Other guests had retreated from Angelini's outside bar, leaving the three settled like a family in their living room.

"Tell him, Ronnie!"

"Okay. Okay. I swear you'll break a glass with that squeal." He lowered his voice in an attempt to reduce Arthur's excitement.

Emmanuel sat easy in his chair—entranced by the sleepy brogue.

"We were home in Blackpool. Arthur wants to party. Needs to party. We had been out with a friend of mine. A good guy. But a bit . . . different. We had a nice meal; seafood. Fresh. No sauce. Simple."

Arthur licked his lips.

"This friend of mine orders his meal. Prawns, I think. Then, when the meals arrive, he gets up and stands behind a palm . . . a big plastic one that some restaurants like. While we eat, he spends the entire time peering through the branches of this bloody palm, at us and the other tables. Full, the restaurant was. I had to ask a big favor to get the table."

Arthur giggled, open-mouthed.

"Then," Ronnie said, "the waiter comes over and says he's disturbing the guests. I said to the waiter, 'He's fucking disturbing me too.'" Ronnie addressed Emmanuel, after drawing a shallow mouthful of his cigar. "You see, he was a voyeur. I had to go over in the middle of my seafood plate and tell him to sit down."

"'Come on, Dave,' I said. He shook his head at me. 'I'm Dorothy,' he says. He even had a different voyeur's name. And he wouldn't come back to the table. We had to leave; me, Penguin, and bloody Dorothy. Like the Wizard of bloody Oz."

Arthur doubled over, tipping off the edge of the lounge like a large chocolate egg.

"You weren't laughing then." Ronnie grinned. "We had to leave a really expensive meal. So after all of this, Arthur announces he wants the girls. He wants me to arrange it. So, I make contact with some . . . Russians; like gymnasts, they were, except taller. We go back to my place, the three of us and the girls, and I hand them some cash." Ronnie's head tilted towards Arthur. "So this guy says he doesn't want to pay the girls. I said, 'Jesus, Arthur, how the hell are you going to get girls if you don't pay them? You're a bloody beach ball.'"

"Don't, Ronnie." Arthur gazed up from his kneeling position.

"Okay, okay. You're adorable." He puffed at his Cuban and caught the waiter's glance. "Fill the glasses," he said, the softened tones nearly disguising the rudeness. "But we had a lovely night. Lots of coke and Viagra. Nothing better, my boy. Nothing." He sipped his port. "My doctor says it will kill me . . . Perhaps."

A cool breeze drifted over the Chao Phraya as they sheltered within an overcoat of alcohol, wet air and cigar smoke. Through the entrance of the bar, an elderly Thai woman carried a package tied over her chest and abdomen. A sleeping ginger-haired baby. Gliding through the maze of lounges she approached the party of men. Arthur glanced at Ronnie.

"Princess ready to go bed," the gap-toothed woman said to Emmanuel.

Arthur's gaze fixed on Ronnie.

"Thank you, Chosita." Emmanuel tabled his cigar and port. "Sleep well, Princess."

The old woman gave a nod, moved back through an artificial exit created by two separated lounges, and away. Ronnie, with eyes down, consumed the remainder of his glass. "Yes. My doctor says it's a real lethal combination."

The waiter placed a small partitioned dish of salted cashews and olives on the table, then refilled their glasses as needed.

"My daughter," Emmanuel said.

Ronnie nodded. "Beautiful. I have two. Both adults now, of course."

"Just the one for me," Emmanuel said.

"One is enough, believe me."

During the six hours nested at the bar, the party of men made no mention of family—women, but not family.

"Are you here with your wife?" Ronnie asked.

"Unfortunately not." Emmanuel's eyes followed the late night river life; vessels of bauble light trumpeted the sounds of old pop hits. Diesel fumes replaced cigar smoke.

"She died, Ronnie," Arthur said, his gaze never leaving the snow-haired man. "Died giving birth."

"Shit... in this day and age to die in childbirth... and in Australia... incredible," Ronnie said. "She was Australian?"

Emmanuel nodded. "I prefer not to talk about it, if that's okay?"

"Sure, sure my boy. I gather you're here in Bangkok to forget... and with that, I may be of some assistance."

Chosita shuffled around the room without sound. Her long hair, kept in a bun with a bone-colored rod, revealed bronzed facial skin with crevices from sun and age carved deep into forehead, brow, upper lip, and chin. Her mouth sprouted three protruding teeth, irregularly spaced, where four had once been. Behind her, large balcony doors were opened, allowing heat to escape or enter at will, though two portable fans were always pointed toward their target.

She moved to the mattress that lay on the timbered floor in one corner of the room and lifted the bundle, the baby's ginger head resting gently in her palm. Then she kneeled in front of the spirit house at the room's opposite corner and placed her down. Within the teak structure, no larger than a doll's house, a half-burned incense stick gave sweet enticement to the spirits. A miniature sky-blue ceramic dog, white orchid, and an unlit candle of red and gold almost filled the house. She positioned the offerings, lit the candle, and wished to the house spirits, wished harder than any time she could remember.

From the black outside, a slamming door broke the quiet. The old woman remained unflinching before the spirit house, her spine straight, legs tucked tightly under thighs, eyes closed, head bowed. At her knees, the baby, also ignorant of the outside din, slept still.

After some minutes, the old woman moved from her crouching position, carried the sleeping baby to the room's opposite corner of humming fans, and placed her down on the mattress, as always, with care.

Emmanuel rose to the day—a timid wake—then drew the curtains to reveal overcast skies. Standing naked at the glass balcony door, he stretched his arms to their full extent. Cigars and port had squeezed all moisture from his morning mouth. A tight band clawed at his scalp.

Desperate for pain relief, he swallowed two capsules with the remaining supply of bottled water. He opened the door, allowing warm air to cloak his body. Showered and dressed. After a light breakfast of fruit and cereal, he exited the Shangri-La Hotel.

And he wandered.

"Taxi, sir?"

"Tuk-tuk, sir?"

Hawkers of all varieties littered the small street below the hotel. He wandered.

"Suit, sir? We can deliver by this evening, sir."

"Massage, sir? Best in Bangkok. Special rates today for first customer."

He wandered. Beyond the hawkers, through tangled streets packed with carts, pulled and pushed, overflowing with the vitals of life, and motorbikes that edged tentatively in all directions. He wandered. Past lottery sellers, small machine shops with blackened walls, floors, ceilings, faces, past shops of jewelry, ceramics, silk, bronzes, teak. He wandered. On wider roads with vehicles wedged in every vacant space, all crawling with boisterous horns. Past twisted limbs of beggars, their heads slumped over cups of scattered coinage. He wandered.

Emmanuel slowed his pace, halting outside a shopping mall whose entrance was flanked by a man sitting cross-legged on the ground, his large, pristine eyes depressed in sockets around old, burnt flesh. Emmanuel placed a two hundred baht note on the beggar's plate. The man's head lifted and eyed the passing stranger, his half-melted lips lacking expression—only his eyes responding with joy. Emmanuel's heart raced. Joy consumed both.

With the morning ache of his limbs retreating, he quickened the pace. Sweat beaded his brow, pearls of salt water met eyes and lips. Turning east from Silom Road, he entered the equally bustling Rama IV; his pace quickened to a canter. His throat was scorched; his shirt, drenched under arms, soaked his back. After a few minutes, he slumped, exhausted.

A grunt came from behind. Again, louder and disjointed. Emmanuel turned, remaining hunched, arms supported on wet thighs.

A young woman, perhaps yet eighteen, brought fingers to her mouth. Grunted again. She was of thin frame, shirt and face soiled with street grime. But the streets had yet to remove the beauty of youth. Her sharp canines flared as she opened her mouth, fingers waving between exposed teeth, then moved her gaze toward the supermarket adjacent. Smiled and repeated the pantomime.

The deaf-mute entered the store, leaving the door ajar. Emmanuel followed, welcoming the cold climate sponged dry of all humidity. She moved further into the shop, he a few paces behind. Pointing to the pre-packed dinners of noodles and chicken, she eyed him with a smile, shark-like canines exposed. He nodded, took the item and a large bottle of water, and moved to the counter, the girl at his side. The store attendant gazed intently at the deaf-mute who lowered her eyes. Emmanuel handed the forty baht and collected his change, then drank half the water bottle before they left the store together.

They dawdled at first, neither showing any clear signs of an intended direction. Soon, though, she took charge, stepping east along Rama IV. Emmanuel followed the girl, trailing a body-length behind, his emotions blurred. They came to a busy crossing, vehicles punching through dodging pedestrians. With experience, she moved forward and, noting Emmanuel's hesitation, lifted an outstretched arm, fingers oscillating, like that of an older sister. As the tips of his fingers touched hers his pulse raced—a thrilling rush—and they moved through the traffic, she turning intermittently to assess his safety. Protective.

The heat of the day radiated from the asphalt. His heart pounded through his drenched shirt. Having crossed the road, the pace suddenly slowed, again in need of direction. Soon the girl moved into a small adjacent lane, smiled at him, and continued, but at a dallying tempo. Emmanuel halted, as if to avoid an invisible obstacle, all his thoughts lacking clarity. Tentatively, he moved further along Rama IV but, as their distance separated, she lifted her hand in final farewell. Then, turning into an adjoining lane, she disappeared from sight.

He moved on forward, closer to the railway tracks and station. This slice of road was crammed with humanity, hawkers and pedestrians squeezed into every crevice, sheltered or exposed. He entered a section of covered walkways that dimmed the ambient light, wrapped the crowds into a swarming tube. With escalating tightness in his chest he tracked back west along the same road and found open air. He entered a small side street cluttered with bars yet lit with the neon lights of buttocks, breasts, and legs flanking both its sides. A few tourists wandered—mostly men, but only stragglers, since the street slept restlessly during the daylight.

He walked its full length of no more than two hundred feet and circled onto a sister street with limbs of bars and clubs—though most, as with its neighbor, proffering entrances padlocked or sealed with fastened shutters. A woman of late middle age with painted make-up approached him, her accent Chinese.

"This is hot day, sir."

Emmanuel panted.

"You need rest. Too hot to be out. Come into my bar. Air-conditioned. You will like."

He hesitated. She met his hesitation with a smile, not pushing him in any direction. The day's heat seemed to build, never ending.

"Just a quiet drink, sir." She moved to a narrow entrance leading to ascending stairs. Emmanuel followed up the poorly lit staircase, trailing within an arm's length of the woman. The end of the stairs opened into a small room. On entering the mouth of the room, he glanced left to view a bar, dimly lit, adorned with dark, timbered fittings and two unoccupied stools. No attendant was present. He glanced right, the vision forcing his head back. A floor-to-ceiling glass wall glowed, with its bright fluorescents the only source of light. Two levels of white-painted seats, reminiscent of a Greek amphitheatre, occupied the full length behind the glassed enclosure.

Sudden, high-pitched shouts pushed Emmanuel back a further step. Bikini clad girls of all sizes and shapes were packed tightly on both levels. The discord began in earnest.

"Hello darling," the pink bikini said.

"Buy me a drink, handsome," said green.

Yellow said, "I do nice massage." And wriggled like a puppy.

"You'll be happy with me," red shrilled, the pulp of her index finger pressing down—opening her thighs.

Competing adulations, promises, smiles, tongues protruding, fingers suggestive. Emmanuel's head drowned under the cacophonous Sirens' pleas.

He turned to his Chinese host, shaking his head, then moved to the exit. As he descended the stairs, screams of last promises intensified from beyond. Contracts of pleasure. Emmanuel stepped out onto the sidewalk and found curious respite from the radiating heat of the sleeping street below. The Madam followed him down the stairs, leaking too onto the charred sidewalk.

"You can take them back to hotel, sir," she said.

"You asked me in for a drink!" He shook his head, trying to restore calm. He failed. "What the fuck do you think you're doing?"

"Any time you want... for as long as you want, sir," said never changing her tone.

An old man limped past with a small plastic bag of ladled foods from a distant vendor. Otherwise, the path, though still littered with rubbish from the preceding night, remained deserted of life. Neon buttocks and breasts unlit. And within this detritus, under a ceiling of scorching sun, Emmanuel turned away, his flushed anger settling, to leave the dozing street to its agitated siesta.

"Any time you want, sir," beckoned the woman from afar.

With street life thinning, Emmanuel walked back westward toward Silom Road, discarding his empty water bottle into a caged bin. In a tired lane nearby, beside a repository of ashen bins that leached trash from their open mouths, a man of thirty years or so sat on a blanket, his clothes, hands and face all crusted with dirt. The man placed a tin can to seal his mouth and nose, eyes drifting upward, showing only their whites, head slumped as he inhaled the glue. And passed the can to the young deaf-mute of recent acquaintance, who raised it to her face and echoed the action.

Emmanuel moved on, without faltering. She never noticed his presence.

They strolled the grounds. Foliage of vivid green hugged the two-story traditional houses, an intimate jungle within Bangkok. Inside, a warm of polished teak welcomed a snaking wind from the hidden klong behind, only revealed by occasional splashes from long-tail boats that needled against the stream.

"I always get my shirts at Jim Thompson's," Ronnie said. He was carrying three bags from a recent purchase. "The best quality silk. Smart." The peaceful surroundings interrupted by his soft English burr hypnotized Emmanuel. "I must show you my tailor... traditional cuts... quality fabrics... takes his time. He's just outside the Oriental Hotel. I'll introduce you."

Emmanuel nodded an approval.

"I love coming here," Ronnie said. "Usually I have a light lunch at the restaurant... fresh produce. Thompson was an architect, you know, before the silk business. Just disappeared in the jungle of Malaysia. Murdered, most likely. Gay, I think."

"No wonder he liked Bangkok," Emmanuel said, grinning.

"Something for everyone here, my boy."

Leaving the grounds of Jim Thompson's, they meandered along its feeding street laid bare and treeless, the cool retreat replaced with a blistering midday sun.

"I'm going for a swim back home, lounge a bit," Ronnie said. The Shangri-La was now his home, a veiled comfort of sorts, though, for the present, it was all he needed. "Let's go out tonight. Have some fun."

A taxi driver leaning against his car acknowledged them with a smile. They entered the vehicle—a sauna, nurtured by the baking sun.

"What about Arthur?" Emmanuel asked.

"Sure, bring him along." Ronnie hesitated, twisting to face his companion. "How long have you known him?"

"I met him when I first arrived. Four weeks ago. Odd guy, but he's been helpful. Found Chosita for me. He obviously likes you."

"Like a pet," Ronnie said. "I've known him maybe ten years."

"You know him pretty well then?"

"I wouldn't say that, but he sits at my feet when I need some distraction from whatever shit is happening at the time."

"Guy times."

"I wouldn't say that either, though it's true we share the same nocturnal hobbies." He raised his brow with a grin. "I introduced him to Bangkok, actually. Feel a bit sorry for . . ."

"For Arthur?"

"For Bangkok."

Both men laughed.

"He lived in Blackpool for a while," Ronnie said, drifting back into his hypnotic brogue. "God, it was a dive of a place. Really, it was straight out of Oliver Twist. He had a room so small you could nearly touch the sides with both hands, and shared the loo and kitchen with another twenty guys. Most of the others were just off the street, yet he had a job. Not flash, but enough to stay in a nice bed-sit near the ocean. I used to drag him away from the place, but it always felt like I was taking the bloody dog for a walk."

Emmanuel stared into his white-haired companion.

"I know what you're thinking." Ronnie looked out the window. "I can be a real fucker sometimes."

"Actually, that's not what I was thinking."

Ronnie turned again to Emmanuel and, mopping sweat from his face with a silk handkerchief, said, in softer tones, "You need to know, Arthur can be a tricky beast. Walk carefully with that one."

The heat within the unmoving taxi stifled, suffocated.

"Where you go?" the driver asked.

"Shangri-La Hotel," Ronnie said.

"Okay. And we stop . . ."

"And we don't want to stop at a bloody jewelry shop."

Händel's *Art Thou Troubled?* resounded splendidly. Marilyn Horne's aria replaced all sound. He floated within the shallows of opera's ocean, no other senses invading. But touch. She straddled his legs; he faced heaven. She was thin, but not emaciated. Young. Her frame was made slighter by full-length black trousers and matching short-sleeved shirt. Bare feet displayed long toes, nails painted pillar-box red. Her tongue flicked the elastics of her braces as she oiled his member. Slow, lingering strokes. Long fingers curled, sliding. One hand cupped his sack, softly kneading.

"You like?" she said, smiling, her voice deeper than one expected from her bird-like features.

He stared into her eyes but gave no acknowledgement. Gave nothing.

"You want more?" Her tongue mopped dribbled saliva. His eyes were piercing, but without emotion.

She added more oil, dripped down its glistening length. Tongue caressed the cheeks of her mouth, exploring gums, teeth, braces, both hands clenched, rhythmic, milking.

He arched his loins—raising himself high—and floated amongst ethereal viola, violin, and bass; floated amongst Horne's sweet, overpowering vibrato. His once shallow panting now crept to a deeper, cavernous expanse, lifting him even higher off the bed. The girl, astraddle his thighs, rose with him. Then, as the aria's crescendo reached its peak, he held his breath, with mouth ajar. And bore down. The finale.

Erupted bowels expelled putrid contents. Mud flowed, oozed filth, all engulfed by the orchestra's sweet angels.

"You fucking animal!" she screamed and moved up, away.

He grabbed her arm but underestimated the strength of the ladyboy, who scratched deep into his chest. As he relinquished his grip, his eyes never left hers, tore deeply in, though again displaying no emotion.

She moved quickly though the dim room, lit only by a slivered opening in the curtains, and twisted her neck to view the man's barely painted form still sprawled on the bed.

"You're a dog," she said, her tone deeper, calmer. Wiping the shit from her soiled trousers, she opened the door, retreating beyond the room's entrance—and proffered again, this time louder, from the barren hallway. "A fucking dog."

Her vermillion lips were glossed. Wrists and fingers in full extension, thumbs reaching skyward, eyes gazing into space, shoulders of bare amber skin adorned with drapes of gold. And all were perfectly still. The hidden xylophones and gongs altered their tune, signaling a change of position. Slowly her fingers formed bird silhouettes, wrists bearing bracelets of crimson and white petals dangling, head tilted slightly. With eyes finding a new invisible target, she steadied her pose. Again—perfectly still.

Emmanuel sipped his wine as the dancers glided to other tables. A relieving breeze drifted from the river.

Three structures surrounded the Shangri-La Hotel's central pool, all facing the Chao Phraya River. Angelini's bar, furthest from the river, was centrally placed. Two riverside eateries, north providing buffet dining and south, Salathip, completed the semi-circle. Salathip consisted of small teak houses and balconies opened to the river's life, with warmly lit palms and potted foliage. Emmanuel's table was cluttered—all positioned with care on gold-lipped serving dishes.

Tonight, as was usual since his arrival, Emmanuel dined alone at Salathip. His table, reserved because of regular patronage, almost hovered over the Chao Phraya. Since he rarely ate lunch, this evening ritual occupied a special place in the day's routine.

"Hello, Mr. Emmanuel," she greeted.

"Hello, Yanisa." Emmanuel beamed, warmed by the near-empty bottle of wine, his mood now hanging within the narrow confines of alcohol's brief spell, that could both dispense charm to the immediate surrounds and ward off inner demons. "I missed you tonight."

She blushed. "I'm sorry. They put me in the kitchen this afternoon to help prepare." Yanisa paused, her thoughts clearly rehearsing her next sentence. Emmanuel's waitress, standing nearby, rescued the somewhat awkward silence by refilling his glass. The two women stood next to each other like sisters, both dressed in ankle-length Ruean Ton of cream silk. Yanisa, the slightly taller of the two, kept her elbow-length hair tied back. Her light skin, rarely unprotected from the elements, softened with highlights of pale pink powder. Her lips, too, were varnished pink.

Yanisa gave a subtle nod, satisfied with the sentence. "Was your day pleasing?"

"Very pleasing."

She nodded. Her friend linked their arms, providing courage with her warmth.

"I saw you last night in the bar . . . with some friends. You seemed very happy."

Emmanuel laughed. "Keep away from those two."

"We waved to you when we left Salathip. But you didn't see us."

"You should've come over." His words were slightly slurred, but hoped this wasn't noticed. He breathed deeply, composing himself. Diesel fumes drifting from a nearby pleasure craft invaded perfumed air.

"Yes. But I need to catch my bus home . . . needed to." Again, a subtle nod. She looked over his head, searching for new banter; an uncomfortable silence lingered. Her sister waitress, detecting anxiety, smiled and fastened her grip, arms interlinked.

"We will wave tonight if you are there," her friend said.

"Unfortunately, I am going out tonight. But next time, please do." Emmanuel detected her anxiety, his pulse also quickening. "But I'll be back tomorrow night. Are you working?"

"No. Tomorrow is my night off from work. But the next night—yes." Words collected carefully and spoken as such.

"We will see each other then, I hope." His eyes cast down to the table. Pulse still racing.

Yanisa smiled.

Laughter cut into the air from the boating revelers beyond. His eyes, intoxicated with wine and the girl's faultless visage, met hers.

"I will like that," she said softly. And her friend pulled her away.

Emmanuel and Ronnie ploughed through the early evening throng of the sky-train passengers, their shoulders wading in an ocean of heads. Emmanuel dressed down in jeans, T-shirt, and shoes of worn black leather; Ronnie in dark blue linen pants, a full-length silk shirt of cream, and matching suede shoes. They changed trains once before arriving at the Plaza station. The approaching road revealing huddled street stalls of delicacies fried, boiled, or ladled.

"I usually like to get here earlier," Ronnie said, "to see the parade of trade." His excitement was palpable, displayed with quickened movements and speech. This was why he came to Bangkok.

Arthur sat at the open bar at the plaza's entrance. Within, rows of customers, slightly elevated from the passing swarm, faced the plaza's opening. The bamboo fixtures of the bar's landscape attempted a tropical atmosphere but failed. This the heart of Bangkok's nightlife, with the holler of shoving street traffic nearby, out of sight but within earshot, the city a pulse of unrivalled energy. Men, young and old, locals and milky castaways—the farang—all dribbled testosterone.

"I've kept us seats . . . kept us seats!" Arthur bellowed. Heads turned to locate the source of the squawk.

"In the front stalls, my boy!" Ronnie said. "You're a bloody marvel."

They straddled their chairs. A woman in the later years of middle age sat nearby, painted makeup failing to conceal her age. Short skirt, light stockings, red shoes, and matching lip-gloss. She brought a cigarette to her lips and smiled at Emmanuel. His eyes drifted to her skirt's entrance, revealed by crossed legs.

"What you gentlemen like to drink?" she asked.

"What'll we have, lads?" Ronnie rubbed his hands. "My treat."

The bamboo bar sat along a corridor before the only entrance to the plaza. Whoever entered had to pass the bar, all on display to the onlooking customers. At the entrance of the plaza, a shrine protected its occupants. Beyond the entrance, three levels surrounded the center in a square, all cramped with go-go bars, clubs, pubs. Neon red, green, blue, and yellow glowed within the plaza's heart, a cartooned circus of a space, welcoming its guests.

"Nice one over there, Ronnie . . . nice one." Arthur followed the slow movements of a passing tall beauty. She halted, facing the shrine. Hands placed with touching palms, she bowed serenely, then moved quickly up adjacent stairs to prepare for the night's labor.

"Too tall for a penguin like you," Ronnie said.

Arthur grimaced, but his annoyance drifted with further distractions of passing finery.

They sat through three rounds of drinks. Despite his stale wine, Emmanuel felt at ease. Fleeting visions mixed with alcohol's softening charm. Then, disturbing the calm, he felt a tug at his shoe. In panic he resisted. Another tug, more forceful this time, nearly managed to remove the shoe.

He peered over the bench. Below, on the facing path, a girl of early teens crouched at his feet, again pulling at his laces through the open bamboo of the bar's cover.

"You need shoes cleaned," the girl said.

"Do I?" He glanced down at the worn leather, washed of its color, and smiled. "Perhaps I do."

"You, too." She aimed her glance at Ronnie.

"These are suede, my dear. They can't be polished," he said.

"Of course. I know. I professional."

Another teen, of slighter build than the shoe shiner, moved over to the scene, displaying her wares: small packets of chewing gum. Arthur and Ronnie paid no attention.

"Thirty baht," the gum seller said.

"No, thanks," Emmanuel said.

"Okay, fifteen baht."

Emmanuel shook his head, still smiling.

"Okay, one hundred baht... one thousand baht... one million baht," she sang, her voice trailing away from the failed deal.

The shoe shiner applied small amounts of black polish from her timber tray and massaged Emmanuel's shoes carefully, drawing out the task to extend its sense of purpose. She applied a second layer of clear wax and polished the shoe with a cleaner rag. Having completed the first she pulled off his other shoe, this time with less force, and began the process again, working slowly, with care. After ten minutes, she placed the buffed shoes together. Smiling, she stood up, her head only just reaching the bench top.

"Two hundred baht." Her voice was confident, never trailing.

Emmanuel grinned.

Ronnie looked over the bench at the transformed shoes. "Nice job."

She nodded and smiled.

"How about one hundred baht," Emmanuel said.

"Okay. One hundred."

He handed her the cash, which she placed in a small bag attached to the front of her waist. Without a farewell, she drifted away, sourcing other shoed feet. And, on the other side of the path, the gum seller sang from within the stream of pedestrian traffic, "One hundred baht... one thousand baht... one million baht..."

Ronnie led, with Arthur and Emmanuel trailing. Wading through wet air, they climbed the stairs to the second floor open balcony of the Plaza. They strolled the balcony's circumference, eyeing the short-skirted and bikini-clad girls. Ronnie sauntered over to one, inspecting every curve. Lifted the skirt; fingers fondled. Out of control.

"Don't touch merchandise!" screamed a voice from behind. With hands on hips, the tall ladyboy moved in confrontation, loving the melodrama. "Who you think you are, the owner?"

Ronnie smiled. Moved on.

"Don't come back here, boss man!" screamed the ladyboy milking the giggling audience, all appreciating its theatre.

"Come in, boys. We have lots of girls to choose," said a smiling madam. She knew once they were captured within, they would be easy to please. But they continued on, the reek of stale beer rising up from the open plaza below. They passed other entrances, enticed by sounds of revelers within. Ronnie chose a doorway of dangled beads flanked by plastic palm trees. Botanic sentries.

"Good choice, Ronnie . . . good choice," Arthur said.

They entered the dark interior of black-timbered floors, walls, and ceiling. Two tiered rows of chairs surrounded a central raised stage that revolved slowly. Phosphorescent colors glowed from the black lights overhead. Bikinis danced in singles or pairs to blaring techno music. Some waved; others ignored, adjusting their makeup.

The three men sat in the front row. Ronnie pointed to a small, sculptured beauty who squealed with clapping hands, dropping into his lap. On other chairs men paired with neon bikinis; caressed.

Emmanuel eyed a tall goddess smiling warmly at him. She was as beautiful as any woman he had ever seen. He nodded tentatively, and she climbed from the moving podium and sat down next to him. Softly kissed his lips. Held his hand. Three older ladyboys in schoolgirl uniforms moved over to join their party. Tongues wiggled, licking open lips. Emmanuel's girl kissed his cheek—so gently.

"Would you like to buy us drinks?" one of the schoolgirls asked.

Emmanuel nodded in submission, again kissed his girl with softly parted lips. How could she be so perfect?

"Would you like to come upstairs with me?" she whispered in his ear. "Or back to your hotel room?"

Emmanuel's head continued to spin.

"Play with all of us," one of the schoolgirls said. "Take us all upstairs."

Emmanuel turned to his girl and stuttered a reply. "I'm just with my friends really."

She caressed his cheek, tenderly held his hand. With thoughts confused, he looked over next to him. Ronnie's girl, her head in his lap, sucked his cock greedily, then looked up at Emmanuel with glossed lips still sealed to Ronnie's member. Eyes all smiling.

"Do you like real ladies or ladyboys?" Emmanuel's goddess whispered.

He shrugged. "Either is fine."

Clearly surprised, she laughed aloud, betraying the restrained façade. She kissed his cheek sweetly. "Then what am I?"

He gently opened the front of her bikini, fingers moving between her thighs.

"Surprised?" She giggled.

He kissed her softly at first, then with increasing fervor, his head spinning from the revolving bikinis, alcohol, and passion.

Suddenly he felt unnervingly detached. Faces that hovered above him were of plastic masks rather than skin. She sensed his reservation; she knew the signs.

"You are so beautiful," he said.

"Thank you."

"But I'm with my friends—really. Just tagging along." He took a thousand baht note from his pocket.

She beamed. "For me?"

"For you."

Emmanuel took out a five hundred baht note and paid for the drinks. The madam nodded her thanks. "We see you again soon."

He moved to the door of dangling beads that allowed wisps of color to peak through from the well lit outside, then turned and focused on the scene: the girl's head bobbing in Ronnie's lap; Arthur, his hypnotized gaze directed to the podium; and Emmanuel's girl, number 23, dancing softly to the techno beat on the ever turning merry-go-round of neon bikinis.

Emmanuel moved down the stairs to the open plaza below. Pushing through the crowd bathed in rainbow light, he found a seat in the bamboo bar beyond the plaza's entrance.

"Having rest?" the manager asked from behind. He turned to see her smiling in the same cross-legged position, cigarette poised between painted red lips. "What you have?"

"Just a Coke, no ice." He needed clarity.

"Your friends gone?"

"Upstairs."

"You don't like?"

"Not so much."

"Then you stay here. Relax. They won't be long. They never are."

The bar attendant handed him his drink. Then a tug at his shoe.

"You need shoes cleaned," the girl said.

He looked over the bench at the smiling cheeks of pristine skin, soiled with smudges of shoe polish. "Again?"

"You best customer. I give you half-price deal... one hundred baht."

"One hundred baht it is, then." He smiled, calmed by the girl's presence.

She set to task, this time undoing the laces before removing his shoe. Hair of ink was pulled back in a ponytail, some strands escaping to forehead and cheeks. Her knee-length shorts were tight over chubby flesh—flesh that promised to reduce as adolescence progressed.

"Where your friends?" she said.

"In the clubs."

"You don't like?"

He laughed. "I don't like."

"Why not?"

Emmanuel paused. He had no idea. "I'm not that sure. Where's your friend then?"

"Gone home," the ponytailed girl said.

"I think you have the better business."

"Not bad. Too many thongs in Thailand. Farang . . . not us."

"What are those on your feet?"

She shone a dimpled smile. Painted toenails of pink gloss oscillated.

"I'm only kid," she said. "Feet always get bigger."

"How old are you?"

"Guess."

"Sixteen?" he lied. She would be pleased.

"You wish!" She pulled his other shoe, this time without untying the laces. Firmer. Applied black polish, then wax with a cleaner rag. And throughout, straggling limbs of the eager open mall glided high above her.

In time, Ronnie bounded down the path with Arthur trailing, his girth finding too much resistance through the swarm.

"Ronnie, wait on!" Arthur screeched.

Ronnie eyed Emmanuel, shaking his head while pushing through the thickened crowd, and approached his friend.

"This bloody penguin is so tight with money," he said. "Tries to bargain with the girls after the event . . . after the agreed price." He chuckled. "Like World War bloody Three up there."

Arthur found safe passage back to the bar. "Ronnie . . . Ronnie . . . don't be mad. This is Thailand. You've got to bargain . . . got to."

"He's mad," Ronnie said, addressing Emmanuel. "You don't bargain after agreeing to a price, you bloody beach-ball!"

Arthur whimpered. "Ronnie, don't."

"Let's go home." Ronnie sighed. "I'm spent."

Emmanuel found his polished shoes neatly positioned at his feet. He slipped them on, paid for his drink, then moved onto the path to meet the three in waiting, the shoeshine girl having squeezed between the two impeding giants. Reaching in his pocket, Emmanuel placed a folded one hundred baht note into the girl's hand. She nodded, businesslike.

He moved on with his two companions, toward the escalating street noise.

"I only fourteen," a voice trailed from behind.

He turned, smiling at her dimpled cheeks. Both grinning. Emmanuel turned back and continued onward with his friends, all the while singing to himself, "We're off to see the wizard, the wonderful wizard of Oz . . ."

And left Dorothy behind.

No breeze found passage through the open balcony doors. Air sat stagnant. The old woman held the naked baby at breast level, gently stroking a cheek with the rubber teat. The baby instinctively found its way, gulping the bottle's sweet nourishment. She fingered the tepid pool, adjusting its warmth with kettle water, and placed the baby down. Folded pink flesh splashed. All smiling.

He entered without knocking. Watched the scene. Turning briefly, she acknowledged his presence, but quickly returned to her precious task; ladled water over arms, chest, crown of ginger hair. She sang softly, in her native tongue, of a mountain child with a little body and white face, where the air was cool without need of fans. The baby giggled, kicking warm splashes.

He placed the swollen envelope next to the spirit house, glancing briefly at the strange trinkets it contained. A small wedge of peeled mandarin sat in a shallow saucer at its entrance. He didn't know what to make of the tiny house—he had never bothered to ask—but it strangely disquieted him.

"You have everything you need, Chosita?" he asked.

She nodded, and continued her song through stagnant, dripping air.

Emmanuel watched the play. But not for long.

"You like it here?" Arthur asked.

Emmanuel nodded.

"Better than Sydney?"

Again affirmed in silence.

They sat alone in Angelini's outside bar, the midday quiet settling them, despite the heat. Arthur pawed at his teacup, his plump finger unable to fit into the cup's ear, though he managed to slurp a mouthful that burnt his tongue.

"Great idea to have tea, Emmanuel... great idea. Perhaps we can have High-Tea sometime? What do you think?"

Emmanuel nodded, though not with eagerness.

"Have you had High-Tea before?" Arthur said.

"No. What is it?"

"Tea with cake, or proper food. But little portions." He paused. "Little portions are better for me. Don't you agree?"

Emmanuel smiled; softened by his friend's awkwardness.

"Chosita is working out well."

"Thanks, Emmanuel. She's a good choice. I knew she'd be." He bent forward to sip more of his tea, this time directing the cup to his lips by holding the saucer with both hands.

"I know what I wanted to ask you, Emmanuel," he said with bright eyes. "Do you want me to get a cheap iPod for you? I can download all my music on it. It would be great to share my music with you... really great."

"It's okay. But thanks for the offer."

"No problem. Just let me know if you change your mind." Arthur twisted his gaze to capture the scene. "This is some flash place hey... really flash."

Emmanuel studied his friend's face as his enthusiasm continued unabashed. Ronnie had said, *He is like a pet,* and he agreed. Glancing at his wristwatch that reassured sufficient time had been spent, he waved at the waiter to close the account.

But pets do have a purpose.

Emmanuel spent the remainder of the day drifting, traversing novel side streets, alleys, markets, grazing on street vendors' morsels, footsore with heat exhaustion. As evening approached, he boarded the sky train—this time alone. Thirsting for the familiar, he alighted at the Plaza station, a tender breeze welcoming him. His spirits buoyed.

The bamboo bar had few customers at this early hour. He found a seat overlooking the plaza's walkway and ordered a Coke. With light fading, and the flickering of neon announcing dusk's end, the beauties gradually arrived—singles, pairs, arms locked, some giggling, everyone composed. All paused at the shrine at the mouth of the plaza and bowed before sauntering beyond on scattered paths.

Emmanuel took a block of ice from his drink and wiped his forehead. He scanned each of the floating women carefully, some in turn noticing his gaze, twisting their necks ever so slowly as they moved steadily on. Eye contact fixed on their target before taking their leave with a smile.

He let the iced water dribble onto his lids—cool tears that soon overflowed onto a cheek. Would he remember the goddess?

"You good customer," came a voice from behind; the bar manager's unlit cigarette rested between her lips of gloss.

"Do I get a discount?"

"Yeah. Cheap Coke." She lit the cigarette. "I retire soon with your big spending."

"Sorry. I only drink wine. No spirits or beer."

"We have wine."

"Maybe later."

"Not what you had before. Special stock for special customer."

He wiped the wet from his face with a broad brush from his hand. "Okay . . . but will you join me?"

"Don't drink with customers." She inhaled deeply, the cigarette's end glowing. "Except special ones." She gave the attendant instructions in Thai and he moved out of sight into the bowels of the bar. She sat on a stool, legs crossed. A fishnet stocking swung.

"I thought you don't like clubs?" she said.

"I don't."

"But you like my bar . . . with shit wine."

Emmanuel studied the woman, charmed by her raw spirit—jagged and underdone—that trickled from her pores. And nodded.

"You meet you friends again?"

"No. I'm all alone tonight."

"Alone good sometime."

Emmanuel pondered the comment, then swept it aside. He liked people—or, rather, disliked his own company. He always had.

The attendant came over, wine bottle in hand. The woman inspected the contents.

"For special customer. Not cheap."

"Nice . . . but *only* if you join me."

"You pay?"

"My shout." He grinned.

"Okay, Aussie boy . . . you shout."

The waiter opened the bottle and poured the contents to the brim of the glasses. Both. Emmanuel smiled at the waiter who acknowledged with a nod. Both knew this would not be cheap, but Emmanuel surrendered to the joy-grabbing moment. A cool breeze snaked its way down the pedestrian corridor lifting him high in his stool.

"You like?" she said.

"Perfect. Really wonderful."

She sipped and shook her head. "Tastes like tobacco to me."

And they laughed together. The fishnet woman uncrossed her legs, watched as his eyes flashed down—only a stammer of a glance—and drew into her cigarette deeply. On such occasions, Achara Songpow sat comfortably in her chair.

A familiar tug at his shoe. Emmanuel lounged over the bench, gazing below. Same lemon shirt, knee-length pants, ponytailed hair, thongs with pink nails glistening.

"Special price tonight for first customer. Fifty baht."

Emmanuel gulped his wine, wanting taste, intoxication, and more. "Fifty baht it is then."

The manager spoke severely to the girl in Thai. Rising on pointed toes, the shoeshine girl rested her chin against the bench and poked her tongue out at the woman. Eyes smiling.

"My daughter is too much for me. Needs two mothers. One for day. One for night." Her stern gaze fixed at the dimpled smile that soon disappeared from view, his shoes removed without laces untied. Contractual obligation confirmed.

Over the next thirty minutes they emptied the bottle steadily as the crowd thickened and the girls paraded. They talked of weather, work, rest, and Bangkok, all well rehearsed bar banter—nothing intimate, but offering a sense of comfort. With only the shallow dregs remaining within the bottle, the woman turned and nodded to the barman.

"Thanks for drink," she said. "You make yourself at home. My shout next time." She uncrossed her legs and dropped off the stool, then curved her back to face him again. "Can you keep secret?" The fishnet woman came over, her face only inches from his—scorched tobacco mixed with lipstick's scent—and whispered, "Our shit wine tastes better after second bottle."

She smiled, then drifted away into the center of the bar.

Emmanuel peered over the bench at his shoes glowing beside socked feet. The girl had resumed fossicking for customers nearby. He watched the unrelenting routine—scavenging seated patrons, tugging at shoes with confidence, shoulders back, though eyes pleading. Usually ignored, she moved on, drifting through the crowd with timbered shoe kit in hand. Worn shoes, only eager for nocturnal treasures, ignoring tugs and begging stares. Having completed the process, she sat against the street vendor's cart on the corridor's path, knees up, face resting in her hands. She caught Emmanuel's eye, frowned, then resumed scanning the passing feet.

The bamboo bar, now with all seats occupied, housed excess revelers standing. Emmanuel sipped his wine, preserving the alcohol's soothing warmth, numbed of all thoughts of future and times past—plans, needs, failings. His eyes followed the hypnotizing crowd, who crammed down the pedestrian lane.

With a tug at his toe, the inked ponytail rose quickly to bench level.

The girl held her stare. "Mum say you don't have to pay."

"That's no good. I see business is slow tonight."

"Only when customer not pay."

"Do you mind passing me my shoes?"

"Are you too drunk to pick up?"

"Maybe."

She bent down, finding a fifty baht note folded in one shoe. Her head bobbed from the surface, chin resting against the bench top, cheeks dimpled with eyes smiling.

"What you do tomorrow?" she said.

"Not much."

"I guide. Professional. I show you sites."

"What about school?"

"School finished, holiday now."

"How much to hire your services?"

"We talk about at end of tour. Very cheap." Her chin remained resting on the bench top. Eyes fixed unblinking.

Emmanuel sipped his wine. "Okay. Where do we meet?"

"Where you stay?"

"Shangri-La Hotel."

"I see you in front of hotel."

"What about in the lobby?"

"No. Might not let me in."

"I'll sort it out. I'll meet you in the lobby at nine in the morning."

She nodded, her chin rubbing against its bamboo resting place. The girl's gum selling companion arrived at her side, displaying her wares. Emmanuel gave her twenty baht for a packet.

"You my lucky first customer," she said.

The resting ponytail fell from the bench. "Mine, too. Double luck for you."

The girls turned away from the bar and chattered in Thai, moving slowly into the flowing bevy.

"Hey. What's your name?" Emmanuel shouted.

The girl turned, and raised her voice over the throng. "Lalana. See you in morning. Don't be late."

She beamed a wide smile, then turned back into the swarm with arms linked—giggles of youth floating above the hum of testosterone's revelers.

Emmanuel woke early, showered, and took the lift up to the Horizon Club for breakfast. Ronnie had organized this upgrade, allowing a more intimate breakfast compared with the larger buffet at the river's border below. He found an empty table by the window with skyline views of Bangkok's sprawl cut in two pieces by the winding Chao Phraya River. He ate a bowl of yoghurt and peeled fruit of pear, peach, lychee, and prune, finishing with some toast and a small pot of tea. A short, neatly sculpted blond man, skin bronzed from recent sun, entered the room. Scandinavian, late thirties, perhaps. On each side, Thai beauties hugged his arms. Both taller. Immaculate.

"Another day in heaven." The bronzed man smiled, acknowledging Emmanuel's presence, who returned the smile. Emmanuel considered the scene.

He understood the man's needs, grabbing life's moment with both hands clenched, so hard you could almost see the knuckles whitening. But his own needs were palpably different—at least where love was concerned.

Nearby, a mother and daughter conversed over omelet and coffee. Americans, sixties and early thirties. The daughter, leading the chatter, stood and moved to the buffet at the other end of the room, never missing a stride in the conversation as if the seated mother followed her. Dialogue of pop's operation and aunt's chest pain, both caused by lack of dietary fiber, filled the room for all to hear. Eyebrows rose from a turbaned head seated nearby; Pakistani, his face consumed by a giant twirled moustache, gray handlebars rising with bites of toasted marmalade. A waitress draped in crimson and blue silk filled his cup with brewed coffee. All adding to the stage.

Emmanuel finished his tea and checked the time, for he didn't want to be late. Leaving the Horizon, he moved along the corridor and found Ronnie alighting from the elevator. Unshaven.

"Didn't see you around last night, my boy."

"Had a quiet one," Emmanuel said.

"No excuses tonight, then. I'll take you to a great bar just up the road. You'll love it. It's up-market. Dress up a bit. No ladyboys. Not that you seemed to mind the other night . . ." He paused. ". . . too much." It was said with a grin.

Emmanuel organized their meeting place, then took the lift to the lobby. Lalana, who was seated in waiting, rose to greet him, her yellow garb replaced with long pants, shoes, and a collared shirt, all in black. Professional.

"Good morning, Mr. . . ."

"Emmanuel."

"Funny name. Emmanuel, where you want go?"

"Anywhere you like. I've only seen the hotel and some bars since I've been here."

"And girls?" She frowned.

"Actually, not that many."

"Yeah, yeah. Let's go."

She led him through the marbled lobby, where the doorman unveiled a wall of warm, wet air. Lalana continued to lead, weaving through the morning's chaos, inked ponytail bobbing in time. Soon they arrived at the ferry terminal. Emmanuel paid for the tickets according to Lalana's instructions; on boarding she steered him through tightly packed commuters to the boat's bow. A cool breeze tickled their faces. Both smiled together.

"You like?" she asked, but knew the answer.

The ferry moved down the Chao Phraya steadily. He had observed the river's life over many hours but never from within. While the ferry loaded and unloaded its cargo, they remained clinging to the bow's point, Lalana giving commentary—identifying wats, churches, hotels. After thirty minutes, they alighted, burrowed through cramped tourist stalls flaunting drinks, smoking foodstuffs, and plastic memorabilia, then beyond to the sun-drenched main road, littered with buses head-to-tail like giant caterpillars. Lalana moved to one of the street vendors, who greeted her with a smile.

"Grand Palace closed for three hours. Just for local people now," came a voice from behind. The man herded map-clenching tourists away from the entrance as sweat dripped down confused faces.

"Oh, thanks," Emmanuel said.

"You come back in three hours," the man said, while continuing to direct stray tourists.

Another man approached from across the road. "Where you going, sir?"

"It's okay. I'm fine."

"Grand Palace closed now," the new man said.

"I know. Thanks."

He showed Emmanuel a map, well worn, with sites circled in thick pen. "I take you to these places, then back in three hours. Only fifty baht."

Emmanuel studied the map before a tug pulled at his shirt.

"Come." Lalana held two bottles of water. He followed, but at her side.

"The Palace is closed now," Emmanuel said.

"Yeah?"

She moved without reducing her stride. After fifty feet, they entered the Palace entrance cluttered with camera-draped tourists, all huddled around guides with colored flags. Emmanuel paid for the tickets, again according to instructions.

"Closed, ah?"

She grinned. They moved into an open courtyard; temples of gold, some smooth with curved surfaces, others intricately carved, sat majestically, all tapered to needle-points directed to heaven. Smaller stupas of stone rested like children at the feet of their glittering parents, adorned with polished tiles of orange, bottle green, electric blue, and garnet.

"The Grand Palace has more than one hundred wats and shrines built for two hundred years..." Lalana began her commentary. Professional.

"Where did you learn those things?"

"School," Lalana said. "We come many times."

The waitress scooped more rice onto her plate. Emmanuel watched, himself unfed.

"You have some appetite," he said.

"I'm growing."

"Of course."

She spooned more duck pieces onto her plate. "You not hungry?"

"I don't eat lunch usually."

"Bad for skin if not eat lunch."

The restaurant had few customers and no locals. Its air-conditioning lured escaped tourists from the midday sun.

"Good food," she said, "but too much money. Street better. You farang spend too much." Lalana gulped her lemonade. "That man with map would take you away . . . you still be out there."

"Where?"

"Somewhere you don't want. You stick with me."

"I promise."

She nodded. Scooped more rice and duck to her mouth.

"You have brothers or sisters?" he asked.

"Two—me oldest."

"Your mum seems nice."

"You like her?" In a noncommittal tone with a mouth full of lunch.

"Yeah, sure."

"She likes you. Can tell."

"Is your father around?"

"Nope."

"Must be hard."

"Nope."

Emmanuel sipped his Coke. "How long have you had the shoe business?"

"Two year. Mum says she keep eye on me better when with her."

"Makes sense."

"You not married?"

The girl's eyes that gave no insight to the purpose of the question. "No."

Bones of duck, stripped of all meat, lay scattered on her plate. She looked coyly at the menu of sweetened ices, held up by metal fingers at the table's edge.

Emmanuel smiled. "Would you like dessert?"

"No. Mum say too fat."

"You look perfect to me. Remember, you're growing."

"Okay." Lalana grabbed the menu. "You don't think I too fat?" she asked hesitantly.

"Definitely not."

"Durudee think I fat."

"The gum seller?"

"Yeah."

"Don't let it worry you. Kids always find something to tease about."

She nodded—though without conviction. "Men like skinny girls."

"Who says?"

"I see them. Who they like. Who they with."

"You mean the bar girls."

She nodded.

"You want to be a bar girl?"

She gave a sharp stare at Emmanuel. "Are you crazy?" And pushed the menu away.

A busload of tourists streamed into the restaurant, some waving bamboo fans across faces that glistened. Emmanuel picked up the menu, briefly scanning its contents. "You know, men like girls who make them smile."

"You *are* crazy."

The waitress ventured back, avoiding eye contact with the waving hands from the large table of unsettled customers. "Anything else, sir?"

Lalana raised her head with defiance. "Ice cream . . . two scoop please."

Emmanuel grinned.

The temple's enclosure hugged its treasure. Its walls—decorated with intricate scenes, colors finely etched into form—embraced the cramped throng, yet were barely noticed. They stood at the end of the two gigantic feet, soles of milk and gray inlaid mother of pearl, each toe-print swirled hypnotically. Beyond lay serenity, all in gold. The Buddha lay in repose, stretched on one side, smooth curves shining. One arm lounged limp, fingers elongated. The other supported the resting head. Eyes half-closed. Lips curled. Smiling.

"Forty-six meters long. Real gold, but brick inside," Lalana said.

They moved slowly down the corridor, toes to head, leaving the reclining Buddha's enclosure, and squinted against the afternoon light that stung at their eyes.

Lalana paused in concentration, then nodded. "No happiness surpasses peace of mind."

Emmanuel stared at her. "What?"

"No happiness surpasses peace of mind," she echoed, slipping into her shoes. "My history teacher say that. Every time we leave. She write it down on board . . . we copy."

"Your history teacher is very smart," he said.

"Buddha smarter . . . he say that."

Emmanuel tied his remaining shoelace and closed his eyes. He felt a wave of nausea deep in his gut.

"You tired?" she asked.

"No. Hot."

"Okay. Follow me."

She led him past shrines of mosaic bedded on a lawn of concrete that sprouted the odd tree, yet provided no shade. Heat radiated. Soon they entered the building housing a single large room. The windows were open to the outside, like a large balcony, capturing any breeze. Fans, mounted against walls and ceilings, purred. Rows of mattresses slightly elevated from the floor's surface covered the room, all occupied by lemon shirts kneading at weary travelers' flesh.

"We rest here," Lalana said.

The attendant led them to adjoining twin mattresses and guided them onto their backs under the cooling fanned breeze. Emmanuel closed his eyes and allowed the masseuse's hands to bend his limp limbs at will—molding skin, sinews, muscles.

"Can this last forever?"

"You like?" Lalana asked, though, again, she knew the answer.

He looked over to see her lying facing him. Unattended. "Don't you want a massage?"

"For old people, not kids."

The masseuse giggled; both exchanged words in Thai. Other lemon shirts smiled.

"I'm not that old," he said.

"How old?"

"Twenty-nine."

"Not too old," she said. "So you don't think I too fat?"

He turned to face her. She lowered her eyes.

"You're perfect. Trust me."

Lalana kneaded the mattress, mimicking the masseuse's actions. "Men always lie."

"Who told you that, your history teacher?"

"Mum."

Emmanuel, with eyes closed, drew breath. Struggled to find an adequate reply.

Lalana fell silent, before whispering "Promise you not lie to me?"

He turned to face her. This time she kept her gaze. And waited.

"I promise," he said. Though he was quite uncertain how to keep it.

They walked from Wat Pho back to the ferry terminal and bought drinks from the canopied lane at the water's edge.

"You stay here," she said to Emmanuel, and moved some thirty feet further down the lane.

He watched Lalana dragoon a boat master. They haggled. Heads shaking. Held her ground. After some minutes, she beckoned to Emmanuel and they moved to a fleet of long-boats, needles of color bobbing on the olive waters of the Chao Phraya.

They entered an empty boat. A real beauty, with its striking timbered hull of lollipop stripes. Overhead, an arched canopy of matching color stretched to protect them from the blazing sun, flowers proudly hanging from the pointed bow. The boatman untied the vessel as they sat together in the center, and departed through the dizzying aroma of diesel fumes. They darted across the large expanse, dwarfed by ships of charcoaled cargo. Soon they entered a smaller arm of the river, and quickly ducked into finer branches some fifty feet in width—then slowed.

Worn timbered houses, held dry by poled fingers emerging from the waters below, sprouted from the canal's edge. Palms shaded from behind; small canoes waited, tied at steps or ladders. These precarious sanctuaries housed men who repaired, women who washed, and children who played and waved. Some sat on balconies, snatching any breeze on offer.

Emmanuel stared with the open-mouthed smile of those entranced by a marvelous vision. A woman paddled quickly over in a canoe filled with fruit. Emmanuel bought bananas with generous payment, bringing a grin to her bronzed cheeks. Then he bought drinks for all. They moved on, slowly entering fatter klongs bearing houses of brick—displaying less life. As their pace quickened, cool air mopped the sweat from their sticky skin.

"Better than bars, hey?" she said.

He beamed. "Much better."

After thirty minutes of drifting through the canals, she turned to the boatman and pointed directions. The long-boat swerved into a smaller capillary, again flanked by timbered houses that were worn but cared for. They approached a larger house of cedar. Two stories. Steps rose from the klong's waters to a central gate flanked by a high fence of gray timber that allowed privacy from the canal life. Potted plants, some with flowers of peach, lined the fence's edge. The boatman switched the motor off and, with paddle in hand, steered them to the steps.

"My house," she said.

"Very beautiful."

She nodded. "We now finish tour. The man will take you back to hotel. You pay him two hundred-fifty baht when you get back. I hope you like today tour." Lalana paused and, with eyes lowered, said "I hope you take my service again."

Emmanuel's eyes glistened. He reached for his wallet. "This has been the best tour I've ever had. How much do I owe you?"

"One thousand baht."

Emmanuel handed the cash to Lalana and counted aloud until reaching the figure. She stood and alighted to the steps at the water's edge. Then turned,

"In Thailand you bargain. One thousand too much. Next time I give you half-price . . . but no bargain then." She grinned back at him before disappearing through the gate to her house.

After three attempts the boatman started the motor, then darted down the klong and into the larger feeding waters of the Chao Phraya. Emmanuel, with eyes closed, wiped the wet from his cheeks—his skin cooled by the canal's breath.

Lalana tugged the rug from under the bed and wriggled underneath, mattress springs catching her hair. She quietly pulled the cut timber slat up. Her hand descended below the floor, eventually consuming the entire limb to shoulder. Fingers stretched to find the brass handle while avoiding the two carefully positioned mousetraps. She took the tin box from its protected home but remained under the ceiling of springs. After entering the code, the plastic lock twisted, allowing entry. She unfolded the worn magazine page and studied the photograph, then took out the baht notes and placed them with the others, also worn.

Then replaced her treasure, timber slat, and rug.

Slumped on her bed, she examined the photograph, then carefully folded it and closed her eyes, contemplating the scene in her mind. And, with the sounds of squabbling neighbors in the klong outside—through lively protests and the drone of longtail boats—she imagined the sweet scent of flower petals.

"Nice, ah?" Ronnie squashed his cigarette in the glass ashtray held by the waiter. "Another two chardonnays as well."

They leaned against the glass railing sixty-four floors above nocturnal Bangkok. Below, the Chao Phraya curled between glow-worms of urban sprawl.

"Service a bit shabby, but a million dollar view."

Behind them, perched on a massive staircase, sat a domed temple ringed by Ionic columns bathed in golden light. Nearby, water poured from fountains of white stone. A cool breeze drifted through the bar, all open to the night sky.

Ronnie answered his phone. Listened with furrowed brow, eyes smiling. "I told you to dress up . . . told you, my boy." Winked at Emmanuel. "Yes, yes. Do that. Good. Good." Ended the call with laughter. "That bloody Arthur. He never listens. They won't let him in. I bet he's in his bloody penguin outfit." Ronnie beamed. "He said he'd call later." Turned toward the bar. "Where's those drinks?"

Emmanuel leaned against the railing with the vista unveiled, waiting for Ronnie to get enough alcohol to relax. The service would be better when Ronnie had a drink in his hand.

Ronnie fidgeted with his cigarette. "I need to give them up. Always hard in bars, though."

The waiter returned with glasses of wine, lit Ronnie's cigarette, and handed him a clean ashtray. Ronnie nodded in approval.

"So . . . you're quiet tonight," Ronnie said. "But I can sense a good mood with you. Am I right?"

Emmanuel affirmed with a smile.

"Well talk, my lad. Entertain me."

"Had a good day," Emmanuel said.

"Mmm."

"Actually a very good day."

"Mmm." Sipped his chardonnay.

"And now a perfect night." He raised his glass.

"Splendid. Let's order a bottle. It's good Chablis."

Ronnie waved at his waiter. For now, he would only be served by this personal servant.

"Spent the whole day by the pool myself. Bought a few things in the arcade. Have you been? Some nice stuff. Good quality. Nice to wind down though. Starting to relax." Ronnie rubbed at his hair of snow. "Good to get off the coke for a bit."

"What about those girls? No luck?"

"They haven't got back to me yet. But good to give it a spell. Gets you down, you know?" Cigarette glowed a moment. "I think that's part of the kick . . . get up then down . . . need the down, too."

"Really? Why would you like being down?"

"A good, healthy wallow in self-pity, my boy." He drew into his cigarette. "But feel a new man here. You know, I really love this city."

"Me too."

Emmanuel studied his friend's face; his cheeks blushed with the tint of recent sunning, his hair neatly manicured; and wondered at the comfort of his stance.

"Ronnie, what do you love about Bangkok the most?"

"My boy . . . in Blackpool I am Ronnie James, scraping to make a quid or two, doing okay, but just plain Ronnie James." He raised his arms with a broad smile. "But in Thailand, I'm a fucking king!"

He swallowed at his glass, splashing the wash into his mouth. "I met a guy in a small town about a hundred miles from Bangkok once. He was a Brit too, and so we had a chat over lunch. He told me he had lived in that little town for more than five years. He was about my age, perhaps a bit younger . . . tanned . . . in good shape. And he tells me about his two girlfriends in the town, you know, all the details. I met one. Gorgeous, she was. As I was saying my goodbyes, just before getting into my car, he looks at me in the eyes and pushes his finger into my chest. You know what he says to me?" Ronnie lifted his index finger into Emmanuel's chest, his gaze fixed into his. "He says . . . you are looking at the happiest man in the world."

Ronnie gulped the remainder of his glass, and grinned.

"And when you're in Thailand, are you the happiest man in the world?"

Ronnie chuckled high into the night sky. "Far from it my boy. Far fucking from it."

The waiter returned with the Chablis, which they proceeded to devour steadily. Couples wandered, hands linked. Evening dresses glided.

"Oh, Jesus . . . look at this." Ronnie's grin transformed into laughter. Emmanuel turned to see Arthur moving down the stone staircase in his familiar black shorts and shoes, but transformed from the waist up. A shirt of fruit, pineapples dominating, was buttoned to the top, his neck squeezed by a tourniquet of thin black tie, and a houndstooth jacket, of olive and beige, that flapped with each descending step.

With the stairs conquered, he waddled over.

"What the fuck have you got on?" Ronnie said.

"Jacket and tie they said. But others don't have ties, Ronnie . . . don't have them."

"Where did you get the jacket?"

"On special, Ronnie. Just down the road. They said the customer didn't pick it up. My luck, hey. Good price, Ronnie, good price. Threw the tie in for nothing, he did. Nothing, Ronnie."

"The shirt . . . what about that bloody shirt?"

"It's the only one I have that buttons to the top." He pulled at his collar attempting to release his folded neck flesh.

Ronnie's head was shaking. "We can't stay here now. This is too much."

"I just got here!"

Emmanuel grinned. "Have a drink, Arthur."

"Don't fucking encourage him." Ronnie scanned the surrounds. "How are we going to meet some nice girls with you looking like a bloody Oompa Loompa?"

Emmanuel emptied the remaining wine into his glass and offered it to Arthur, who gulped it down in one swallow.

After two hours, the alcohol had taken its full effect. The three paid in cash with generous tips, except from Arthur, who now slumped with his tie unfastened.

"Where to, Ronnie?" His words were slurred.

"Plaza best at this time."

"The Plaza. Great choice Ronnie."

They entered the lift for a long descent. Traffic bustled on Silom Road as Ronnie waved a taxi.

"I might leave you guys to it," Emmanuel said.

"No!" Arthur squawked.

Ronnie glared. "Don't leave me with this overgrown parrot."

"Don't leave . . . don't leave."

"Don't feel like the girls tonight," Emmanuel said softly.

"Okay. Next time, though." Ronnie grinned. "It takes training to become a true degenerate. But don't worry, we'll have you in fighting trim in no time."

The two entered the taxi. Arthur's bulbous head, framed by the open window, beckoned. "Talk to you tomorrow, Emmanuel . . . tomorrow." Then they departed, curving into the torrent.

Instead of moving toward the Shangri-La Hotel minutes away, Emmanuel turned in the opposite direction up Silom Road. Gradually his pace quickened, pulse raced—swimming in alcohol's warm bath. After fifteen minutes, the crowd thickened, their faces lit by candy-colored neon that clung heavy to walls and overhead signs—that dangled from invisible twine fastened high in the black sky. Girls and boys hustled on the pavement, displayed their wares to mesmerized tourists—amused, titillated—with crinkled menus of shows, detailed inventories of bananas, balloons, ping pong balls. Displayed their wares with skirts high, shorts of denim, Lycra, tight against pussy, buttocks, cock. His pulse escalated, yet he moved on at a steady pace, turning right into the wider Rama IV, with its sea of traffic flowing. Drops of water splashed from the sky, then cupfuls. Emmanuel hugged a building with a sheltered canopy and waited with fellow travelers, dripping, warm, then moved on with a faster tempo gained from the unscheduled respite.

With familiar surroundings in view, he slowed his pace, carefully scanned limbed alleyways, side streets, beggars with empty bowls, huddled together or sitting alone on the asphalt that glistened with its detritus now washed away. He walked this slinking trail—littered with the deprived. Then stopped.

She sat on the top step of the supermarket. Hair stuck against wet cheeks. Her shirt molded against arms, back, breasts. He met her eyes. Both smiled. She placed waving fingers to her mouth, sharp canines flashing. He nodded, still with breath held. The deaf-mute rose and ventured toward the market's entrance. Emmanuel shook his head, met her questioning eyes. Quickly he turned and hailed a slowing taxi to halt. She remained unmoved at the market door. Uncertain. He smiled at her, held out his hand. And waited.

Sheets of rain suddenly fell—yet he remained still, his arm extended in welcome. The girl moved slowly at first, then quickened her step as the heavens descended. On approach, wet fingers and palms touched skin softly. He smiled with apparent tenderness—tenderness that seemed genuine to her. And then, with rain drumming overhead, they departed together within the taxi.

At first, the girl's eyes widened at the regal environs, found chandeliers, brass sculptures, manicured women in silk, all clean, all perfect. Soon her eyes lowered to the marble and carpet—pristine under her bare feet with toes black from street grime. Emmanuel moved quickly to the elevator-in-waiting. Both entered, but not alone, and found middle-aged eyes that poked and prodded. He turned to face the girl, encouraging comfort with a smile, though her head remained bowed. Reverential, as the elevator continued its slow ascent.

They drifted in silence down the corridor and entered his room. Emmanuel moved to the table and found the all-night menu, mimicking her gesture with fingers in mouth. She nodded, her eyes scanning as she moved further into the room. He dialed and ordered a mix of dishes. Satisfied, he gave an encouraging smile. She echoed his smile, tentative.

Emmanuel moved to the bathroom and turned the faucet on. As water steamed, he added scented oils, adjusting the temperature of the water with care. Bubbles frothed. Then he took one of the paired dressing gowns of white cotton and gave it to the girl. With eyes lowered, she disappeared within the steaming bathroom.

Emmanuel slumped on the bed and listened to the splashes and giggles that filled the room—and with them, a wave of joy engulfed him. After thirty minutes, the dinner arrived. The waiter arranged the plates of food on the outside balcony table. Emmanuel moved to the bathroom and opened the door. Slowly. Splashes ceased, replaced with silence. Sliding his hand around its edge, while shielding himself behind the door, he waved a fork and spoon. The girl giggled, a flat, arrhythmic sound. Emmanuel grinned and returned to the balcony.

With no breeze, the evening managed to retain its early warmth. Pleasure craft and ferries now docked, only occasional long-boats and the Oriental's cross-river crafts gave life to the sleeping river. The girl, with dressing gown fastened, sat at the table. Following a confirmatory nod as he went from dish to dish, Emmanuel spooned the food on to her plate, and for the second time that day enjoyed the dining of others. But dining of need, not want. As she ate, he moved into the room, found the largest T-shirt he had, and neatly folded it at the end of the bed. At all times the girl followed him with her eyes, yet continued to raise hand to mouth. An innate and mechanical chew.

He moved to the bathroom and showered. Replaced damp clothes with dry. As he re-entered the balcony, the girl's eyes met his, then lowered, mouth curled in a grimace, uncertain, as all plates lay bare. Emmanuel grinned, and when she sneaked a glance to gauge his reaction, she mirrored it with a beam. He offered her his hand and, with soft skin touching, led her back into the room, propped pillows, slumped on the bed, and ignited the television. She let out a deep grunt when cartoons appeared—Tom and Jerry scampering. The girl nestled against him, her arms wrapped softly, head cushioned on his shoulder. Warm.

Emmanuel followed the cat's futile attempts to catch the mouse—a chase through bleary eyes—and heavy lids—as slumber soon found him.

TWO

The boy moved briskly. Past Chinese banners, some with English subtitles, most without, past dangling lanterns of red and lamp posts encrusted with golden dragons, past boxes stacked with goods delivered by rushing trucks, obstructing pavements, through jade-colored arches traversing narrow roads bejeweled with open-mouthed fish. He entered the building and opened the small post office box with his key, one of only three fastened to his key ring, took out the large envelope and felt inside the empty box to ensure he had removed everything. Then he tore the package carefully and pulled out a smaller envelope and one hundred dollars in cash.

He pocketed the cash, placed a stamp on the smaller envelope, and left. Walked quickly, crossing roads, dodging the building afternoon traffic, then jumped on the cable car, which jerked and staggered, slowly climbing the steep incline up California Street, slowly revealing San Francisco's signature vista.

As the car slowed, approaching Van Ness Avenue, he jumped and continued with brisk pace until posting the letter minutes later. Then he returned home.

Jill Abbot didn't like to be called Jillian. Old gray Stephen—Stephen the second that is, her husband was the third—liked to call her that. She was Jill though, no matter what pomp or fuss or fat cigar breath said otherwise.

"I don't think you appreciate the delicacy here, Jillian," said old gray Stephen.

She turned her head away.

They sat in a huddle. The Stephens, second and third, on the big black sofa, a lounge of hard hippo leather, shot by Old Gray—so the family story went, though she doubted it. But it was real hippopotamus, corrugated overlapping plates of thick, charcoaled hide from a single beast—so the family story went. Though she doubted this too.

"*Extremely* delicate," Old Gray said to her turned-away head.

She sat opposite the Stephens on her comfort chair. An old recliner, the fabric original, the pattern frayed on the seat with little yellow strands twisted and clumped and connected, the springs maybe rusted, because they squeaked like a mouse. Her mouse chair. This was her aunt's and the only heirloom she had in the house.

The fog had started to drift from the harbor. The tinted blue-scape of the sky peeking through the haze, the glimmer of silver-white pylons, and the olive pines sharp-edged in front. All this she saw from her mouse chair. Jill sighed into the hot air—the fire ablaze nearby, even though it wasn't that cold outside. But old gray Stephen felt the cold. So they all sat in the heat.

"What do you suggest, Dad?" her Stephen said.

"Let's keep playing the game to his rules . . . for now."

Her husband looked over to her. She could see his face from the corner of her eye. But she kept watching the drifting fog.

"That's what Buck says to do," Old Gray said. "I rang him. That's what he *strongly* suggests."

She turned her head back to the black lounge and spoke to the hippo. "He has experience with this?"

"Buck has been around for a long time. And knows people. He made the calls all day yesterday. We pay him serious money to make these decisions."

"Well, as long as he *knows* people," she said to the hippo.

She lifted her gaze up to her husband. He was a little boy compared to Old Gray. Thirty—but still a little boy. She liked this about him.

"What do you think, Jill?" he asked.

She usually liked it when he asked her advice, something old Stephen never did. But somehow she wished he hadn't asked the question right now. She wanted to mull on it some more. Without old Stephen around.

The maid brought the tea and placed the tray down on the wide teak table. She was glad for the intrusion. "Thank you, Hattie."

Black Hattie. 'What family has an African-American maid called Hattie?' her father often asked. 'Why don't they just call her Mammy and really get into the part?' Not said when old Stephen was around, of course. Her father was a tie-dyed Haight-Ashbury liberal, a reader of the Howl—he could quote pages of it—which he liked to do in front of old Stephen. 'How's Mammy on top of old Telegraph Hill,' he would say to her Stephen—who laughed at that. This she liked about him too.

Jill sipped her tea, then looked up at her husband. And sighed again into the heat.

"I don't know," she said. "I really don't know."

"Let's take Buck's advice then, for just one more time." Old Gray lifted the cup and saucer with his brown-blotched hand. From age not sun. His face was white and pink and remarkably wrinkle free. Old Stephen was an indoor man, had been all his life. And he had some work done on that face. 'Why does he keep his hair gray with his face pulled as tight as a baby's ass,' her father often said, though only to her.

"You haven't told anyone, Jillian?"

"Only my father."

"I wish you hadn't," Old Gray said.

She turned her head away again. "He has as much right to know as you."

"Then let him pay like me." He raised up his creaky voice.

"Take it easy, Dad," her Stephen said. "He had to know. He comes here once a week. How could he not know?"

"And Hattie knows obviously," she said.

"Not the details I hope," said Old Gray.

"No, not the details."

"Hattie can be trusted," the old man said. "Your father, I'm not so sure about."

She watched the fog drift. A white cotton blanket easing itself from one silver-colored tower. And the blue of the sky and the blue of the water.

"Hattie," she called out.

The maid came out from the kitchen into the sun-drenched room.

"Can you turn off the fireplace, please? It's boiling in here."

Hattie stood waiting for her at the foot of the stairs.

Jill moved down the stairs. "Hattie, I found Josephine's door shut again."

"It's the wind, Miss. With the window and the curtains open in that small room, it closes some time."

"Why don't we get one of those magnets that attach to the door and wall?"

"I'll go down to the hardware tomorrow, Miss."

"Thanks, Hattie."

Jill moved into the living room, and the sparkly night lit along the high glass wall. She sat down in her mouse chair—her Stephen upstairs in their bed, trying to read a book. She never liked to read in bed—her paperback on insomnia told her not to. She picked up a hardcover that sat on the coffee table—an abridged selection from the *Diaries of Samuel Pepys*, a gift from her father. 'If you get bored just skip to the bits on the Plague and the Fire of London,' he had said. She had already read these—the slow unfolding of the real, as it happened, before it was really thought about. *The plague, it seems, grows more and more at Amsterdam*—this off-hand note after eating a good plain dinner with Mr. Cutler and a couple of old women. Plain like the dinner. She flicked the pages to his first notes of the fire. *About 7 rose and there looked out at the window and saw the fire not so much as it was.* Notes scribbled at the dawn of tragedy, the first glimpses of the impending, where eventually seven of eight lost their homes to the great conflagration and two of ten were dead of the plague. She read now from the start when she couldn't sleep. She read most nights.

Jill put the book down. She stood up from the chair that gave a squeak and moved over to the hallway and checked the door was unlocked. Checked the latch was unfastened. Checked the burglar alarm was off. Then went on back to her comfort chair and comfort book. 'Peeps, not Pepys' her father had said to old Stephen, 'you pronounce it Peeps.' 'Those Brits should write it as they say it then. So in my house, it's Pepys,' old Stephen said. They all had laughed at this. Even Josephine—which made old Stephen laugh as well, his great white false teeth flapping out loud.

She read about Pepys' painful testicle—*by a stroke I did give it in pulling up my breeches yesterday over-eagerly*—and thought about writing her own diary. She used to as a girl. Especially when they travelled. Her father had kept them in his safe, these old diaries, little tan leather books with yellow stained pages written in pencil, erased if mistakes were made, impressive penmanship for a youngster he always said, and still does, of hikes in Yosemite, or visits to the big Sequoia, a picture drawn of Dad and her holding hands next to General Sherman, Dad nearly as big as the General, of a mule ride down part of the way in the Grand Canyon, before a dust storm blew up.

She looked out at the string of pearls that strung across the harbor. The black silhouette of the trees. And the glitter bunched and sunken lower down.

She wasn't a superstitious woman. Few were at her age. Though she wondered if she did begin to write a diary, would her story run the course like some of Pepys'?

If she started now though, tonight, there would be no offhand comments before a tragedy. No going back to bed at the first glimpse of flames, because it seemed far enough off, to see how it was in the morning. Ablaze. Out of control. Her blaze was already well lit—a rushing furnace. But nobody yet had succumbed.

She stared into the sparkly black night. She wasn't a superstitious woman. But she wouldn't write just in case. And flicked the pages over to one marked with a long dog-ear crease.

Great fears of the Sickenesse here in the City, it being said that two or three houses are already shut up. God preserve us all.

THREE

Emmanuel woke fully clothed with his mouth parched. Light flooded the room through the open curtains. The girl lay prone on top of the covers, propped on pillows and elbows, her head at the foot of the bed, intently studying prancing cartoon characters. She wore Emmanuel's long gray T-shirt and nothing else. His eyes followed from feet to legs—thin and smooth—to the crease of her buttocks. Her legs lifted as the duck and rabbit danced. Shoulders giggled.

He touched her foot—and she turned, beaming, and darted back to his side. Nestled in his arms.

They lay together for an hour, perhaps more, sharing laughter while the frantic cast scuttled. When Emmanuel rose, the girl followed, then moved ahead to the bathroom, pointing with a nod to seek approval, which was granted by his smile. As the girl splashed through rising bath foam, he left the room and took the elevator to the ground floor—to the hotel's small arcade of shops—and entered a fashion store attended by a lone woman.

"Can I help you, sir?"

"Looking for a few things for a friend. A girl . . . woman . . . eighteen. A Thai girl."

"Of course, sir. Something casual?"

"Casual will be fine."

"What size, sir?"

"She is tiny, but I don't know her exact size. Is it possible to exchange if they don't fit properly?"

"Is possible, sir."

The shop attendant moved to one rack of clothes. "This is our smallest size. Brown skirt . . . looks nice with Thai skin. Simple design.

Young women like more simple style. Not like older ladies." She browsed through the rack. "This top would go nicely. Black and white easy to match."

"Very nice." Emmanuel scanned the remainder of the store. "Do you have sandals?"

"Yes, sir, but difficult if you don't know size. Could your friend come to store. It would be better."

"Yes. Perhaps." Emmanuel hesitated. "But maybe if you show me your smaller sizes, I can return them in the next hour if they don't fit. You see ... my friend is not feeling well today."

"Of course, sir." She moved to a small selection of sandals in black leather. "I would recommend simple again."

"Lovely. Perhaps if you give me two sizes, I can return one of them in the hour."

She nodded. As he scanned the shop he pointed to a T-shirt with "I love Bangkok" printed on it, a red heart replacing the word 'love'.

"Could I get this as well, in the same size ... and can I charge these to my room?"

"Sorry, sir, we cannot do that."

Emmanuel took out a wad of cash, and on leaving, turned. "You don't sell any underwear, do you?"

"No—sorry, sir. Try the market just down the road." Like many of the staff at the Shangri-La, whatever she may have felt did not reach her eyes.

They stood in the elevator. The girl scanned the others, this time with her head slightly raised. As more entered the lift she clutched the arm of Emmanuel, who stroked her hand. After many stops, the elevator descended to the ground floor, and they strolled to the buffet at the river's edge.

With only half an hour before closing, just a few late breakfast diners were seated. They moved to an isolated table by the window, remaining within the confines of chilled air. Emmanuel ordered a pot of coffee and gazed at the drifting girl, adorned in her new outfit. She moved from dish to dish, feasts of fruit, cereals, cold and warm meats, eggs of all varieties, and more. She paused to watch the omelet chef in mid-preparation, then continued on, her plate remaining empty. Emmanuel stood and moved to the girl's side. She lowered her eyes. Gently, he took her plate in hand, spooning up delicacies after receiving approval with a nod, smile, or soft murmur.

They ate together, slowly consuming their banquet long after the remaining guests had retired, while tables were cleared and new cutlery laid. A grazing, sluggish feast—for those with time on their hands.

A tap at the window. A broad grin flashed just inches away, only separated by the thin pane. Ronnie stood in his bathers, a towel draped over glowing pink shoulders, then moved inside.

"My boy, my boy."

Emmanuel smiled. His thoughts unclear.

"Didn't feel like any girls last night, hey?" A soft English drawl. "Hello, my dear. We haven't been introduced." He took her hand. "Ronnie James."

The girl smiled.

"What a night. Very late . . . very late. Will make a nice story over drinks later. Also, I made contact with my friends. You know . . . that business we discussed." He brought one finger to his nose and sniffed in pantomime. "Might be fruitful if you're still up for it."

"Sure." Though not entirely sure.

Ronnie rubbed his yet-shaven cheek. "I need to sun my old body, after a bit of a dip."

"Sounds good."

Ronnie eyed the girl. "Have you a swimming costume with you, my dear?"

The girl glanced at Emmanuel.

"No matter. I'm sure the hotel can oblige, my darling. I didn't catch your name."

She gave a brief guttural grunt and, with hand gestures, revealed her trouble. Ronnie glanced at Emmanuel, briefly, and returned his gaze to hers.

"I'm sorry, my dear." Then he paused, realizing further conversation would only add to the farce. The girl smiled, appreciating his embarrassment. "But you are a beauty my dear." His eyes scanned her legs, then breasts to face. A drawn out examination.

The girl blushed, his meaning received.

Emmanuel held his breath—disquiet jarred deep in his guts. "We'll catch up, Ronnie. Have some stuff to do today. Might see you at Angelini's later?"

"Angelini's." He rubbed his cheek and tried to assess the situation. "Absolutely, my boy. Absolutely. As always." And then retreated poolside.

Arthur rearranged the objects. There were only two. With curtains drawn, the room was bathed in a soft yellow light from the naked bulb dangling above. Perhaps not enough light.

He took out the camera, an old-fashioned Polaroid, and held it steady over the arrangement, while checking the angle carefully with his legs braced taut. And shot. Pulled the film and waved it sluggishly, wiping his face of dripping sweat, and carefully peeled the cover to display the picture.

Not enough detail.

He moved to the curtains and parted them a fraction to allow entry of further light. Stood closer this time, again with braced legs, and repeated the procedure. This time successfully. Then, after opening the curtains to their full extent, he tucked the photograph deep in his pocket and left.

"You're here early, little one."

The vendor tossed strips of beef that crackled against the heat of the wok.

"I've made a study, Mr. Intalak," Lalana said. "The farang are more likely to get their shoes cleaned at this time... before they get too drunk."

"Same with eating."

"Maybe. Perhaps I could do a study for you too. My rates are extremely competitive."

"I'm sure they are."

"I can count the number of dishes you sell every hour... from the start of your day until closing time. Better over a week, you know, for statistics. Take the average and graph it for you... a full report, bound, all in color. Though color costs a little more."

"So I pay you for something I already know, since I've worked this spot for the last five years, and it hasn't changed a bit around here."

"Ah, until you see the report you only *think* you know Mr. Intalak. And speaking of business..."

"I wasn't."

"Have you thought about us having a deal of offering a free shoeshine with a bowl of noodles? 'Free' of course would be built into the price."

"I have enough trouble selling the food by itself."

"Let me work on this idea. I'll get back to you with a proposal. I'll include it in the report... no extra charge."

Lalana wiped her mouth with a broad brush from her forearm, her lemon shirt bulging tight against her chubby arm.

"How are you going at school, little one?"

"It's holidays now, Mr. Intalak, but pretty good."

"You're the best student in the class, I bet."

"That's debatable. Bapit is better at math, and maybe science."

"I was never good at math either."

"That's why you need me to do this study for you, Mr. Intalak."

The vendor grinned into the climbing steam. "What's your favorite subject then?"

Lalana scrunched her face. "I'm not sure, but I like role play in drama."

"We didn't have that in my day."

"It's great, Mr. Intalak. The teacher gives us a scene, and the first line, and we make it up from there." She scooped the last of the noodles into her mouth and kept talking through the chew. "The last one was about two boys who were fighting. We weren't told what about, but I had to find a way of stopping them."

"And did you succeed?"

"Yeah, I told them girls don't like boys who fight, and if they didn't stop, all of the girls would get together and ban them from future dating until the end of high school."

"And that worked?"

"Yeah. Most of the boys in our class goggle eye the girls . . . the pretty ones, that is."

"Like you, hey?"

"Not really." She lowered her gaze to the fried strips of beef. "More like Durudee."

"You don't have a boyfriend? I can't believe that."

"Well, believe it. Anyway, I think I prefer them older."

Lalana picked up her cleaning kit, scanning the shoes dangling down from the open bar.

"We could use some of that role play to work out how to stop the fights around here," Mr. Intalak said.

"Yeah. I told mum about the class and asked her what she would have done."

"Nobody I know has more experience in stopping fights than your mother."

"She said if they didn't stop fighting she would get Narai—you know, the bouncer upstairs—and he would smash their heads together like melons."

The vendor laughed loud into the neon-lit dusk. "Yes, that tactic has been used more than once by your mother. I'm guessing your teacher would prefer your way."

"I think you're right. Durudee did the same role play the next week and used the watermelon line . . . it didn't go down well." She grimaced. "But Narai is as big as a mountain. Have you seen his fists?"

The vendor handed a plate of noodles to a customer. "He is a big one. But he rarely needs his hands. He just stares them down, and they soon scamper away."

"I saw him throw a farang over the bar once," Lalana said.

"There is more than one way to skin a cat."

"That's a bit freaky. Where did you hear that?"

"Maybe it's one of your Buddha sayings?"

"I don't think the Buddha would really be skinning cats, Mr. Intalak."

"No I guess not. Perhaps it was Confucius?"

"Have you ever eaten cat?" she said after a moment.

"Only when I was hungry." He smiled and ladled more noodles into a bowl.

Lalana gave the man a playful slap on the arm. "I'd better get back to it since this is my peak hour of business. Let's talk some more about that report I'm going to do for you . . . maybe over a bowl of noodles later, Mr. Intalak?"

"Maybe," he said, and handed another customer a plate of Sen Yai.

He tapped on the table. "Like that they were. Buttocks as hard as this marble." Ronnie slumped back, the lounge comfortably molding his bulk.

Angelini's bar was at its busiest at twilight, and on this evening, if not for their reserved table, the men would be drinking within, beyond the intensifying colors of river life, beyond its soporific breeze.

"But the fact that she was a guy makes me feel a bit . . . held back."

Emmanuel laughed loudly. "I've never noticed you holding back before."

"Have some respect for your elders, my boy."

The two men lounged back in their chairs, cradling glasses in their palms, and watched a gliding bather wade slowly in the pool ahead. Further afield, an old-fashioned steamboat churned its massive wheel, its wake raising a splash on the river's embankment, and chugged gray clouds as it wandered by. And unbeknownst to Emmanuel, as a man near death reminiscing on past joys, he would cherish drinking in Angelini's at dusk with as much fondness as any time of his life.

"So, tell me ... the lovely young lass this morning ... details ... details."

Emmanuel sipped his wine. Smiled.

"Ah, you don't kiss and tell ... such gentlemanly restraint ... a rare quality, indeed. But this is Uncle Ronnie, my boy."

Emmanuel emptied his glass and recounted the discovery of the young deaf-mute in detail.

"How you manage to keep a doll like her in your bed without tasting the trimmings is almost beyond belief. You're an unusual one indeed, my boy. One of life's special characters."

"Nothing special here, I'm afraid."

"And where is the young lady now?"

"In my room." He bent forward easing his glass onto the table. "You see, she loves the television. Cartoons, mainly."

Ronnie nodded, but demonstrated no understanding. "Don't like them staying in my bed ... for any extended time, that is. No offence, my boy, no offence."

Emmanuel smiled.

"Not wanting to pry ..." Ronnie sipped his wine, but shifted forward on the lounge. "But your wife ... it can't have been easy ... and your daughter ... this—"

"Don't, Ronnie." Yet said in softened tones, as not to offend.

"Sorry. None of my business."

"Ronnie, I'm just here to escape. And forget."

Both men retreated into the wine's relief. After an uncomfortable pause, Ronnie lifted his glass. "Unwritten rule number one. The past is the past in Bangkok. Live only for the present."

Clinking glasses affirmed the mantra.

Nearby, in fading light, murmuring lovers embraced, their table littered with cocktails barely touched. As Emmanuel soaked in this scene, a voice came from behind.

"Hello, Mr. Emmanuel."

He turned to see Yanisa, arm linked with her sister waitress. Both smiled.

"We are starting work now. Will we see you tonight?"

Emmanuel hesitated. Words churned in his mind. "Perhaps . . . not sure yet. But it's good to see you, Yanisa. Really good."

Ronnie turned. "I'm offended, ladies. You haven't asked whether you'll see me tonight."

Both giggled. "Mr. Emmanuel is our best and favorite customer," Yanisa said.

"And what does he have that I don't, my beauties?" Ronnie eyed both, from legs to face, as was his custom. The girls remained grinning, well versed in the manners of the farang.

"If you are his friend, we like you too."

"Then I might see you both later. What time do you finish work?"

"Very late." Both girls laughed, then conversed in Thai.

"Perfect. I'm a night person." Ronnie rose, pulled out a card from his pocket, and presented it to the women. "Here is my phone and room number. If you two ladies would like to go for a few drinks after work, please call. Maybe to the Sirocco bar. Have you been? Wonderful views, and just a few minutes walk. Very classy. Perfectly suitable for beauties like yourselves." All delivered in his gently crafted brogue.

Yanisa took the card. "We finish very late. But thank you." She smiled. Her friend tugged at her arm, beckoning her to move on.

After a few steps, Yanisa turned, still drawn in the performance. "Would Mr. Emmanuel be coming with you?"

"Mr. Emmanuel?" Ronnie laughed. "He might have his dance card full. But I think we could persuade him." He turned, winking at Emmanuel.

"Remember what I told you about my friends, Yanisa."

She grinned as their eyes met. Emmanuel's pulse raced. Then she turned, arm in arm with her girlfriend, toward the Salathip restaurant and labor's tasks.

Ronnie gulped his wine. "Nice girls, my boy. She likes you, that's for sure." He frowned. "I'm supposed to meet our penguin friend tonight. Wants to talk in private." Ronnie chuckled. "I can't get rid of the bugger. He's the pet I never wanted."

The waiter returned, refilled their glasses, and placed a fresh dish of olives and cashew nuts on the table. Nearby, the Scandinavian man who nestled between his two beautiful companions ordered more cocktails of raspberry and peach. Giggles echoed from tables further along.

"And you, my boy, what is on your dance card this evening. Cartoon capers, perhaps?"

Emmanuel leaned back on the lounge. His skin tingled, head and limbs light, floating in wet air.

"I have no idea. Absolutely no idea."

Arthur handed Ronnie the film container. From its light weight, he knew it contained something other than its original contents. He unsealed the lid, removed a paper tissue, and unfolded it.

"Well, well, my boy. What a surprise."

He rolled the stone in his hand. Then went to his chest of drawers, removed the magnifying loupe, and moved to the window's natural light.

Arthur picked his skin to remove the scab off a nearly healed sore. "Well, Ronnie, what do you think . . . think, Ronnie."

"Where did you get this?"

"Is it okay, Ronnie?"

"A bit more than okay." He continued to examine it, then glared at Arthur with a hint of a smile. "Five-plus carats, near colorless, only very slightly included." Ronnie scratched his scalp. "And probably close to an ideal cut."

"That's good then, Ronnie. Ideal is good."

Ronnie smiled, almost fondly. "That's bloody good."

"How much . . . how much?"

He continued to examine the diamond.

"To sell or buy?"

Arthur scrunched his face in a grimace as Ronnie ceased his examination and placed the diamond back into the container. "If I bought this as a punter, the price is higher—retail. If you want to sell to a merchant immediately, then you get less. Wholesale. They need their profit margin, my boy."

"Immediately, Ronnie. Immediately."

"Now, I'm only guessing. Needs better eyes than mine."

"Yes, yes, Ronnie. A guess is fine."

"This is no quote, Arthur."

"Yes, Ronnie, how much, though . . . how much?" His pitch rose higher with each word.

"About one hundred. US dollars."

"One hundred thousand, Ronnie . . . thousand . . . thousand." Arthur heaved himself from the chair, arms opened in embrace. Ronnie staggered against the mass.

"Calm down, my little sumo friend."

Arthur stepped back and lifted his shirt to display a black plastic pouch taped to folded chest skin. "Pull the tape off, Ronnie."

"What the fuck is this?"

In answer, Arthur wrenched at the tape awkwardly, leaving welts as he tore it from his skin, and fumbled before opening the seal. Ronnie stared—open-mouthed—thoughts clouded. Fifteen or more diamonds of equal size to the stone just examined, glistened before him.

"Well . . . I'll be damned." He peered into the face of the grinning behemoth, who stood shirtless, a band of proud welts ring-barking his chest.

The retreating sun lit the room, only gray sky visible from the bed. The kind man lay beside her, warmed by her warmth, and gently kissed her forehead.

She had spent the afternoon soaking, pampered by clear water. Nice smelling water. Then watched the late afternoon river life swarm, ant-like far below, and dozed under sheets of cotton. Cool and stiff.

She turned her head to focus on the bowl of unfinished fruit that lay on a shiny wooden table. An apple sliced in half, its bare, white flesh now bruised with brown spots. And the glass of cola with all its bubbles gone. She had watched the fruit spoil over the hours, and would let it rot to a green and black froth, if she could. But she didn't know why.

She thought of the others—and saw his dark brown face. She had never been gone so long as this. He had, but not her. He'd be worried of course. She saw his worried face, saw him wandering with his worried face—looking in the places they slept or ate or begged. He'd be hungry of course—and saw his hungry face.

She lay with her full belly. All silent in the clean.

The man lifted his head to gaze at her, his face painted with an easy grin.

She smiled at him, and looked back at the brown-specked fruit. This life she knew from magazines, and never questioned why such marvels had come to pass. Never questioned the reason or future. Just bathed in the moment. Protected. Cared for.

"I'm going to make some assumptions."

"Yes, Ronnie."

"But I don't want any answers, unless I'm wrong."

"Yes, Ronnie."

"These are not your diamonds."

"No, Ronnie."

Ronnie grimaced. "Arthur, are you a moron? I don't want you to answer unless I'm wrong, do you understand?" He clutched tufts of snow hair, as if to wrench them from his scalp.

"These are not your diamonds." He glared at Arthur, who remained glued to Ronnie's aura. Open-mouthed but silent.

"You want them moved for you." Cigarette glowed. "In cash."

Arthur remained silent, only occasionally stirring to allow shifting mounds of fat some relief against the chair's skeleton.

"I assume the real owner would like to get these back. Some are marked . . . but that's no problem."

Arthur coughed. Put up his hand.

"What the fuck are you doing?" Ronnie chuckled. "We're not in bloody school." He picked up a stone and examined it with his magnifier loupe, then replaced the stone and examined another.

"Here, look at this." He handed the diamond and loupe to Arthur. "At the edge of the stone, a number is engraved. GIA report number. This diamond has been graded. The number is unique."

Arthur's head, with breath held, became violet with rage.

"Don't burst a blood vessel." Ronnie drew at his cigarette. "It takes two seconds to polish that number off."

A loud hiss of air left Arthur's lungs—deflating his ballooned bulk.

"We—and I say we, since I am assuming you don't have other contacts in the diamond industry." He glanced at Arthur to confirm his opinion. "We need to get these graded again, since nobody I know will give money for stones of this quality without a report. Now, as you may be aware my boy, there happens to be a GIA office in Bangkok."

Arthur nodded, grinning.

"We would want to get the purchaser to get the report in their name. Keeps my account pristine . . . if you know what I mean."

Again Arthur nodded.

"And I would highly suggest to that purchaser not to get the stones engraved. Makes tracing them more difficult without a mark." Ronnie stubbed out his cigarette. "For safety I would suggest moving three or four a year—and to various outlets scattered around the world. Not all in Bangkok, my boy."

Arthur coughed. Went to raise his hand.

"Speak . . . but with a question, not a statement."

"What if I want . . . need . . . to sell more . . . sell more, Ronnie?"

The snow haired man gazed at his companion, before stubbing out his cigarette. "Not wishing to seem rude, my friend, but what the hell do you need more money than that for? You don't have what I would call an expensive lifestyle."

Arthur picked at his skin.

Ronnie tried to assess the situation before him, but failed. "Then more travel will be required. I gather this is the entire lot. There are no more?"

Arthur lifted his eyes, a smile slowly invading his bulbous head.

"There's more?" Ronnie said.

Arthur's grin gave the answer.

"Shit. But I don't want to know anything else." He rose from his chair. "I'm going to have a few drinks at the bar. You get yourself taped back up. I hope you have a safe place for those things. You shouldn't be walking around with such a stash."

Just before leaving his apartment, Ronnie turned. "Just one question. I assume you didn't get these in Thailand. How did you get them into the country?"

Arthur cleared his throat and, with his characteristic high-pitched cry, announced, "Up the bum, Ronnie . . . up the bum!"

The snow-haired man closed his eyes, his head slowly shaking. "I wished I'd never asked."

As the phone rang, Emmanuel gently lifted the girl's head from his shoulder. He picked up the receiver and heard the words spoken in an English accent.

"Have a surprise. Those two young waitresses from downstairs just contacted me. They'd like to join us for a drink. How you placed?"

Emmanuel glanced over to the girl under cover of bed linen. They had dined on the balcony that evening, and soon after burrowed back into their sealed shelter. The girl shifted over, gazing at him.

"Okay, I guess."

"Wonderful, my boy. You get yourself ready and we'll meet you at Sirocco's."

He replaced the receiver and smiled at the girl, then moved to the bathroom, shaved, and changed into a full-length shirt of blue and white stripes. He moistened his palm with hair cream and fingered through his tufts until satisfied with the result, then moved back to the bedside. As best he could, he motioned with his hands that he would be leaving—clearly without her. She nodded with a faint smile as he kissed her cheek. And left.

He moved steadily along streets littered with the bustling traffic of vendors retiring and arrived at Sirocco's some minutes later. Though perched on Bangkok's ceiling, the open bar retained the sticky warmth of the streets below, only occasionally invaded by a relieving breeze. Emmanuel skipped down the white stairs, the area comfortably cramped with late night revelers. Ronnie, as usual, held court, leaning against the circular glass railing at the bar's furthest point, the nocturnal vista beyond. Emmanuel smiled as the now-familiar waiter attended to Ronnie's cigarette.

"And here's our boy," Ronnie said.

Yanisa looked up and greeted him with a warm smile.

"My man has prepared a nice bottle of bubbly for us. My treat. I feel in a celebratory mood tonight."

"Arthur not around?"

"Alas, no. He had other pressing matters. And perhaps for the best... would have unbalanced the situation a bit." Ronnie winked, waving at the waiter to deliver Emmanuel a glass of champagne, and to refill his own.

"These girls drink like pigeons," Ronnie said. They giggled, reaffirming the buoyant mood. "Drink up, my beauties... drink up."

Her friend hugged at Yanisa's arm. "We can't get too drunk. We need to stay alert around you, Mr. Ronnie."

Ronnie eyed the girl with his customary slow scan from legs to breasts. "You are safe with me, my dear."

Emmanuel laughed. "Safe?"

"Well... let's say in good hands." He brushed his finger along her forearm.

Emmanuel glanced at Yanisa's friend, yet couldn't read a reaction in her eyes. The Bangkok training.

"This is wonderful view," Yanisa said. "You can nearly see where I live." She moved slowly over to the opposite hemisphere of the perched bar. Emmanuel followed.

"Over there, I think."

"Nice," he said, not knowing where the directed finger was pointing.

"I... we missed you at dinner," she said softly.

"I ate in my room. Just a hamburger. Every now and then, I feel like one."

She smiled.

"Do you live alone?" he asked.

"No. With family. Brother and sister. Younger," she paused, checking her words. "... and my parents."

"Nice." He faltered. "You're not married?"

She sipped from the champagne flute, its contents barely touched.

"No," she said softly. "And what about you?"

"No."

Yanisa smiled into Emmanuel's eyes. His skin prickled. Limbs floated. While such a feeling of elation had been felt only a handful of times in his past, it now seemed to him ever-flowing—an emotion on tap—its faucet turned almost at will, gushing liquid bliss.

"You have been at Shangri-La for long time now," she said.

"Yes. It feels like home."

"You like Bangkok . . . yes?"

Emmanuel beamed. "Oh yes, Yanisa."

"I like, too." She sipped from the flute. "But it is hard life." And paused, almost in embarrassment. "But I like my job . . . have . . . I have a very good job."

His eyes followed her every gesture, slight movements of fingers, brow, cheeks, and lips. Lips that pouted in pink gloss.

"Will you be staying in Bangkok for long time, Emmanuel?"

For the first time, she addressed him without the title of mister. Emmanuel looked out at the city's lights. Glow-worms sparkled.

"I don't know." And he didn't. "But I hope so, Yanisa." He lifted her hand gently, cradled childlike fingers in his palm.

"More champagne, my boy." Ronnie nestled up to both. "This waiter is not doing his job . . . again." He filled Emmanuel's glass, yet balked at Yanisa's near-full flute. Her eyes met with those of her girlfriend's, who had followed. The girls gently conversed in hypnotizing Thai.

"My father is taking us home soon," Yanisa said. "He drives a taxi. He will pick us up from the hotel."

Emmanuel glanced at Ronnie, whose face was flushed with disapproval.

"I'll come down with you," Emmanuel said.

"No." Yanisa blushed. "Is better to not . . . not to. My father is . . ." She paused, trying to find the correct expression.

"Her father . . . is her father," the girlfriend said.

All three beamed, leaving Ronnie alone to gulp champagne—his affect noncommittal.

"But let's do this longer next time," Emmanuel said.

"That would be very nice." Her eyes found his. "I am sorry I haven't finished the wine." She handed Emmanuel her glass. "I hope to see you tomorrow." And with eyes lowered, she turned, arm linked with her companion's, and moved away.

Emmanuel watched the girls' ascent of the wide stoned staircase—and marveled at their gentle poise.

"God, I hate teases," Ronnie said when the girls were beyond earshot. "What a waste of time, and good champagne." He scanned the bar's lingering contents. "But the night is young, my boy."

"More champagne, sir?" the waiter said, returning.

"There you are," Ronnie said. He drew deep into his cigarette. "I thought you were bloody dead."

Emmanuel smiled.

He slowly opened the door—the room illuminated only by the dancing television screen—and crept in to see her lying, eyes closed. Lovely.

He staggered to the bathroom and stripped the clothes from his skin. Showered. Warm water rejuvenated, transfused with alcohol's charm. Still wet, he moved to the bed, peeled back the sheets to expose legs of long, smooth, bronze glazing; her shirt hunched up, exposing buttocks and glimpses of pudenda. Slowly, he buried his face between her thighs, tasting every crevice. And, as her moans increased, so did his want.

Emmanuel turned the faucet fully on. Ecstasy flowed. Unchallenged.

They spent the next few days together, shuffled with bags of clothes through densely-packed malls, baked skin at the pool's edge, plunged in tepid waters, sipped cocktails, rubbed lotion on warm flesh, made love at will, hands held, grinning as young lovers do. And at night, they feasted on their balcony, overlooking the Chao Phraya's bobbing life below. All intimate. All hidden.

Emmanuel departed the room, leaving the girl propped against a mound of pillows, her gaze fixed at the television screen. He descended in an elevator jammed with smartly dressed guests of the early evening. Then moved to the direction of the glow of Salathip's entrance. Xylophone teeth sang as festooned dancers glided past tables of brightly colored dishes. He scanned the area, but failed to see her.

"Hello, Mr. Emmanuel. A table for you outside tonight?" the manager asked.

"Not tonight, thank you." He scanned around.

"Are you looking for someone?"

"No . . . well, yes." He faltered. "Is Yanisa here tonight?"

"I'm not sure. I will find out for you." She moved toward the kitchen area and returned some minutes later.

"Unfortunately, she is not here tonight. Would you like to leave her a message, Mr. Emmanuel?"

"That's okay. No message," and moved back toward the lobby's entrance.

"Emmanuel!" squawked from afar.

Arthur sat in Angelini's bar, waving both arms, as might a drowning man. Ronnie sat adjacent, studying a menu through thin-framed spectacles. Emmanuel walked over.

"Join us, Emmanuel . . . join us," Arthur said.

"Yes, my boy. We've missed you these past days."

Emmanuel entered the bar and nestled on the couch, glad to be in the company of his friends.

"Have a glass of white Burgundy. It's very good," Ronnie said. "We're just about to eat. Will you dine with us?"

"I've just eaten, but glad to have a drink."

"Then let's stay out here. More relaxed." Ronnie waved to the waiter.

"I'll have a steak," Arthur said. "Well done. No blood . . . and a big one."

"He's a growing boy." Ronnie winked and placed the menu down on the table. "I'll have a small piece of veal. And some vegetables. Carrots, cauliflower, zucchini . . . sautéed . . . with some garlic, sugar, butter . . . a little salt. And perhaps some potato . . . mash . . . do you do mash?" The waiter looked confused as he tried to keep up with the detailed instructions. "If not mash, then don't worry about the potato. But I am sure, in what is arguably the best restaurant in Bangkok, that your chef can do mash."

"I'll have that too . . . with the steak." Arthur said.

"And perhaps a nice bottle of red with all this meat. Nothing too heavy, not outside in this heat. Perhaps a nice pinot . . . Burgundy to match the white. And could you bring some mosquito coils . . . three or four. It's like the bloody Amazon out here tonight."

Emmanuel smiled at the drama unfolding before him. The waiter looked visibly distressed, beads of sweat dribbling from his brow. He repeated the order, leaving out the cauliflower and sugar, but was soon corrected. Then scurried back into the restaurant of ruby goblets and polished timber.

"I hope you give him a nice tip," Emmanuel said.

"When earned, my boy . . . when earned." Ronnie sipped his wine. "We were thinking to visit our old haunt tonight. Our home away from home. Care to join us?"

"Okay . . . why not?"

They merrily consumed their meal, paid the waiter with a generous tip, and made for the lobby. Just before departing, Emmanuel returned to his room and found the girl asleep. He brushed his teeth, then revisited the main room, turned off the television, and quickly departed.

Since the evening had entered its late phase, with traffic easing, they took a taxi and walked down the corridor of the Plaza just before eleven. Emmanuel saw Lalana from afar, seated beside the familiar street vendor whose steaming noodles, at this late hour, failed to snare passing trade. Lalana's elbows rested on bended knees, scanning feet for worn leather.

"I'll leave you two to get on with your debauchery," Emmanuel said.

"Nicely put, my boy. If we see you later, depending on the treats that await, maybe a game of pool?"

The two men disappeared within the bowels of the plaza, Ronnie leading. Emmanuel walked over to the vendor's trolley and stopped in front of Lalana, feet together, ready for inspection. She looked up and smiled, then frowned and retreated to her scanning position.

"Aren't you pleased to see a valued customer?" he asked.

She shook her head, chin resting on palms.

"Okay. I'll be at the bar. If you have time tonight, I would like to get my shoes polished." He headed toward the bamboo bar, then turned. "And discuss another tour . . . if you're available, that is."

Lalana lifted her head abruptly, all signs of sulking vanished. "Okay. I plan now. I come over soon."

He moved up onto the bar's platform and found a stool overlooking the pedestrian traffic. Emmanuel turned to see Lalana's mother attending to quarrelsome customers, a pair of loud farang draped in Thai beauties. The scene displayed the best and worst of humanity. Muscled limbs waved as the party left. Obscenities trailed.

Emmanuel caught the manager's eyes as she handed the barman cash from the departing storm. She moved to a vacant stool, legs crossed in familiar style, as she lit a cigarette.

"These tough guys say they didn't have so many drink. Feel sorry for those girls."

"Did they pay?"

"Yeah, they always pay. Tough guys not that tough." Smoke poured from her crimson lips. "Some wine for you?"

"I've had a fair bit already tonight. Just a glass. Will you join me?"

"Yeah, will do me good to forget those . . . pigs." She shouted instructions to the barman, her voice still thick with disquiet.

The barman returned with the same wine from their previous meeting. Carefully, he removed the cork and pulled it past his nose. Pleased with the result, he poured two large glasses.

"Wonderful." Emmanuel beamed and lifted his glass in salutation. "Here's to paradise."

She frowned at him in silence, sipping at her wine; then drew into her cigarette. "If this is paradise . . . I in big trouble."

He laughed, catching a glimpse of a smirk camouflaged through a haze of smoke.

"So where's the perfect place for you?" he asked.

"Somewhere no men."

He grinned. "You sound like your daughter."

"She learns. Thinks she here to clean shoes . . ." Smoke oozed from the corner of her mouth, ". . . but this is night school."

"And you're the teacher?"

She gulped more wine. "These are the teachers . . . all of them." She pointed to the bar's debris of boisterous customers, and the passing crowd of the walkway, that all ventured eagerly into the night.

Lalana's head bobbed from below. Her dimples grinned as she rested her chin against the table's edge. "I have plan. Not much money."

"Half-price, I seem to remember."

Lalana scrunched her face. "We talk money after."

Her mother watched the interaction. Silent.

"And can I bring someone?" he said.

"Two means more money. Not half-price."

"Sounds reasonable."

"Who is it?"

"A friend."

"Girlfriend?"

"Perhaps."

"You not know?"

Emmanuel laughed. "I guess she is."

"Is that why you not come back?"

"Not really . . . well, maybe . . . but I'm back now."

"She from Australia?"

"No."

"Thai girl?"

"Yes."

Lalana's mother slowly sipped her wine, her gaze fixed on her daughter's eyes.

"Bar girl?"

"No."

"Where you meet."

"At the supermarket, actually."

"You buy girl at supermarket?"

Emmanuel grinned. "Yes... on special. Half-price, next to the vegetable section."

"What her name?"

Emmanuel glanced at Lalana's mother. "Is she always like this?"

"Daughter number one student. At day school... and night." She spoke softly to her daughter in Thai, Lalana's head falling below the bench. Emmanuel felt gentle fingers untie his laces.

"My shout tonight," said the manager, who gulped the remainder of her wine. "Must go back to work now." And, with legs unfolded, she drifted off the stool.

Emmanuel slowly devoured the wine, savoring its perfume that cut through the stale beer and cigarette smoke. He watched the passing traffic. The customary women with arms linked. Men in groups, both farang and Thai, with eyes on fire, some staggering, some steady, some alone. Couples both old and new, arms wrapped, with smiles broad and genuine. Though mostly on the men.

After some minutes, Lalana's head bobbed up. "All done."

"Still fifty baht?"

She nodded. He pulled a note from his pocket and handed it over. Lalana's head dived below, but soon resurfaced.

"We start early," she said. "But not tomorrow. Next day, okay?"

"Okay."

"Five-thirty okay?"

"What?"

"Five-thirty at hotel."

"In the morning?"

"Yes."

"Well I'm glad it's not tomorrow, then."

"And don't have breakfast."

"That won't be hard . . . at that time." He grinned.

"What girlfriend name?" she whispered.

Emmanuel consumed a last mouthful of wine. Rubbed his stubble. "Has anyone ever told you that you ask far too many questions?"

The lovers spent the following day as before—sun drenched dozing, waking to bite-size delicacies and cocktails of pink and orange, while finding broken relief within the pool's cool waters. During the morning, Emmanuel attempted to discover her name. The wall imposed by deafness and lack of mutual understanding of written English or Thai made the task somewhat lengthy, a process finally solved by the bemused staff at the Horizon club, who transcribed in Thai and made the final translation back to English.

Hom.

Communication continued through hand and facial gestures, pointing to objects, sketches quickly drafted, often comical, but usually effective. Such is the effortless conversation bathed in new love.

Emmanuel had reserved his table at Salathip earlier than normal, and for two. He had searched for Yanisa in the late afternoon, but without making an effort. So, when at half-six in the evening they strolled out in the still warm night for dinner, Emmanuel had not seen Yanisa since their nocturnal meeting four days earlier.

"Hello, Mr. Emmanuel, welcome." He was softly greeted by Yanisa's girlfriend at the restaurant's entrance. Her face displayed no emotion as she led them to his normal table at the most exposed corner of the open veranda.

"This is Hom," he said.

"Hello, madam." She pulled out Hom's chair. The girls' eyes met briefly. Hom smiled but quickly lowered her vision to the tabled coverings.

"It's a very warm night," Emmanuel said.

"Very warm. Would you prefer an inside table tonight?"

"No, no . . . this is fine."

"Can I get you some drinks?"

"Some water to begin. A bottle of white wine with the meal would be good."

"The Italian wine, like usual?"

"Yes, thanks." He paused. "Perhaps bring the wine out now."

"With pleasure, Mr. Emmanuel."

He twisted and scanned the restaurant. Only six or so tables were occupied at this early hour. Half were seated within the adjacent, air-conditioned teak pavilion.

"Is Yanisa not working tonight?"

"She is."

"Oh, good." He paused, fingering the yellow and gold plate. "Good."

"Anything else, sir?"

"No, no . . . that's fine. Thank you."

She moved to task, as Hom beamed, rubbing her stomach. Emmanuel smiled and nodded, but behind the façade, an all too familiar shower of emptiness soaked his skin.

The waitress returned and poured two large glasses of wine. Emmanuel quickly gulped the nectar, hoping to ward off invading demons. Paraded dishes of tom yum goong, curry of roasted duck with grape, pad Thai, spooned with steaming rice—all slowly consumed in silence. A second bottle of wine was ordered, Hom having finished only one glass.

"Hello, Mr. Emmanuel." This was softly spoken from behind. Yanisa stood in her uniform of cream and crimson silk. Emmanuel twisted, mouth open, searching for words.

"Hello, Yanisa . . . I missed you tonight. I looked for you before. And on other nights, too."

She spoke without eye contact. "I started a bit later tonight. Working mainly inside tables."

"Oh. I guess it's cooler for you. It's very warm this evening."

"Yes, a very warm day today . . . it was."

Emmanuel faltered before announcing, "This is Hom."

"Hello, Miss Hom." Yanisa only briefly glanced at the seated girl who nodded.

"She cannot speak. She is deaf, Yanisa." These jarring words announced an end to previous awkward pleasantries.

"Oh. I'm sorry." She looked more closely at Hom's silent figure. "But she is very beautiful."

Emmanuel bit his lip, agitated. Yanisa, sensing his anxiety, continued. "Hom is a pretty name. It means nice smell."

"Nice smell. I didn't know that."

She moved slightly closer to Emmanuel, enabling him to sit facing her without twisting his shoulders. In this way, he was facing both Yanisa and Hom. He had preferred the previous position.

"Have you been well?" he asked.

"Quite well."

The initial sense of disquiet had crept back.

"And you, Mr. Emmanuel. Have you been well?" she said softly.

"Yes. I have been busy lately."

"I hope busy with good things."

"Yes, good things . . . mostly." Emmanuel's face strained with unease.

"I should be getting back to work. We have many customers now."

"I enjoyed our night at Sirocco, Yanisa. Very much." The words were blurted out with alcohol-fueled courage. "We must . . . or I would like . . . to do that again. Soon."

Yanisa paused. Her brow wrinkled, as if trying to solve a difficult computation. She took one of the empty plates from the table, drawing out the silence.

"Can I get you any dessert?" she said.

The still-wet air suffocated. He gulped with ever-deepening breaths.

"Dessert . . . Yes . . . Perhaps dessert would be good."

"I will get Chailai to attend to you."

Before he could compose his thoughts and respond, Yanisa had moved away. Emmanuel slumped, lifting his glass to finish its contents, then spooned some rice and duck onto his plate but never ate it. The overcoat of despair remained, worn and tattered, heavy on his shoulders.

And, as the xylophones timbered, announcing the arrival of the dancers, Hom looked on, through his eyes, and beyond.

He woke with a tap on his shoulder.

"Where is girlfriend?" Lalana asked.

At five-thirty in the morning, Emmanuel sat alone in the marble lobby. He lengthened his back, yawning.

"Good morning, Lalana." She stood before him in her familiar black uniform. Emmanuel noticed the lipstick and rouge of painted adolescence.

"You look very beautiful this morning," he said.

Dimples smiled. "Where is girlfriend?"

"I let her sleep. So just one customer today. Is that okay?"

"Okay. We go now," said in a manner that gave nothing away.

She led him through the quiet streets, still sleeping, to the nearby ferry terminal, and found seats on the half-full vessel carting its weary cargo. After fifteen minutes they boarded the same long-boat as their previous excursion. The boatman greeted both with a broad smile, happy with the prearranged early trade. Soon they needled across the river's wash, with imposing silhouettes of the Grand Palace's temples drifting past. Emmanuel dozed as the inky sky slowly transformed to the bruised lavender of early dawn.

Again, he woke to a tap on his shoulder, and found himself drifting in a narrow corridor of water, at most six or seven boat widths, flanked by overhanging open verandas. The diesel motor had been extinguished, replaced by the boatman's effortless paddling. Multitudes of canoes and small long-boats jostled for position; some tied to the canal's edge, some free floating. Most were attended by women with broad straw hats resembling lampshades, surrounded with full baskets of eggplants, ripe mangos, bananas—both miniature and as thick as wrists—custard apples, lychee, and rambutan. Lalana beckoned to the boatman, who eased toward a nearby craft. The woman nodded in recognition, said something brief that trailed into a toothless smile, and handed a selection of the giant fruit to Lalana. They drifted further, and nestled against a larger long-boat, with hats of all varieties stacked in mounds. The boatman pointed to a straw hat decorated with splashes of color matching those of his painted craft—and soon modeled a variety of sizes, styles. Lalana conversed with him in Thai as he displayed the options. The seller joined in with suggestions—and they all giggled like a family at Christmas dinner. After some minutes, the boatman navigated the craft further, clearly pleased with his new garb.

Nearby, a monk in saffron robes paddled by. Vendors scurried to give offerings in his shiny dishes and woven baskets. Lalana beckoned again, and the boatman arched his back to steer the craft to the monk's side. She carefully positioned fruit in the monk's basket, and bowed with gentle hands placed on touching palms. They drifted on. She opened a timber box at the rear of the boat containing plastic plates and napkins. And, as the sky glowed orange with the awakened day, they feasted on the soft, sticky flesh of sweet fruit.

Emmanuel slumped against two cushions and wiped his fingers. "Lalana, you're a genius."

Lalana poured tea from a thermos flask into three small mugs and distributed them to her two male companions. The boatman, yet to sweat from his labor, paddled slowly down the full length of the klong, easing through the cluttered vessels.

"Bang Khu Wiang is best floating market," she said. "Real one. Not for tourists." She sipped her tea. "Girlfriend sleepy?"

"Yes. I guess. She was asleep when I rose. Like most people."

"Market people start early." She frowned.

"It's okay. I wouldn't have missed this for the world."

She nodded. "Does girlfriend show you Bangkok?"

"We mainly hang around the pool. And shop. And eat. She eats more than you."

"She fat?"

"No. Skinny." He paused. "Like you."

Lalana reflected. "She pretty?"

"Yes . . . like—"

"I know, like me, yeah, yeah."

Emmanuel fixed his gaze on the girl. She sat slumped, with one hand supporting her chin. "Are you tired?"

"I worked late last night. Durudee want me to stay."

"Durudee, your gum selling friend?"

"Yeah. I told her I go to bed. But she get lonely without me."

"Why do you girls work so late?"

Lalana lifted herself higher on the seat. "Save our money. Durudee wants . . ." she paused, then moved over to Emmanuel's bench and lay facing upward, with her head resting on his thigh. "She wants teeth straight."

"Oh, braces. Are her teeth very crooked?"

"Not bad."

"And you? What are you saving for?"

"That secret," she whispered.

"I thought we didn't have any secrets?"

"No . . . we not lie. Secrets different." She lifted her head, seeking a visual response.

"True." Emmanuel watched as another paddling monk received alms from scurrying merchants.

"Only mum and Durudee know secret." She repositioned her head to gain maximum comfort. "Would you like to know?"

"Very much." He grinned at her—and felt his overcoat of melancholy slip off as her dimples smiled up at him. This sadness of his came in waves—usually for a reason, but sometimes without. Like a knock at the door.

Lalana sat quickly upright and gave instructions to the boatman, who reignited the motor. Soon, cool air stroked their skin as they sped through branching canals of varying widths. In time, passing bathers began waving at Lalana, and within minutes, the boat approached her klong-side home. Lalana opened the timber gate as the boatman supported Emmanuel onto the steps that ascended from the canals depths.

The teen opened the main door and brought her finger to her lips, gesturing for silence.

"Mum still sleep," she whispered.

They walked through a dimly lit corridor, whose details remained veiled as Emmanuel's eyes slowly adjusted to the light. The girl moved to the end of the passageway, then tiptoed up a narrow staircase that led directly into her room. And entered.

Emmanuel sat on the small bed as Lalana slid under the mattress springs. Legs and thighs dangled out from the enclosure. Her room was tidy and clean. Timbered walls freshly painted in yellow reflected light from the dangling, naked bulb. A small portrait of the king was dwarfed by posters of slender, guitar-clad youths with flirting eyes. Uncluttered floorboards, stained and polished some years past, showed wear at the door. At one corner of the room, the shoe shining equipment rested in its pine tray. A small desk and chair sat in another corner. Photographs in colorful plastic frames sat on the desk. Emmanuel recognized her mother, flanked by Lalana and probably two smaller siblings. A separate picture of a Thai man, perhaps in mid-twenties, sat adjacent. A handsome, smiling man, baby in arms. Content. Emmanuel guessed this was a portrait of Lalana and her father. A more recent photograph of her and Durudee with arms linked, both clad in their lemon uniforms, sat framed in pink.

Lalana crawled out from under the bed.

"This is some secret," Emmanuel said softly.

She lay face up on the bed, again using his thigh as a pillow. In her hand, she had a folded page cut neatly from a magazine. She handed it to him, with her eyes fixed on his. Emmanuel unfolded the photograph. A landscape. Snow-capped mountains framed the background. In front, but some distance away, a carpet of olive green encircled a small mountain lake of brilliant aquamarine. And, from the edge of the lake, occupying the entire foreground, was a vast field of purple flowers.

"So . . . not much of secret, ah?" she said.

"Depends. Tell me more about it."

A sound of footsteps rushing down the stairs.

"My brother and sister wake."

Emmanuel noticed for the first time that Lalana's makeup matched the color of the purple petals.

"It nice . . . yes?" she asked.

"Very nice. Where is it?"

"Not sure." She frowned. "But not Bangkok."

"No, it certainly isn't."

"It cold. See snow."

"Yeah, I see."

"It smell nice. Look how many flowers."

"It's beautiful."

"No smell of petrol. No smell of smoke. No smell of beer. Just flower smell."

"I've never seen so many flowers," he said.

"Daisies. Mum say they purple daisies."

"They're beautiful. So, are you saving to go there?"

Lalana nodded. "Durudee say she might come . . . might."

"What does your mother say?"

Lalana flipped over and rested her chin against both hands, and peered up at him. "Mum say they don't smell nice."

Emmanuel adjusted his slumped position on the bed, allowing his gaze to meet the girl's.

"I don't understand," he said.

"Daisies. They don't smell nice." She paused, pulling at an exposed thread of the bedcover, avoiding eye contact. "Mum say they smell like shit."

They strolled through the gardens, the morning yet to submit to the impending tourist flow. Before them was a large, two-storied, L-shaped mansion of fawn-colored teak, its evenly spaced, powder blue shutters opened to invite cool air. Both slumped on the lime lawn facing a row of palms nested at the mansion's feet.

"Where I would live if I was queen," she said.

"Very nice choice."

"Biggest teak house in world."

"You would like to be queen?"

"You crazy. Everyone wants to be queen. Your girlfriend wants to be queen, you ask her." Lalana flipped over and met Emmanuel's eyes. "But sometimes not good to be queen." She jumped to her feet. "Come," and led him away, past smaller buildings—other tourists yet to venture to these outlying, painted teak children. After some minutes, they entered into one sibling, washed in sea blue pigment, then up stairs of polished timber. Lalana scanned photographs mounted on the wall, and moved to one with her hand held in open invitation. Fingers touched his softly.

"This one." She examined closer. "Yes . . . this one."

An old photograph, black and white, of a young woman seated, without comfort. She was leaning forward with her hands in her lap, holding something unidentifiable. Her thin frame was draped in the traditional attire of wrapped silk, with one shoulder bare. Her face glowed with a hint of a smile. No—a definite smile. And she was beautiful, very beautiful.

"Queen," she said. "Number one queen of King Rama V."

"She's young . . . and looks happy."

"She is queen." Lalana removed her hand from his—an awkward adolescent fumble. "In those times, only king can touch queen."

Emmanuel moved his gaze to Lalana. She was, perhaps, the same age as the framed subject.

"She fell in water. No one pick her up. No one allowed to touch queen."

Emmanuel stared back within the frame at the angelic face with the world at her command.

"She drown." Lalana gently touched the black frame of the photograph. "Sometime not good to be queen."

"I take you back to girlfriend now."

They had finished the hour tour of Vimanmek mansion. The festering heat of noon manacled their legs and slowed their pace.

"Let's get a taxi," Emmanuel said.

"Tuk-tuk cheaper."

"It's too hot."

Soon they entered the lobby of the Shangri-La, an oasis of dry chilled air. Emmanuel moved to a vacant lounge and slumped. Lalana sat at his side.

"What a great day." He sighed, with eyes closed. Lalana nodded. Both content.

"Rama V great king," she said. "History teacher say next to our King, Rama V is second best." She tapped on Emmanuel's shoulder. "You awake?"

He opened his eyes to a beaming grin.

"Rama V stop slaves." She giggled. "Mum say still many slaves in Bangkok."

Emmanuel lay on his side facing the girl.

"Is girlfriend here?" she asked.

"I would think so."

Lalana chewed at her lip. "You know name yet?"

"Hom."

"I have older friend at school with name Hom. She fatter than me. So not same girl." Lalana pulled at a cushion of embroidered cotton.

Emmanuel gazed at the girl's dimpled cheeks, eyes, furrowed brow.

"But might be same girl . . . could be," she said. Her eyes lowered as she patted down a loose thread of the cushion's case.

"Would you like to meet her?"

"We could eat . . . together." Said with the hesitation of uncertain youth.

"Yes, we could. I would love to see you two eat together. I hope they have an extra chef."

Lalana struck him with the cushion playfully. "I still growing."

Throughout the morning, Emmanuel's draping overcoat of gloom had slowly shed its fleece, in layers, as peeled from an onion. He now lay unburdened, enthused, life again revealing all of its joys. From a distance, he saw the snow-haired man with pink shiny skin. Both waved as Ronnie quickened to the couch.

"I've been looking for you, my boy."

"I've been the tourist all morning," Emmanuel said. "Do you remember Lalana?"

Ronnie's eyes slowly scanned without recognition.

"She cleaned my shoes, at the Plaza."

"Yes, of course. Nice to see you again. Nice." He rubbed his stubble. "Can I see you for a minute, my lad?"

Both men moved to a quieter corner of the lobby, out of earshot.

"Got some gear for tonight," he whispered.

"Gear?"

"Those girls came through. Not coke. Anyway coke is rubbish here. Ecstasy. It'll be a nice break from the booze. I've put on some pounds . . . need to shed some of these handles." He gripped his gut.

Emmanuel smiled, Ronnie's whispering drawl hypnotic.

"So we have enough for the three of us, your girlfriend, and the two lasses, of course."

"The three of us?"

"Our penguin friend. Can't leave him out, he would be shattered. Though he needs twice the quantity."

"Okay, I'm up for it," Emmanuel said, buoyant mood still hovering.

"Excellent. We are meeting in my room at eight."

Ronnie moved toward the lobby's exit—then he faltered and returned, placing one arm over Emmanuel's shoulder. As would a caring parent.

"Don't eat after four. No booze either. Have a nap if you can." And with instructions given, he left.

Emmanuel moved back to Lalana who sat comfortably in the lounge, studying the hotel guests.

"This good place for shoe cleaning," she said. "Double money here. Easy."

"I'll go and find Hom." Then paused in brief reflection. "Oh, and I forgot to tell you . . . she's deaf . . . and can't speak."

He fixed his gaze into Lalana's eyes—who merely shrugged.

"How you talk?"

"Pictures mainly, and lots of pointing."

"Deaf. Not same girl then."

Emmanuel smiled with relief. He wanted Lalana's approval even if the reason was somewhat murky.

"I'll be back soon."

As he moved away, Lalana resumed scanning the drifting shoes; imagined a queue of tattered leather, a calm trail waiting with cash in hand. *Even triple money here—easy.* And grinned wide into the ambling shoes.

They sat at the table. Hom, dressed in the "I love Bangkok" T-shirt, gazed at her plate, avoiding direct eye contact with the stranger. Lalana twisted to see the awaiting buffet behind.

Emmanuel grinned. "Your lunch is ready for you. Take your time."

"You take time . . . I eat now." She alighted with plate in hand.

Hom lifted her eyes to his, gave a tentative smile. Emmanuel held out his hand, bringing soft fingers, only pencil thick, to cradle in his palm. She beamed, then also twisted to view the feast. Soon food, both hot and cold, formed hillocks on large plates. The girls giggled as they swapped from each other, comforted in each other's dining etiquette that muddled and spilled, with sticky staff all close to meet their needs. Lalana spoke Thai to the waitresses, who laughed, attracting others. Soon, a family of waitresses and waiters circled the table, Lalana the central attraction. And, throughout, Hom followed the theatre with dancing eyes, laughter a contagion.

The manager brought over a pen and pad used for taking dinner orders and handed it to Lalana, who scribbled some text in Thai and pushed the pad to Hom. Her scribbled reply led all to giggle loudly.

"Better food than aunt's wedding!" Lalana said.

"Thank you," the manager said.

Lalana scribbled further, and showed it to Hom and the manager. The later penned a brief reply. Both girls stared, open-mouthed.

"More cost than aunt's wedding!"

Two chefs with mountainous white hats came to the table, spoke in Thai, and shook hands with all. Bemused guests reflected on their special attention, and, throughout, Emmanuel ate some sashimi, drank some tea, and sat in what he knew was undeniably paradise.

The girls nibbled desserts arranged in one large plate at the center of the table. Their consumption slowed, not from lack of appetite, but from greedy message writing, the table now a litter of discarded scribblings. Giggles mingled with silent frowns, paused thoughts—eyes that wandered down. In time, diners slowly departed, until finally, after some hours of grazing, their small table at the window's edge alone was occupied.

"You talk now," Lalana said.

"Sorry?"

"You talk now with Hom."

Lalana stared at Emmanuel. Hom's eyes were directed at her plate, lap, hands. He scratched his scalp.

"I guess that would be sensible, with you here to help."

Lalana nodded, pencil in hand. She tore off the facing page of the pad to display a clean sheet. Emmanuel sipped his tea.

"You need help?" she said.

"No. Just time to think I guess."

"Ask how old."

"Am I?"

"Her."

"Okay. That's a start. Ask how old is she?"

"Eighteen," Lalana said immediately, her gaze fixed on him.

"Okay . . . " He frowned. "Where does she live?"

"On streets." With gaze remaining fixed.

"Yes, I guessed that. Does she have any family?"

"Brother. Older. Can't speak, like her. Parents gone long time. Not sure where."

"I certainly won't need another pad of paper. You seem to know all the answers."

"Not all. Not yours."

A shawl of unease gently settled on his shoulders. "Does she need to see her brother . . . to tell him where she is?"

Lalana transcribed the question and Hom read. Then wrote a reply, crossed out some words, then added more text. Lalana, as if not accepting or understanding the answer, wrote a further message. The process continued some minutes.

"She scared to."

"Scared of him?"

"No. Scared you not here when she come back from visiting brother."

Emmanuel's heart raced. Hom's eyes remained downcast.

"Tell her I will take her this afternoon."

Lalana nodded. Wrote the message and pushed the pad toward the deaf-mute, who lifted her eyes and smiled. Tears welled.

"Tell her we are going out tonight with friends."

"Man in lobby and other man at mum's bar?"

"Yeah."

"Don't like them."

Emmanuel grinned. "They grow on you."

Lalana transcribed a lengthy message. Hom read and giggled, wiping the wet from her cheeks.

"What did you write?"

"Told her you and her and dirty old man and very, very fat man go out tonight."

Emmanuel grimaced. "How inviting." He scratched his scalp. "You have taught me one thing, though. I really must learn to read and write Thai."

Lalana grinned. "I teach you. Cheap."

"Hom might like to ask a question," he said.

Lalana turned over a clean page and pushed the pad to her friend, who scribbled a short note. Lalana glanced, and repeated with a longer message. As before, this exchange continued some minutes before Lalana read the last note.

"This is some question," he said.

"Not question. She has no question."

"What was all that writing?"

Lalana tore the pages from the pad and placed them in her moneybag. "You learn Thai and find out."

The pedestrian traffic of late afternoon swelled. She had scanned the usual places—well-known eyes, hungry, slumped on street corners, on cushions of cardboard, peering at her clothes, skin, all clean. Occasionally she nodded, smiled almost, yet confused guilt always restrained her. Throughout, Emmanuel remained at her side, but not touching. Intimacy hidden from envious eyes. She thought it best.

Hom found him with his trunk and head arched over to meet his knees. The tin can of glue at his side. He looked up with eyes crusted, lines of blood drawn on their whites that took time to focus. Then anger, shown with hand gestures even onlookers could understand. She placed her palm on his shoulder but was immediately swatted away. His other hand pushed, grabbed at her shirt.

She accepted his anger. Well-deserved. He needed her for food—young girls stronger magnets of charity than men, old or young, even though they shared the same wants. He needed her for companionship, of sorts. He needed her.

She pulled out a wad of cash and placed it in his hand. Quieted his anger. Then spoke slowly with fingers and palms. Occasionally he peered at Emmanuel, who stood back some yards, but glances only, for he knew his place. And, after ten minutes of busy hands, nods, and grimacing smiles, peace was restored. They hugged briefly, then Hom moved away, Emmanuel following—down the wide avenue that gradually settled, as they eased themselves away from the horde.

The man returned to his resting position, with the tin can of volatile nourishment sealing nose and mouth, and slumped with chin to chest before searching for his sister—whose now-fading presence formed only a faint outline sketched in the distance. Emmanuel turned, watched the hunched man who moved like he was wading through a vat of molasses. Yet Hom continued on. And never looked back.

"Let's take them now, Ronnie . . . now!" Arthur screeched.

Ronnie's room bulged. Two girls, both dressed for clubbing, flaunted denim shorts baring butt creases. Their chests wrapped tightly in Lycra, one in yellow, the other red. Their faces painted with thick rouge. Hom stood apart, clad in sepia—baggy brown shorts, a black short-sleeved top, unadorned skin—and hugged at Emmanuel's side.

"Okay, settle, big boy," Ronnie said.

He beckoned to Emmanuel, and they entered the chocolate-marbled bathroom. From a plastic pouch, Ronnie produced a dozen small white pills, like aspirin, yet scored with a small heart at their center.

"Plenty to make the night go around." he said. "You haven't eaten?"

"As instructed," Emmanuel said.

"Good. Don't want any gut ache to ruin the fun."

"You sure these are okay? I've never done this before."

"Trust Uncle Ronnie. The girls have had these before. They say they're the best. Clean. Nothing smacky." He rubbed his scalp of snow. "I would suggest you and the girls have a half of one tablet each and the other half in three hours."

Arthur entered the bathroom, habitually attired in black shorts and T-shirt. He squeezed between the two men. "Look at these. Perfect, Ronnie . . . perfect. How many for me?"

"You, my pretty penguin . . . you get two."

Arthur's balloon-hand clawed at the tablets.

"Shit . . . wait a moment, we all have to take them together."

Ronnie took one of the tablets, placed it on a small sheet of aluminum foil, and carefully cut it in two halves with a penknife. Then he repeated the process with three others.

"Let's get the girls," Ronnie said, and they went back to the room. Hom sat on the bed watching television, the others sipped gin procured from the mini-bar.

Ronnie shook his head. "You leave five minutes and the bar is raided. Ladies, don't drink booze with ecstasy. It has the opposite effect. Didn't your parents teach you anything?"

"We like," said yellow top. "It relax us."

"Come with me, my pretties," Ronnie said. He escorted one on each arm. "It's time to party."

They all entered the bathroom. Emmanuel took Hom's hand, and they smiled together, though somewhat nervously. Both peered at the tablets, each distributed on six squares of foil.

"Now take your medicine, like Dr Ronnie prescribed. We must come up together. One big happy family."

Ronnie opened a bottle of water and swallowed one of the tablets, then folded the other tablet in the aluminum foil and put it in his pocket. He handed the bottle to Arthur, who repeated the process. The girls followed, well versed in the procedure, both securing their unused half-tablets in the cup of their bra.

"That's no hiding place, ladies. That's the first place I like to feel when I meet beauties like you." His eyes fixed on their breasts—for he lacked the knowledge that these women usually dressed for themselves and less for the pleasure of others.

Red top giggled. "We lucky not all men like you."

Emmanuel took his half-tablet, bitter as quinine. "Yuck." He sipped more water to remove the taste, then handed the bottle to Hom. During the afternoon, he had not communicated to her what they were planning—her glue sniffing providing a justification of sorts. Emmanuel looked into her eyes, beckoning her to continue, but felt uneasy. She nodded with an empty expression.

"Last but not least," Ronnie said softly.

Emmanuel handed her the half-tablet. Without pausing, she swallowed it with a brief mouthful of water. Then he folded the remaining half in foil and put it in his pocket.

"Off to get our kicks on route sixty-six," Ronnie sang.

"Great choice, Ronnie . . . Route sixty-six . . . great choice," Arthur squawked.

The two candy-colored girls eyed each other and giggled. Arthur oblivious. Seemingly.

They descended in the lift together, took two taxis, and soon entered the club identified with splashes of vivid neon as "Historic Route 66 USA."

Within the club's blackened interior, couples scattered, singles scanned, and some danced on the open floor with techno music blaring through warm, wet air.

"Still early," Ronnie said. "Drink plenty of water, my boy. And no booze."

Emmanuel nodded. "Not feeling anything much."

"Give it time, my boy. The night is but a pup."

The Lycra girls chattered to the barmen. Hom clung to Emmanuel's side. Arthur, nearby, eyed the scene—of amber Thai, clad in tiny shorts, skirts, tops—and waited. In time, the crowd distended like bubble bath, the intervening space slowly constricted, squeezed air between writhing skins. The girls brought bottles of water for all from the bar; Ronnie saluted the barman, who nodded his thanks. Then, within the swelling crowd, they danced, insidious energy building with smiles all beaming. Hom moved with the masses, her deafness no barrier, dancing to a beat that reverberated in her ribs.

"This is lovely!" Emmanuel screamed above the music. Stroked Ronnie's shoulder.

"You feel it?" Ronnie asked.

"I feel it."

And they danced. Arms, legs, heads moved to the beat. Flesh collided with others, shirts sucked moisture from sweat that dribbled without heat; their rhythmic movement ceased only long enough to replenish the supply of bottled water. And they danced. Danced for hours.

Ronnie focused on his watch and signaled to the group.

"We aren't going?" Emmanuel shouted over the loud techno.

Ronnie raised up his hands. "Time for our second dose," he bellowed. "Follow me."

They tracked a path with arms on each other's shoulders, needled through bobbing, glistening flesh, led by Ronnie. When nearing the center of the dance floor, he carefully took out the aluminum foil from his pocket, unwrapped the tablet, and gulped it down with water from shared bottles. Others followed, one at a time. After all had completed the task, they began to move as one, arms resting on the shoulders and hips of others, hands stroking skin. Permanent grins beamed, their energy slowly building. And they danced.

Then it happened.

A wave of energy—of light, of joy—from his toes moved briskly to his legs, up to thighs—cool electricity sparkled to groin, upward to chest, heart—exploded, moved up—fast now—to neck, mouth, and finally eyes. Eyes that saw everything—look at the light—eyes that saw the crest of a wave of pure unadorned ecstasy. He floated. Unrelenting energy poured from all orifices, vivid light, clearer than ever before. Hands floated in laser beams, bright as the sun without glare, fingers moved through crystal, sweat poured in cool air, skin prickled, touch exquisite.

Fuck . . . this was life, this was life.

He looked at Hom, whose smile shone. He kissed her, tongues flicking deeply, swallowed her, loved her, he fucking loved her. Saw Arthur's eyes closed as he bopped to the beat, enormous body gorgeous—then his eyes opened and met his, grinned, kissed him, held his bulk, loved his friend, the Lycra girls his sisters, shared grins, water, shared this wonderful fucking life, yellow and red bopped, he loved these breasts, not sexually, sisterly. The three danced in unison, together—neon lights glowed pink, green, yellow, blue—look at the colors, look at the light. He caressed Ronnie's white hair, fucking beautiful hair; he moved to him, danced with arms on hips, caressed his chest, shoulders, cuddled him like a sheep, loved him.

"I love you, Ronnie!" he shouted, and kissed him gently, lips wet, glistening, as music blared—"I can feel the heat, can feel the heat, can feel the heat." Cool air sucked into his floating lungs—fuck, this is life. They danced with hands held, his brother, his beautiful friend, the six beaming grins, music played for them, for him alone—don't stop this fucking wonderful life—and they danced. Danced for days.

"Look at your eyes, my boy!" Ronnie shouted. "Your pupils are like watermelons."

Pulsed movement of unrelenting energy—couldn't stop. I cannot stop. Never let this stop.

He drifted to the past. His loves. They were all loves, great loves. He saw them all, danced with them all. Loved them all. Glanced at Hom, whose arms swayed, held high, eyes dazzling, reflecting his joy. Loved them all. Who did he love the most? It didn't matter. Danced with Lalana, he loved Lalana, why wasn't she here? Closed his eyes, arms reached for the heavens. Fingers flicked at laser light. Fingers glittered. Look at this wonderful fucking light. Loved them all. "You don't have to be the lonely one, you don't have to be the lonely one," the music blared. "Come on, come on, baby..." Danced with Yanisa, serving him delicacies with ruby lips, loved Yanisa. Loved her gentle hands, tiny fingers. Loved Yanisa. "Take me higher... higher and higher." Images of Princess's baby cheeks flashed. Chubby limbs. Ginger hair.

He held his breath.

Sudden paranoia—a consuming dread, hung heavy down. The baby's giggles an open-mouthed scream. A wave of nausea gurgled with the scream—with eyes of nearby strangers that pierced deep their stare.

They know, they know. God they know.

And yet they danced. The light a rising bright electric. What paradise was this? What fucking paradise.

And they danced.

Lalana re-read her diary entry, neatly penned.

> *Yesterday spent with E. Wonderful time. Very romantic. Lay on his lap. Then met his girlfriend—my new friend. She cannot speak but we laughed a lot. I like her very much but we shared sad secrets. Maybe will tell diary someday but promised I wouldn't yet. Her name is Hom. I think I would rather go to the field of purple daisies with her, not E.*

Emmanuel's ears were filled with a high-pitched whistle—the remnant of swimming in an air of constant, loud techno. They tore off their clothes, pulled back the white cotton sheets, and fell onto the bed that drank them whole. A painted film of crystallized sweat clung to their skin, skin that licked and kissed—but gently—both cocooned in an odor of exhausted pores and soft joy; not sparkly or dazzling, but like waxy fleece. A balmy shroud.

As slumber swallowed them.

"What a night."

Emmanuel slumped in Angelini's outside bar that was colored orange by the resting sun. Hom nestled at his side. Arthur and Ronnie sat adjacent in single sofas.

Ronnie poured the champagne. "Some get a little down after ecstasy, but I feel like a million dollars."

"No complaints here," Emmanuel said. "The night seemed to last two days."

"You were grinning the whole time, my boy. This is your drug of choice, no doubt."

"But I don't crave for it. I don't want any now."

"That's the difference. With coke or speed you need more and more. But not with ecstasy. I swear—it's a bloody vitamin." Ronnie prodded Arthur. "You're quiet, my friend. Have some champagne to ease into the night."

Arthur shifted his bulk to the edge of the sofa. His fat hand held the flute like a pen, and sipped the wine.

"Okay gang, let's go out somewhere," Ronnie said. "We need to keep the momentum up. What about the Plaza?" He glanced at Arthur, who gave no response. "Come on, big boy. The Plaza! We have family there."

Arthur nodded, with a faint smile.

The four caught a taxi, since none had the energy to push through the throng of the early evening sky train. The swollen traffic that hampered their travel also extended their rest. In time, they waded through the cramped surroundings outside the bamboo bar.

"We'll leave you guys to it." Emmanuel said.

"Hope to see you later, my boy." Ronnie departed through the crowded entrance to the plaza, Arthur some steps behind.

Emmanuel led Hom to the bar holding her hand. The familiar low-level buzz of the bar soothed him. They found stools overlooking the walkway and sat to watch the passing trade.

Durudee caught his eye and wandered over. "Lalana not here yet."

"How's business?"

"Bad. You first customer."

Emmanuel laughed at the well-worn line, one echoed throughout Bangkok from dawn to rest. She held up two packets of gum, one spearmint, the other flavored fruits. Emmanuel gestured to Hom, who chose the latter.

"Forty baht," she said.

"How about twenty?"

"Okay. First customer discount."

Emmanuel handed her the cash. She neatly folded the notes and placed them in the bag strapped to her waist.

"How's your savings going?"

"Bad."

"What do you save for?"

Durudee lowered her eyes, aimlessly rearranging the gum in her case. Then lifted her head and grimaced—showing both upper and lower teeth, irregularly placed, but well manicured.

"Nice smile," he said.

"Teeth crooked."

"They look all right to me."

"You dentist?"

He laughed. "No."

"What your job?"

"I sell shoes."

"In Bangkok?"

"Sydney, Australia."

"You have lots of money for shoe seller."

Emmanuel smiled.

"Do you own store?"

"No. Just sell them."

Durudee frowned. "In Bangkok, shoe seller not rich like you." She paused, then said with excitement, "Perhaps you get Lalana job. She expert in shoes."

"It is not a great job, believe me. So why do you want to get your teeth straight?"

"Your girlfriend pretty."

"I think so too."

"Lalana say she not speak."

Emmanuel twisted in search of the manageress; champagne's blanket waning. Only the barman was in view, busily tending to customers.

"She not here yet," Durudee said.

Emmanuel's skin flushed. Some yards behind Durudee, she glided past. Soft pink powder brushed on high cheekbones of pale coffee. Pink lip-gloss of past gentle kisses. Their eyes met and she smiled, yet kept moving steadily toward the plaza's greedy mouth. The ladyboy bowed to the shrine and slowly turned her head to gaze back at Emmanuel, then mounted the stairs out of view.

Durudee studied the scene.

Emmanuel turned back toward the bar and waved at the barman, gesturing his need. Soon the barman returned with a bottle of chilled white wine—cheap Australian—and poured two large glasses.

"Can I have some?" Durudee said.

Emmanuel drank large swallows of wine, his thoughts mixed, but not his intentions.

"I don't think Lalana's mother would be thrilled by the idea of me handing booze to young girls in her bar."

"I've had some before. Many times."

He grinned. "Many times?"

"Well . . . some times."

He quickly finished his glass and filled another to its brim, topping up Hom's, who had only drunk a shallow slice. He shifted on his stool, as to avoid a stone in a shoe, and gulped more wine as the Plaza girls paraded. Gulped more wine.

After no more than fifteen minutes, he gazed at Hom and pointed to the entrance of the Plaza. She nodded and started to leave her stool.

Emmanuel placed his hand gently on her shoulder, easing her back onto the chair. He motioned with fingers the likely time he would spend away with Ronnie and Arthur. Not long. He waved to Durudee, who had resumed her gum selling with some success, finding a string of first customers. She counted the money and strolled over.

"Could you do me a favor?" Emmanuel asked. "I'm going to meet up with my friends for a while." He shifted on his stool. "Could you look after Hom . . . keep her company . . . while I'm away."

Durudee nodded.

"Thanks. You're the best."

He kissed Hom and eased himself off his stool, staggered briefly, then found his balance. He waved to the barman indicating he would return, then handed Durudee a one hundred baht note.

"You're the best," he repeated.

Emmanuel moved away through the throng and descended the steps of the bar, whose cramped patrons spilled onto the walkway below. Within the crowd, Durudee sang softly, "I simply the best . . . better than all the rest . . ." twirling within the sea of pedestrian traffic that dodged her floating arms.

And throughout, seated at the bamboo bench, Hom stared into vacant space.

Emmanuel moved through the entrance flanked by plastic palm trees, parted the dangling beads, and entered the dim interior. He scanned the surrounds but found no trace of Ronnie or Arthur, yet he continued to drift into the room's innards. And sat. The unhurried podium displayed its wares; slowly dancing bikinis jostled for attention. His eyes focused on the pink lips of number twenty-three; her beauty mesmerizing.

Without instruction, she drifted off the stage and moved to Emmanuel's side. She kissed him gently on his cheeks, eyelids, lips. A taste of strawberry lip-gloss. Then, without a whisper, she took his hand and led him to the waiting room upstairs.

The girls giggled together, their backs resting against the vendor's cart. Lalana scribbled on a pad and showed it to her friends, creating more laughter. She held Hom's hand. Durudee took the pad and began writing a more considered prose—showed the pad to Hom, who read with a smile that dissolved away. Hom took the pencil and scribbled some notes while Durudee rested her head on Lalana's shoulder. They had continued this game for over thirty minutes. Never speaking once.

Emmanuel stood nearby, watching for a bit, then moved over to the girls. All looked up with smiles. Hom gently caressed Emmanuel's leg, then continued writing.

"Looks like I'm at a disadvantage here."

Lalana and Durudee nodded, yet maintained their silence. Hom pushed the pad to the girls, who read with interest, all nodding with smiles born from an intimate understanding.

Emmanuel moved away to settle his account at the bar and found Lalana's mother sitting in familiar garb, cigarette in hand.

"I've come to pay the bill."

"Ah. My favorite customer." The barman handed her the order. "What was wine like?"

"Cold and wet. But it did the trick."

She brought the cigarette to her lips. "Not our best, ah?" She twisted to the barman and gave brief instructions in Thai. "Next time we give you better."

Emmanuel smiled.

"You don't want another now?"

"I'm pretty well done." He took out a wad of cash and handed it to the barman. A handsome tip nearly doubled the account.

"My daughter say you like her tour."

"Very much."

"You take two tour." The fishnet woman peered deeply into his eyes, swinging her stocking to bring his gaze briefly down. "My daughter young girl." She kept her stare. "You like young girl?"

Emmanuel held his breath, could feel the woman's razored probe in his guts. "Not like that." Shook his head, his mouth arid. "I like your daughter very much . . . but not like that. Trust me." He considered his words, words that didn't seem to sit right at all. Of this he had generous insight. Insight that bulged.

The woman broke her stare, gazing instead over at the girls who huddled against the vendor's cart, and grinned as the spiral whiskered chef handed the trio a bowl of noodles. She sucked heavily into her cigarette, and returned her gaze back to the man before her—watched his unease—though with eyes that seemed to sell themselves well. Achara Songpow had faith in her instincts—the reading of the eyes a well-versed skill practiced over many years. That rarely failed her.

"Okay, I trust you." The cigarette bobbed with her words. "Anyway, you tip too much for bad guy."

Emmanuel grinned, drawing back a deep breath. And watched two clouds ooze from her nose.

"You come back soon."

He exited the bar and needled his way through the swarm and back to the girls. Behind, the vendor's cart puffed a chili-flavored haze that sprinkled down and over them.

"So what's news, ladies?"

Durudee lifted her head from Lalana's shoulder. All three seemed lost in reflection.

Lalana broke the silence. "You have baby?"

Emmanuel gazed at Hom, who studied his face.

"I guess so. Yes."

"But mother not here."

"No. She is *not* here." He spoke these words severely, but no more severely than he intended.

Lalana ignored his disapproval. "You married?"

Emmanuel grimaced. "I'll do you a deal. If I answer this question, I *don't* want any more said about . . . about the past."

Lalana took the pad and scribbled some words; handed it to Hom and Durudee. All nodded in apparent agreement.

"Okay. Deal," Lalana said.

"No, I'm not married."

Durudee snatched the pad and scribbled the note to Hom. Tears welled. Durudee placed her head gently on Hom's shoulder. Then Lalana announced with conviction, "We want to play with baby."

"She is not a toy."

"She got wrong words," Durudee said. "We good baby minders."

Fractured thoughts shot from all directions through Emmanuel's mind. Alcohol's warm breath added to the confusion. Perhaps Chosita could do with a break. Perhaps.

"I mind sister's baby," Durudee said.

"I help her many times," Lalana said. "We do it for no money."

Durudee grabbed the pad and scribbled words in large print. Handed to Lalana.

"We do it for half-price," Lalana said.

Emmanuel scraped his fingers across his scalp. Hom took the pad and wrote a message, the girls hugging at each arm as she wrote. Then, with back straightened, Lalana announced,

"We do together. The three of us."

FOUR

The people die so, that now it seems they are fain to carry the dead to be buried by daylight, the nights not sufficing to do it in.

Jill closed Pepys' diary and sat alone in her own night. She looked at her translucent reflection in the glass wall, with the lights of the harbor blotching her face with yellow clumps of brightly lit freckles. She turned her head to the side a fraction—to move the spots to an ugly position, branding her face with a birthmark that burned on her cheek. And stared at this new view of herself for a while.

Her mouse chair squeaked as she stood up. She wrapped her dressing gown strap tightly and moved on through to the hallway, softly lit by little blue-white LED's evenly spaced on the skirting. She pressed the alarm button on and off, a flicker of red then green then red. She had thought about dismantling it permanently, but the power source was hidden away and was needed for the night-lights as well. So she would have to break the console, which she knew was going too far.

She walked over to the front door and opened it. Outside, the porch light threw orange into the dark. Her eyes focused through this bright to the slate path that curved a shallow incline until reaching the wooden steps that fell steeply down to the lane. Sometimes she walked out of the house and down to the top of these stairs, following the trail of the little LEDs that flanked the path like an airport landing strip at night. Sometimes she went further down to the lane itself, lit by a solitary lamppost, an old fashioned gaslight, that had been turned electric.

She closed the door and went back down the hallway, then left to follow the blue-lit way up the stairs—the plush carpet soft on her feet—and onto the landing that drew open through three doors along the wall. She went past the first and heard her Stephen's labored sleep coming loud out into the passage. They said he should have his tonsils out, but Stephen said he hated ice cream, so he preferred them in.

Jill continued down the passageway and stole into Josephine's room that was lit with hanging flowers strung from the ceiling—with mauve petals and golden eyes, some lime and carrot, sapphire and scarlet. The flowers dropped their gentle light down onto the little bed—and she stared at the colors for a bit—at the white quilt painted by the light—and the pillow too. She moved over to the window and felt the cool air rush against her skin. Josephine's bed was placed away from the window, so the air wouldn't blow over it, but during the winter the air-conditioning fought hard against the opening, even though the window was only kept up a few inches or so. Stephen and she had fought about the open window before, but her will was stronger. About this at least.

She went out and back down to the last door, which was closed. Hattie couldn't sleep with the door open. She even locked it before bedtime. Hattie was nervous at night, had been since she was a child, she had told Jill. She said she was sorry but she couldn't sleep unless it was locked. Jill understood this.

She walked back down the blue-white passage, and the plush of the stairs. Her doctor said it might be a sign of obsessive-compulsive disorder, this wandering on the same lit route every night, two or three times, sometimes more. But she didn't think so when she looked it up on the net, because it wasn't irrational, this wandering. It might not be healthy, but it wasn't irrational. It all made sense.

She returned to the long sitting room and her mouse chair that gave up a squeak—the freckled lights settling back on her face—and tilted her head so the birthmark flushed proud. She used to have a friend at school who had a great portwine stain on her face—a romantic name for something that wasn't—of dots of purple and crimson stuck all together. It couldn't be hidden even through makeup, so eventually she couldn't be bothered to hide it at all. Jill knew if she had her friend's face she wouldn't be sitting in her mouse chair this evening. And probably wouldn't be wandering in the still of the night.

She picked up Pepys' diary.

My Lord Mayor commands people to be within at 9 at night, all that the sick may have liberty to go abroad for ayre.

She shifted her gaze up from the page and back to her reflection, and turned her head again so the bright yellow birthmark from the harbor lights smoldered high on her cheek.

The day stood a clear blue murmur through the high window, the silver wake of the harbor boats etching snail trails into the distance.

"Miss?"

Hattie stood at the opening of the hallway, holding a clump of mail down by her side, her other arm stretched out with a single envelope in her hand.

Jill looked over her shoulder and saw the maid standing there and time stood still for a second or so. Hattie moved over with her arm kept outstretched, but she stopped a few steps before her mistress, to allow Jill the final move.

Jill nodded and Hattie handed her the envelope. She studied the outside, recognizing the font of the typed address, and the post-mark stamped in town, and carefully tore it open and took it out. Hattie stood back, but not too far and saw it too. And the women looked at each other with knowing eyes and time stood still for the barest of moments again.

"Do you want me to call Mr. Stephen?"

"Thanks, Hattie. If you can't reach him, I'll phone him on my way." Jill's eyes were now fixed on the contents of the envelope. She felt a brief thrill rise as she studied it more, and, without shifting her gaze from the study, hollered to Hattie who had moved away to the kitchen, "I'll take the car."

The women kept on their raised up talk from separate rooms.

"A taxi might be better, Miss, parking isn't easy around this time. Let me call one."

"You're a 49ers fan, aren't you Hattie?"

"Who isn't?"

"When did they sign Tuckson?"

"He's that new coach?"

"Might be."

"A week ago. Or around then."

"Tell the cab I'll wait out front."

"You want me to pack a sandwich for you?"

"Don't bother."

"I'll bring it outside to you, Miss. If you're already gone, I'll eat it myself."

All this yelled—an excited bellow—through the thick dividing wall.

Jill sat in the back of the taxi and stared down at the photograph. She wasn't a 49ers fan at all. Her father had taken her to a few games when she was a girl—at elementary school age. She had liked the color and the helmets and the rush of the crowd, but the stop and start of the game dragged on too long for her. Her father must have seen her eyes wander away, all asquirm on the hard plastic seat, so he kept on funneling hotdogs and ice creams and drink until her stomach ached. So they stopped going after a while. Still, she thought she had heard something about the new 49ers' coach last Wednesday or thereabouts.

When she arrived at the library it was 2pm. She paid the driver, who grinned and kept his stare long into the smile. She was used to this by now, these drawn out ogles, men nudging elbows into each other, the women just as bad, but today she didn't care much. She moved inside and took the lift to the fifth floor and over to the newspapers hanging on their timber rods. She found today's edition and began to slide the papers back further into the week—reversing time with her hand—until she found the one dated last Monday, eight days ago.

Jill sat down at the table directly opposite an old man who was reading a *Sports Illustrated*. He nodded to her and went back to his reading. She found old men rarely stared at her—which was why she sat where she did. Jill gazed down at the newspaper and briefly read about the Tuckson signing. His face was the same as in the photograph; she didn't even have to take it out of her bag and check. She confirmed the date again, eased herself back in her chair and tried to remember what she was doing on that Monday. It was a Chanel shoot, she remembered; a couple of hours with Horst—who did most of Chanel's shoots with her these days. She tried to remember what she did in the evening, what she had for dinner, but couldn't. She wondered what the old man with the magazine was doing on that day as well.

Jill turned over the pages of the newspaper, glancing at the headlines as she went. On page five she saw a photograph of the Mayor at an opening for a bronze statue of Herb Caen. It was in Washington Square Park because the twin steeples of the Cathedral jutted ornate into the skyline behind. Stephen—both Old Gray and hers—knew the Mayor, and her father had known Herb Caen. She remembered him coming over to dinner on occasion; around the same time she had been to the 49ers' games. She remembered listening in bed to the sounds of their laughter, remembered them swearing a lot, probably drinking a lot, and taking turns at reading some poetry or something like that. And when he died her father said that the city could still see, but had lost its voice.

She read the story to confirm that the opening of the statue had happened on the Monday—eight days ago. And she saw herself and her Stephen and her Josephine all sitting in the park on a checkerboard rug, her father and Old Gray chatting with the Mayor in front of the statue of Mr. Caen, and her Stephen lifting Josephine up in the air, waving her around like an airplane, with the zoom sound effects whooshing from his lips.

And she saw and heard all of this, because she knew it could have been true.

FIVE

"You pay one month in advance. Every month." The man stood with hands on his hips; a thick bracelet of gold dangled; a bulbous sapphire ring squeezed his plump finger. "Okay?"

Emmanuel surveyed the room. It was freshly painted, yet failed to conceal the blistered paint of rising damp. A small bed with a plain spread was in one corner, an unstained pine dressing cupboard opposite. The kitchen was small, but functional.

"Can fit little table. I organize for you."

Against one wall Hom stood next to her brother. Since entering, the brother had only occasionally lifted his eyes to catch glimpses of the room, as his pulse and breath quickened in waves of unease. He had soaped dirt away from all exposed skin, wore a new shirt and shorts, and smelled the smell of the cleansed—yet remained subordinate throughout. He couldn't risk failure.

Emmanuel eyed Hom to seek her brother's approval. She tugged at his shirt and communicated with fingers to palm, the sapphire man looking on with a blank expression. Then her brother, with head still bowed, raised his eyes to Emmanuel and nodded. A hint of a smile flickered.

"Okay. How you like to pay? Can organize bank transfer, but cash easier." The sapphire man grinned.

"Then cash it is."

"How long you need room? Might make a special deal if you long stay."

Emmanuel looked at Hom and her brother. She was beaming, her brother stealing longer glimpses at the kitchen.

The sapphire man held out his hand to conclude the deal. As they shook hands, Emmanuel felt the calm rising inside of him. It was about time he did something good in his life.

The men sat facing each other on a small table set for two. Assorted plates of dumplings steamed in baskets of woven bamboo.

"It's great to be here, Emmanuel," Arthur said. "Just the two of us. I like Hom though. Like her a lot. But it's great to be here. Just us." He looked up, with shining eyes.

Emmanuel nodded, sipping his tea.

"This reminds me of the first time we met, Emmanuel. Remember?"

"Yes, Arthur."

"The banquet. A minimum for two people they said. You sat on the next table . . . by yourself. Just like me."

Emmanuel smiled.

"I bet you can't remember what we ate. I bet you can't."

"You've got me there."

"Try and remember, Emmanuel. Try."

"It was some time ago, now, Arthur."

"What type of soup? Go on try. I bet you can't remember."

"I've got a terrible memory, you know that."

"Shark fin. God I thought you would remember. Shark fin it was."

Emmanuel nodded.

"Ten dishes there were. Shark fin soup, san choy bou, prawn toast . . . "

"What's san choy bou?"

"A lettuce wrap, with pork usually. Ours was pork." Arthur interrupted his chatter by swallowing a dumpling with a single chew, and wiped away its juice from the corner of his mouth.

"Just think, Emmanuel, if you weren't starving, or didn't like Chinese food, we may never have met. I can't imagine if we hadn't met,

Emmanuel. Can you imagine?" he said in a whisper, the voice softened to enhance the intimacy.

Emmanuel smiled.

"Try those gyoza, they're the best. I've left them for you, Emmanuel. Go on, try them."

The waiter moved to their table and poured the tea, the close attention made easier with only a few tables occupied. As the waiter moved out of earshot, Arthur moved forward and beamed at his friend.

"Just think about it, Emmanuel! What would we be doing now . . . both you and I . . . if we had never met at that Chinese restaurant in America?"

Emmanuel stared vacantly through his vast companion. He rubbed at his eyes, unable to hide tired musings, and crept into his invisible shell— a thick ribbed breastplate that wrapped easily around. And stayed there.

Chosita's toothless grin radiated as Durudee tied the last band in the baby's scalp. Upright tufted fingers of ginger hair sprang up like mini antennae.

"Isn't Princess beautiful?" Durudee said. "I wish I had red hair like hers. And look at her big blue eyes . . . just like a doll's."

Lalana bent down and kissed the baby's cheeks, then looked up toward Chosita, who gave final instructions before departing. For the last couple of days, the old woman had finally trusted them enough to leave the baby without feelings of anxiety. She bowed to the spirit house that perhaps had granted her wish, then left to visit her sister, planning only to return by the early evening.

The girls sat together in the wet heat.

"How many babies are you going to have?" Durudee said.

"Not sure."

Durudee wrote the question on the pad and pushed it toward Hom, who lowered her eyes.

"Why are you asking so many questions?" Lalana said.

"You lot are no fun." She lay down on the bed—a single mattress that slumped directly on worn floorboards in one corner of the room. The balcony doors were flung open, allowing entry of heavy air and the occasional shouts of neighbors. In the communal space below, clothes hung, brooms scraped, bikes lay in disrepair and the approaching midday sun sweltered.

"Well, I'm having three," Durudee said. "I love babies."

"With three different husbands probably," Lalana said.

Durudee poked her tongue out at her friend. Hom looked on, then pushed the notepad to her companion. Durudee snatched it to examine the message. "Two. Very nice." She smiled at Hom, then wrote a message back. Hom read the note and blushed in a deep shade of crimson.

"What did you write?" Lalana asked.

"Does two include Princess?" Durudee grinned, and faced the baby held in Lalana's arms. "Is Princess hungry?" she cooed. "Does Princess want Aunty Durudee to give her some nice apple juice?"

"I might have no children," Lalana said softly.

Durudee flipped over on the mattress, her chin cupped in her palms, and examined her friend. "How can you say that while holding such a beautiful baby? Don't listen, Princess. Don't listen to naughty Aunty Lalana." Screams from a neighbor's toddler invaded the calm. "Listen to that naughty baby. Princess never cries." She sat up and moved to the basket that sat shaded from the direct sunlight. Poured some juice into a bottle, then sucked the teat briefly.

"Why do you always lick it before?"

"To clean it before giving to my Princess," Durudee cooed.

"Give the bottle to Hom. It's her turn."

"I made up the bottle."

"It's her turn. And she should practice more with the baby."

Durudee grudgingly obeyed her friend's command. Hom moved over to the baby and kneeled before her, tenderly stroking folds of plump skin, kissing little fingers, little toes. The baby responded with giggles.

Hom gently lifted Princess off Lalana's lap and cradled her in a warm bed of arms, trunk, and thighs; she found the warm juice eagerly.

The girls waded in the serene, only interrupted by the screaming toddler in the courtyard below. Hom kissed the baby's forehead while the drink bubbled down.

"Princess . . . your new mummy really loves you," Lalana whispered.

"Why Switzerland, Ronnie?" Arthur said.

"Because you can open an account there by number. No name is connected, at least for transactions. And there is no limit on the amount of cash you can bring into Switzerland, although getting it out of the country can sometimes be tricky."

"The country?"

"Thailand. Can't take much cash out of the country, certainly not in the quantities you're talking. But there are a few tricks. And when you take out cash from the bank, no personal records are kept of your transactions—at least, not if it's done directly at the bank in Switzerland."

"Perfect, Ronnie, perfect. What about the diamonds?"

"Easy. You just need to open a safety deposit box with the same bank." Ronnie gulped more champagne. "You know, diamonds are the perfect commodity for this. Small, individually packaged, and worth a fucking fortune. When you need some money, sell a few."

Arthur slouched back in his chair, exhaling stale air mixed with Bollinger.

"You just need to make sure you open an account that has no branches in your country of residency, either the UK or Bangkok, as you like." Ronnie emptied his glass and twisted his neck to scan the few occupants of Angelini's bar. "But you do need to have some proof that the cash is legitimate."

Arthur's shoulders slumped. "Legitimate!"

"A bit louder next time, my boy . . . some of the people on that ferry didn't hear you."

"Sorry, Ronnie, sorry. But *legitimate*, Ronnie."

"You need to have a business. A real business. With proof of real transactions." He eyed the waiter, who refilled both glasses.

"Another bottle, sir?"

"Maybe later."

When the waiter was out of earshot, Arthur said, "I don't have a *real* business."

"Then perhaps I can be of assistance? There is always a way, my boy. Always a way."

"Oh, Ronnie, you're a real pal."

"For a minor commission, of course."

"Of course, Ronnie. Of course."

Both men nestled back in their lounges, flutes in hand. Sweat seeped from skin attempting relief from the wet air.

Ronnie swallowed a larger mouthful of champagne. "I might have a buyer for a couple of the stones."

Arthur sat upright, spilling champagne on his pineapple shirt.

"Even with my agreed commission, you should come out pretty much as planned."

Arthur's bulbous face developed tinges of violet—breath-holding an unfortunate habit of his when excitement lacked an escape. He glared at Ronnie without sound, then sucked air, restoring color to his cheeks. "How much, Ronnie?"

The snow-haired man scanned for eavesdroppers, then whispered, "Two hundred, my boy. Two hundred."

Emmanuel propped himself up against the cushions. Hom lay next to him, prone, baking bronzed flesh. Two children flashed past, plunging with bended knees into the pool. Emmanuel finished his Coke and cooled his chest with dribbling ice cubes, then focused on his two friends' cozy chatter at Angelini's. From the serendipitous position of potted palms, he remained concealed from both, but saw Arthur squawking in excitement, saw him spill his champagne, saw him wrapping his arms around Ronnie, saw the unrestrained joy in both men's faces.

Emmanuel adjusted the deck chair to its horizontal position. And closed his eyes.

Durudee switched the fan to full speed and directed the cool to the sleeping baby.

"She'll catch cold," Lalana said.

"Babies get too hot, and she has a sheet over her." She moved over to fully cover their beloved, who slept at one end of the corner mattress. "This is the best job we've had . . . and good money, too. Shame we'll have to go back to school soon."

"I miss school," Lalana said.

"That's because you're smart."

Lalana scanned the room. "This place isn't that great."

"It's okay . . . but it's too hot."

"And noisy."

"Where isn't it noisy? This isn't so bad. You're lucky you live on the klong. My place has much more noise."

"That's because you live above a shop." Lalana hesitated, unwilling to voice the question. "Why doesn't he take Princess to the Shangri-La?"

"Where would Chosita live?"

Lalana moved over to the mattress and lay next to the baby. Through the open balcony doors, the defiant shouts of children's games barked loud from the courtyard below. "Chosita could look after Princess during the day, then leave her overnight with them."

"I guess so, but he goes out at night. Remember?" Durudee grinned, catching her friend's gaze. She moved over to sit at the foot of the mattress, her back resting against the wall. "Did you tell Hom what I saw?"

Lalana lifted herself gently from the bed and lay with her head pillowed in her friend's lap. "No. She doesn't need to know."

"Wouldn't you want to know?" Durudee said, stroking Lalana's crown. She took out the hair band, releasing tufts that danced from the fan's breeze, gently moved them from her forehead, cheeks, lids.

"You don't know what happened. If you knew for certain, I might tell, but you don't."

"I guess so. But I still would want to know if my boyfriend liked boys."

"Kathoey, not boys. Anyway, you said he was beautiful. Emmanuel might not have known he was a ladyboy."

Durudee continued stroking Lalana's hair. She understood the mixed feelings Lalana was developing for Emmanuel, understood her negative feelings against all farang. All men.

"I like him, and your mum likes him," Durudee said softly. "But if he did like boys . . . what would you do . . . if you were Hom?"

"What do you think!"

Durudee smiled at Lalana while carefully twisting her hair into a neat plait. "Mai likes Alak, even though Alak's younger sister caught him sucking his cousin in their bathroom."

"Does Mai know this?"

"Of course she does. Everyone knows it. His sister made him do it again in front of her. Told him she would tell everyone if he didn't."

Lalana raised a heavy sigh. "Well, Mai is not going to marry Alak, and she likes all boys, even Tai, who stinks more than the toilets at the Plaza."

Both girls muted their giggles with the sleeping Princess so near.

"How do you know Hom will marry Emmanuel?" Durudee said.

"He bought her brother a place to stay. Even farang don't do that for just a girlfriend."

Durudee finished the twisted plait and inspected it for flaws, then gently lifted another mound of ink black hair to repeat the process. Lalana purred.

"I like Alak too," Durudee said coyly.

Lalana flipped over on her abdomen, the baby rising with a wave in the mattress.

"Careful . . . you'll wake her," Durudee whispered.

"Even though he sucked his cousin's dick?"

Durudee shrugged. "He makes me laugh."

"*You* make me laugh."

Durudee pulled at her friend's hair, inducing a playful squeal, then wrapped her arms over Lalana's shoulders to position her head back to her lap, gently wiping a bead of sweat from her upper lip.

"Tell me about the purple daisy field again," Durudee said.

"Only if you'll come too." She closed her eyes, waiting for a response.

Durudee committed with a gentle kiss on her forehead.

"There are only small villages around," Lalana said. "But you can live in the fields, in cute little wooden huts."

"Where do you buy food?"

"In the village. You can stock up and store for at least a month. These huts always have big storerooms. In the winter, it might snow. Can you imagine? We will have snowball fights, then come in and sit by the fire to warm up. We can take turns cooking. Fishing in the lake in summer. And it never gets hot. Never."

"How do we get money to buy the food, to pay for the house?"

"The same way other people do in those villages. We work like the others."

Durudee grinned. "Our husbands can do the work, while we look after the house . . . and the babies."

Lalana giggled. "Yeah, and they'll be at work while we play."

"What will your husband be like?" Durudee said. "Mine will be strong, with big muscles, handsome of course, sporty, doesn't have to be too smart, funny, laughs a lot, likes babies—loves babies—not lazy, taller than me, but not too tall . . . and loves me more than anyone in the entire world." She flopped a spiraled plait down. "What about you?"

The screaming toddler bellowed in the heat beyond as Lalana pondered the question—but not for long.

"Gentle . . . he has to be gentle."

Händel's *Ombra mai fu* resonated from within the dimly lit room; the tenor's sweet voice dancing amongst the shadows.

He took the sheets off his bed, first the top, then the fastened bottom that shed easily from the mattress; unfolded a clear plastic sheet and spread it over the base, patting down the dimpled folds to flatten the creases, sliding the pulps of his fingers over its clean surface. Unsoiled for now. He lifted the mattress with ease and tucked in each side of the plastic as best he could. Then replaced the cotton cover over the wrapped base leaving the top sheet discarded on the floor—and sat at one edge of the bed, arching his shoulders down to bring his chin near to chest—waiting—while Plácido Domingo crooned.

In time a knock on the door. She entered cautiously through the door left ajar with a shoe wedged between it and the frame. As the door retreated back, a sliver of light shone through, slicing the darkened room in two. The air sat still and heavy.

The woman peered at the man slumped on the bed's edge. As he tilted his head toward her she held her breath. *Fuck, what place is this? What place?*—and remained at the door's entrance, clutching her handbag with knuckles stretched taut; her short skirt riding high on wispy thighs—white panties clearly visible from the man's sunken position; who beckoned with a hand for her to loom deeper into the room.

She curled her spine toward the door, weighing up her options, then curled back to face him.

"Money first," she said.

He shook his head—slow, pendulous.

"Money first . . . I go."

The man peered into her eyes as she sucked in stale air. "You know what I like?"

She knew.

"Money first."

He lifted himself from the bed and moved over to a writing desk. From the top draw he took a roll of cash fastened with an elastic band, and handed it to her.

She slowly counted the baht. "Need more. One thousand more."

"After you do what I like. *After.*"

She glanced around the room, then back to her client who hovered close. A waft of liquor leaked from the man. "Show me money."

He moved back to the desk and displayed another roll, yet quickly tucked it back in place. And closed the drawer.

"You know what I like," he said.

The girl moved to the door, bent down, and squeezed the wedged shoe away from the frame, the blade of light extinguished with the closing door; the room now painted with barely formed gray outlines. She ventured closer to the man and pushed softly into his chest; controlling his gentle descent onto the bed, a plastic sheet scrunching under the cotton cover. He lay flat, facing her, as she peeled his shorts away—displaying naked flesh that hungered limply.

"You know what I like!"

She took her handbag and unbuckled the latch, removing a large bottle of oil, and rummaged further producing a bouquet of latex gloves, spongy-fingered petals blooming.

"No gloves!"

She fastened her gaze at the sprawled man lay bare, she now buoyed by a fleeting whiff of domination. Yet only fleeting.

"If no glove, will cost thousand more."

The man bit his lip, yet nodded. She will earn it, he thought. She will earn it.

The dark shadows snaked coyly on the bed; jostled warily at first. He flexed one hip, then the other, lifting his legs high with bended knees that arced towards his chest, holding them in place with locked wrists. She took the bottle and twisted the cap, pouring oil over his buttocks and hole. Inserted one finger slowly, then another.

Then another. And more.

Inch by inch she moved deeper inside him, misshaped wanderings greased further within, his rim now pouting at her wrist; then twisted her neck violently away from the soiled ooze that caked her forearm and gagged aloud, a pool of saliva rising in her mouth.

The man released one arm from behind his knee and folded his pillow to increase its bulk—his raised head now settling to an easy view of the scene. He squinted to fine tune his focus on the girl's eyes and lips—before bearing down his load that splattered out.

"Fuck." Hurled vomitus sprayed from her neck onto the bed.

"You know what I like . . ." he softly murmured.

He repeated the words, now with closed eyes.

His thoughts meandered away, drifted on a tortuous path of branching rivulets, flashing faces surfaced from below, swatted away, yet soon replaced by others, laughing heads, swatted away, *keep them away,* children's laughing heads, always back there, these freckle-faced poltergeists of pigtails with bright ribbons, white teeth bared with ruddy gums. He saw them all, as despair struck its heavy blow down.

"You know what I like."

The mantra now lost of all meaning.

The girl wiped away the sick from her mouth with one hand, the other still inside him. A shallow puddle of vomit settled near her knee, fashioned by the plastic under-sheet. And infusing the ashen silhouettes of the dimly lit room, Händel's aria continued to swell within the stench.

The sheet soaked in the bath, tainted bubbles frothing at the murky surface, leaving a bronze scum on the tub's enamel. His hands, squeezed tight in yellow gloves, smarted within the steaming water, as he released the plug that gurgled the brown liquid down. He replaced the plug, and turned the faucet to repeat the chore—the rising tide now fading to the color of straw; an acrid perfume floating high—as Luciano Pavarotti performed his arioso.

Care selve . . . sunk his gloved hands below the froth,

ombre beate . . . closed his eyes,

vengo in traccia . . . the acrid steam dripping from his face,

del mio cor . . . and thought:

Oh, what if I could sing like you then? Then my life would make sense. He straightened his back, pinching at a tight muscle near his loin, and looked at his own image reflected from the bathroom mirror. *Oh, how I would make sense then.*

He turned off the tap and squirted more detergent into the swill before struggling to raise himself up from the floor, tile marks the size of postage stamps now etched into both knees. After repeating the process twice more—the sluice now cloudless—he stretched the sheet over the bedhead to dry slowly in the tepid air.

And, in time, just before retiring to bed, he lifted the now dry cotton and scrunched the sheet into his face, sniffing deeply—and found a faint trace of feces—the scent of daisies—that stubbornly lingered.

And probably for the best, he thought. Probably for the best.

The shop's front room was small. On both sides, a library of folded fabrics hung on the walls; blends of linen, cotton, silk, wool both cashmere and Italian, in traditional tones of washed charcoal, olive, and chocolate; pinstripe, plaid, and check.

"Take your time, sir."

Arthur flicked through the pages of the catalogue, others discarded at his feet. "Help me, Ronnie."

"We need to make him look classy, Mr. Tam. The businessman. A banker perhaps. Savile Row." He broke into a cockney accent. "You know what I mean?"

"I suggest a double-breasted suit, sir. Perhaps a dark gray. Where will you be wearing the suit? England?"

"Switzerland."

"Something warm, then." He moved over and fossicked through the folds of textiles, unraveling one with a nod. "Like this—cream pinstripe on gray, wide and thin; always in fashion and traditional."

"I don't know. What do you think, Ronnie?"

"I like it. I might get one myself. Although, just single-breasted for me. That Versace cut. You know my style, Mr. Tam."

The tailor nodded. "Some shirts, sir?"

"Yes," Arthur said. "Two should be plenty."

"He's a light packer." Ronnie winked. "Now, have you got a tape measure big enough for my boy, Mr. Tam?"

"Don't, Ronnie . . . don't!" The final decibel was almost inaudible.

"Settle down . . . you're so touchy of late. A couple of silk shirts, Mr. Tam. Cream perhaps, to match the pin stripe. We can choose some ties with the final fitting, although I think that pink tie would look very dapper. Very dapper indeed." Ronnie moved over to the door. "Now, you finish up here and meet me back at Angelini's in a few hours. I need to run some errands." And he left without waiting for a response.

"Okay, sir. I take measurement now."

Arthur repositioned his iPod earpiece and shuffled behind the screen; the tailor some steps behind with his dangling tape-measure necklace.

"Take off shorts please."

Arthur struggled with the task of removing his ballooned pants while juggling to keeping his iPod in function.

"You like rock band, sir?"

Arthur fumbled to catch a falling earpiece; the small space became bathed in music.

"Oh . . . opera, sir. Very nice. Very nice."

The tray tapered from its point, fanning down in gradually expanding tiers to a broad base garnished with macaroons, tiny cups of chocolate mousse, finger sandwiches of cucumber, tuna and prawn, scones with rose petal jam and cream dollops, sweet mince pies with castor sugar sweating in beads on soft pastry—all draped like baubles on a Christmas tree. A large pot of tea sat nearby.

"How will we eat all of this?"

"Don't worry, Emmanuel." Arthur grinned. "It won't go to waste."

They sat within the lobby lounge, a cool reprieve from the midday furnace that scorched beyond the floor-to-ceiling glass. Other tables were splattered with patrons leaning as well over tree-layered trays—High-Tea at the Shangri-La.

Arthur poured the tea into both cups. "I'll be Mum."

Emmanuel studied his wide-eyed friend, whose excitement touched him.

"You can have the tempura prawns, Emmanuel. I know you love prawns. I'll stick with the sweets . . . I'll . . ."

"Have you had many girlfriends, Arthur?" he interrupted, though softly.

Arthur lowered his head to his plate, began swirling a pattern with his finger in the cream covered scone. "Nah . . . Who'd have me, hey? Who'd be that stupid?"

"What about in Bangkok. Ever had a girlfriend?"

"Nah . . . Girls the same here as back home . . . all the same."

Emmanuel took one of the prawns from the tray. "Things might change now?"

"Might. Probably won't." He bit into the scone, teeth marks scalloping a large cove in the pastry.

"Have you ever tried to lose weight?"

"Yeah . . . did once. More than two stone. Couldn't keep it off . . . couldn't." He studied the morsel-gilded table, and grinned. "You see, I love my food . . . love it."

He smiled. "I've noticed."

"Perhaps I could try again though. But not until we finish all of this!"

Arthur took a mince pie from the table, and picked at the folded lip at the pie's edge. He took a small wedge, nibbling it away.

"Emmanuel, can I ask you something?" He waited for approval, which was offered with a nod, and gazed into his friend's eyes. "Do you believe in God?"

"Why do you ask?"

"Just wondered."

Emmanuel took another prawn from the tray, dunked it into the tempura sauce, then devoured half in one bite. Wiped his mouth with his napkin. "Shit, Arthur, I reckon I'd be fucked if I did." And consumed the remainder of the prawn as the waiter poured more tea. "What about you?"

"Well I'm fucked already, hey . . . fucked already."

At mid-evening, he kissed her sweetly on the lips, then lifted the cotton sheet over her naked body—like a child, she thought—and moved to the entrance, departing without noise. Always without noise. Her heart pounded with the closing door, she could feel it tapping on her ribs. Usually the panic drifted away after a short while, but on this night, her empty needed mending.

He was kind. He gave the beggars money—more than most—gave the girls both money and time. He gave her brother more than that; gave him hope.

He was soft. Soft with their lovemaking, his hands like the skin of her cheeks. She loved to hold his hand, when they walked or sat or lay.

He cared for her. She had not been cared for by many before—cared for with clean and pretty clothing, with food that heaped on plates, with shelter away from the hot. Out of harm's way.

He was handsome. She liked his height, thin legs, arms, chest; liked his long nose and soft brown hair.

He was happy. He smiled when watching her eat; laughed at her open mouth of lunch; smiled at the dance house; smiled with his friends.

She loved him.

Bathed in the blonde glow of the softly lit room, her pulse settled. She switched on the television, scanning through the channels, but the visions now tired rather than amused. She liked the animals, birds, insects, yet rarely found them; the painted vistas of cartooned monsters, grimacing cats and dogs and mice and fat-cheeked boys suffering—all floundered within an ether of declining interest, scenes of unintelligible farang in blue suits and red ties, the silent mouths of almond eyes just as meaningless. And always silent.

She tossed the television control aside and moved to the door, pressing the *Do Not Disturb* button. Then moved to the bathroom, turning both faucets to full flow; added the bubble lotion that frothed its welcome warm. She could—would—spend hours submerged, wrinkling skin, though seemingly never clean. Spent hours baking her flesh by day, deep fawn and oiled, then gave moisture back at night. And entered the bath.

She loved him.

Her pulse quickened, then breath; soon tingling of fingers, toes, lips. She swatted the froth away from her face, and dunked her head down beneath the shallows.

He was selfish. She could smell them on him. Smell their perfume, their juice, their sex. He was selfish. Left her alone at night, in darkness. He was selfish. Left the baby, his Princess, his flesh—unloved. He was selfish. Came back late sweating alcohol on skin, lips, and breath. He was selfish.

She mopped her face with the warm, dripping cloth, massaged under eyes, over temples, forehead; added more water with swelling steam, bubbles rising into mountains that hovered down. And sighed.

She gave him her love. She gave him her heart. But when could she give him her hurt—hurt that sucked her breath away? When could she give him her pain?

He was selfish.

Arthur waddled around the sticky room. Chosita, having just tested the temperature of the bathwater, began to peel a jumpsuit off Princess's skin, while nearby, Lalana and Durudee slumped on the bare mattress and followed the man's footsteps with stabbing eyes.

"You sure he can't understand Thai?" Durudee whispered.

"None of them can. Even Emmanuel can't remember the simple words I've taught him."

"You would think they'd make an effort and learn some Thai. We learnt English."

"Yeah, they're lazy. Emmanuel as well."

"Let's do a test." Durudee sat upright, faced her friend, yet kept her slantwise gaze on Arthur. "Would you like some food, fat man?"

The girls held their breath—yet he remained unmoved, facing away at the open balcony doors, watching a washerwoman hang clothes in the courtyard below. Both teens strained to mute their giggles while Chosita, having just placed the baby in the tepid pool, aimed a scowl in the girls' direction—restoring order.

"Why is he always here?" Durudee asked.

"He's Emmanuel's friend."

"Still, it's strange. He's here more than Emmanuel . . . and he gives me the creeps."

"He's all right. He brought money for Princess." She pointed to the bulging envelope nested in the spirit house.

"Why didn't Emmanuel bring it?"

"I guess he wants to spend more time with Hom."

Durudee poked at her friend's thigh and pointed to a large paper carry-bag placed against the opposite wall. "What does he do with that old camera in the bag? He had it out before you came and took a picture of a newspaper on the mattress. I swear, if Chosita wasn't around, I would have run off. He is *so* creepy."

Arthur took out both iPod earpieces from the pocket of his shorts and squeezed them into his ears; flicked away sweat that dripped from his brow. He fumbled with the controls as he twisted his neck to stare at the girls. As their gaze met his, he lowered his eyes and quickly turned away, again to face the courtyard scene. Durudee poked her tongue out at the man's back, and, with a feigned shudder, continued without lowering her voice.

"And how can anyone eat so much? If I took a pin to him, I'm sure he would burst!"

Chosita again directed a grimace toward the girls.

"Sorry, Aunty," Durudee said; 'Aunty' being the new pet name for the old woman; and resumed the chat, now with barely audible whisperings.

"Could you imagine being *his* girlfriend?"

Lalana's gaze moved back towards the man's bulk. "He's okay, I think. He just seems a bit lonely to me."

The inside restaurant at Angelini's was another oasis within the Shangri-La; two open floors, layered like a rice field, connected by a central staircase. Crystal goblets sparkled on tables spaced for intimacy, chairs of soft cream cotton comforted, and all surrounded by surfaces of polished chocolate, beige, and brass; bathed in dry and cool air.

The three sat on a table set for four. Hom rested her hand on Emmanuel's thigh; Ronnie studied the menu of Italian fare.

"I feel like some veal tonight," Ronnie said.

"Your recipe or theirs?"

He peered over his spectacles. "You're getting cheeky, my boy."

"You look quite distinguished in those glasses."

"And when do I not?" Ronnie grinned, then pulled his spectacles to the tip of his nose and focused some distance behind Emmanuel and Hom. "And speaking of distinguished . . . I think Yves Saint Lauren is back in town."

Arthur moved slowly, with a beam broad and fixed. The gray pinstriped jacket of cashmere sat comfortably, adorned with a pink polka dot kerchief of silk and matching tie. Pristine black Italian leather shoes, yet to yield to his bulbous feet, pinched with each step, though the ache was anaesthetized by the rest of the splendid vision. He glanced at seated customers to compare attire, glanced at their faces to seek some response, with head held high. And approached the table.

Emmanuel twisted his neck to watch Arthur's parade, and greeted his friend by standing with an outstretched hand. "You look fantastic. Unbelievable."

"Mr. Tam has done the job," Ronnie said, still seated. "Sit down, my friend."

"Can I take your jacket, sir?" the waiter said.

"No . . . no . . . I think that's okay." Arthur looked at Ronnie for approval.

"Eat with the jacket on. I want to dine with the full ensemble."

Arthur squeezed into his seat and adjusted his jacket that resisted the move. When he was settled, Hom gave him a smile and issued an appreciative grunt, inducing the ballooned head into a staccato of shy shallow nods; his broad grin a glued appendage stuck to freshly-shaven cheeks.

"A bottle of the very best to celebrate," Ronnie said. "The butterfly has transformed from the greedy grub."

Emmanuel glared at Ronnie with censuring eyes. Arthur seemingly ignored the quip.

"What to drink?" Ronnie scanned the menu, though knew the wine list by heart. "Perhaps Italian would be most appropriate. If everyone is having meat, I might suggest the Brunello di Montalcino. You can't do much better than that." And beckoned to the waiter. "The Brunello thanks . . . and can you give it a good double decant?"

The waiter nodded without completely understanding the request; practice had taught him to nod to Ronnie's multitude of demands and ask questions later, as necessity dictated.

"You remember, Ronnie," Arthur whispered. "Remember?"

"Yes, yes. Tonight our friend wishes, if I could borrow an expression from Emmanuel, to shout us dinner."

Arthur sat tall in his chair.

"Thanks, mate," Emmanuel said.

"More slang from the colonies, hey, Arthur."

Emmanuel scribbled some symbols, and, with the addition of hand gestures, indicated to Hom the benefactor of the evening's meal. She reached over to touch Arthur's paw. His gaze lifted to meet hers, as both smiled. And throughout the feast of three courses and copious wine, they flourished—even Hom, with alcohol's encouragement, joined in the banter through quickly penned sketches. Laughed to experiences shared of old, titillations new, and futures planned.

"I'll tell you all a funny story," Ronnie said. "Before I arrived here I had been travelling in China. My first. Managed to get to Tibet . . . it's bloody high up there. Anyway, I had been travelling around the touristy sites, getting no action, and found this blind massage joint in Lhasa." Ronnie propped himself up on his chair, leaned forward, and reduced his speech almost to a whisper. "So I get the oil massage, at a good price, from this blind woman . . . mid forties, absolutely professional, and bloody good. She's massaging away, managing not to bump into the furniture, and is working on my thighs. I'm lying face up. I had this towel over me, small, like a tea towel, and I don't know whether it was the altitude, but I got massively horny . . . even for me. She's rubbing on my thighs, absolutely professional . . . no hint of hanky panky . . . and I've got this rock hard stiffy under the towel. But she's blind and has no idea." Ronnie turned briefly, confirming they had no eavesdroppers. "And I'm lying there, starting to feel this heat in my cheeks, realizing I'm going to cum. I couldn't believe it! I start thinking about anything to stop the impending bloody flow . . . mother breast feeding, parish priest mid-sermon, my old sports master caning me. But I couldn't stop it . . . and I came in the fucking towel!"

"This could only happen to you," Emmanuel said with a beam.

"Anyway... she doesn't have a clue about it... just keeps massaging away, and when she moves to my feet, I start to wipe the cum up with the towel. At the end, she starts wiping the oil off my skin with this bloody cum soaked tea-towel. I start getting the giggles... and she thinks I'm a fucking fruit cake." Ronnie leaned even closer, hugging his table of friends. "And the climax to this little anecdote, pardon the pun,... as I'm leaving, I notice she's folding the towel in a nice neat little square at the foot of the bed. Ready for the next customer!"

The boys erupted; squeezing restrained laughter to muted whimpers.

"I'm surprised you went to Tibet, Ronnie," Emmanuel said with a grin.

"Do you doubt that I have a spiritual side?" He chuckled. "But I can find my spiritual side in old Bangkok, if the need arises." He lifted his head, gazing at the ceiling. "You know something, I can't say I want to be anywhere but in this town with all of you."

"Me, too, Ronnie, me too," Arthur said.

"To best of friends," Ronnie raised a toast. Glasses clinked. "You know something else?" He wiped his lips of crimson grape. "I hadn't had the best of years, before coming to Bangkok. Had a bit of a stint with the old suicide watch, back home in sunny Blackpool."

Silence enveloped the table. Hom sensed unease in the eyes of the others.

Ronnie noted it. "This poor beautiful girl can't understand what I'm so gloomy about. Pass me that pad, my boy." He penned carefully on its surface, then pushed the pad back to Hom; her puzzled frown rising from the neatly-drawn stick man hanging from a noose.

Ronnie pointed to himself and said with a cheerful note, "It was me."

Emmanuel leaned forward with elbows resting on the granite table. Arthur's gaze never left Ronnie's eyes. All were silent.

"But feel like a million dollars now." He smiled, bearing teeth stained with clinging tannins. "The girls here... all just for a bit of a laugh, really. Not sure of their medicinal qualities though, but damn good fun."

His slurred utterances were slow and deliberate. "No doubt about it . . . damn good fun."

The waiter moved to the table and placed the evening's bill in front of Ronnie.

"Thao rai?" Arthur bellowed.

The waiter apologized and handed him the docket. Arthur glanced at the bill's total, and then delivered slurred words, "Lot r aa-khaa nawy dai mai?" His request to reduce the price remaining hidden from his companions. The waiter shook his head, and gave a carefully crafted apology, also in Thai. Arthur took his wallet from the inside pocket of his jacket, and settled the account in cash; the transaction hidden below the table's surface.

"You speak like a bloody local, my boy," Ronnie said. "Better every year. I myself haven't learnt a word. Anyway, it's probably best that I don't understand what some of these women say to me."

"Since when do you read the *San Francisco Chronicle*?" Ronnie asked.

Emmanuel turned his head to gaze at Arthur, who quickly tucked the newspaper under his arm. He removed the iPod earpiece nervously, squeezing it within the pocket of his black shorts.

"I might move there, Ronnie," Arthur said.

"To San Francisco? Do you have family there?"

"No family, Ronnie. I like the people, Ronnie. I like . . ." He paused, frowning.

"Yes . . . spit it out."

"I like everything about it, Ronnie. Everything about it."

"It's bloody expensive."

"Haven't decided yet, Ronnie. Just thinking."

"Well, to each his own. I saw you more as a Bangkok boy, myself. But you're always full of surprises."

"Surprises. Yes, Ronnie."

"There's more of that opera music you love there, I suppose."

"Yes, Ronnie. None here, Ronnie . . . none."

But for the three men, Angelini's outside bar would be unoccupied, with the promised relief from the sticky heat of the day yet to arrive. Ronnie, glowing pink from a lengthy poolside soak, slumped in shorts and singlet. Arthur in conventional black garb.

"But you're going to need a bloody lot of opera to fill in those lonely nights, my boy. None of the nocturnal delicacies found here. Unless you get a taste for the boys, that is." He grinned.

"Yes—true, Ronnie."

"What? You've developed a taste for the boys, my chubby penguin?"

"No, Ronnie, not the boys."

Ronnie lifted a cube of ice from his empty glass and caressed his sweating forehead. "Mind you, you're not actually in a desert here, if you're that way inclined. The whole silk industry of Thailand probably wouldn't exist if it wasn't for the boy talent around this place." Icy water dripped over lids onto warm cheeks. "But if you like the hairy boys, then San Francisco is the place, not Bangkok." He chuckled. "You have a taste for the hairy bears, my boy?"

"No, Ronnie . . . no taste for the hairy boys."

Ronnie eased himself off his chair and arched his back. "Well, I'm off. I might squeeze in a foot massage before dinner. I'll catch you lads later." He climbed over a pot-plant and followed the path inside the hotel.

Emmanuel's gaze remained fixed on Arthur, whose beads of sweat funneled onto his chin, some drops finding an escape into his water glass that finely trembled.

"You been here long time, Mr. Ronnie. You like Bangkok?"

No reply.

"You tired today, hey. Just relax. You want tea?"

No reply.

She rubbed the oil into his calf, kneading softened muscle and sinew. He lay fully reclined on the chair of imitation leather. Eyes closed.

"You not chatty today. No problem. You sleep."

She gently lifted his extended leg, then let gravity settle his foot slowly to the floor. Placed the other foot into the bowl of liquid, caressing his dangling limb with the warm washcloth. Then lifted the soaked leg slowly to her lap, and softly dried the pampered flesh, encircling each toe, under arch, heel, tenderly rubbing leg hairs up to knee.

She spoke softly to her colleague, who brought him a small cup of green tea. She pumped the oil into her hand and began again, kneading flesh that greedily drank the unguent warmed by her palm, and conversed with her colleague throughout; soft murmurings hypnotizing, drifting him into another space, away from intrusive thoughts of sadness and doubt. Away.

The hour passed too quickly. Ronnie slipped on his sandals and sipped the now-lukewarm tea, then handed her twice the agreed amount.

"We see you again soon," she said.

He stretched his neck and shoulders that stiffened a tight band. "Actually, my dear, I will be going away for a bit."

"You go home?"

"No . . . for some business . . . to Europe."

"When you go?"

"Tomorrow."

"Ah. You come back soon."

"We'll see, my dear. We'll see."

Dusk had begun to dispense its charm, of marmalade light and gentle wind, that seemed to drag even the swarming river to a languid dawdle. Emmanuel sat on his balcony alone, looking to the river to distract him. But it hadn't for a while.

Was it a sickness? Did others think this way?

He saw his mother's face. His father's too. He had seen them as they waved goodbye at the airport. He had the big family suitcase, the red hard plastic one that they bought at the Christmas sales. They didn't have much really. Bits and pieces that wouldn't amount to much, even if you added it all together.

His mother asked how long he'd be away. He said he wasn't sure. She looked worried. She could niggle away when she worried. He thought she even liked to worry sometimes. *Don't worry*, he had said. What else could he say? But if you added it up—the house, a timber cottage in Annandale, the paint flaking away on some of the boards, it would need doing again before it was sold, that was the problem with timber houses, the agents never tell you about it when they sell it to you of course, you need to paint the whole thing every seven years or so, the furniture old but in good condition, best sold with the house he thought, her jewelry, which he didn't know much about, the value that is—if you added it all up, it really wasn't that much.

But what type of person thinks about these things?

He looked down at the Chao Phraya. Pri-ya, not Fray-ya, Lalana had laughed. Could he ever be able to speak Thai? He doubted it. Not well, at least. He practiced some of the simple words in his head but came unstuck like usual.

The car didn't count. The trade-in value a better way to go. The mortgage was paid off. He had no idea of the amount in their accounts. His father had just retired. His mother hadn't worked since before he could remember. But they weren't old. They were not at a dying age. So why think of it? And why now? This made no sense. And they loved him. He loved them. So why did he think about these things?

Did others think this way?

The Peninsula looked like it was made of blue and yellow Lego from where he sat. The same color as the sky and the clouds. The sun was bright on it—it was that time of the day. He lifted himself to the edge of the chair and took up his glass.

Hom didn't have a cent to her name. This was better. Clean. It made him feel good about himself. That wasn't why he was with her of course, but he enjoyed the feeling nonetheless. He had never caught the Oriental's boat across the river. He watched one drift across, its wash cutting the river in two pieces. Sometimes Ronnie went across on these coffee-colored boats to have dinner at the Peninsula. He watched the boat's wash dissolve away into the blue-brown. It would be like a nest egg.

Anyway—he would have to split everything with his brother.

Lalana loved this place. Loved the memories of gorged feasts, spooning food between laughter with her family of waiters, waitresses, chefs, and managers; loved meeting her new friend, discovering secrets not yet known to others. Plates of food clamored for space on their table, and, as before, the ritual of swapping mouthfuls from dishes met with giggles at the table and from waitresses hovering.

"*Khawp khun*" Lalana said.

Emmanuel frowned.

"*Khawp khun, khawp khun.*"

Emmanuel shook his head.

"Thank you . . . *Khawp khun.*" Lalana took a swig of her juice. "Were you good student?"

Emmanuel bit his lip. *Would I be here if I was.*

"No worry," she said, sensitive to Emmanuel's poorly hidden angst. She twisted her neck to inspect the scene. "This good to have wedding." Scribbled on the pad and pushed toward Hom. Lalana had developed the habit of writing to Hom any spoken communication of importance, always carrying a pad and pencil whenever she met her friend.

"I'll keep that in mind," Emmanuel said.

She eyed Hom with a mischievous nod. "Good, I get good price for you."

"First customer of the day?"

"That right. Can Durudee come?"

"Do you want to finalize the list now?"

She looked at him quizzically.

"Of course she could come. But you're really getting ahead of yourself."

Lalana ignored Emmanuel's worry. "I know monk who do wedding. Bring good luck to you."

"I could use good luck."

"You like wedding. You get very, very drugged."

"Drunk?"

"Yeah, that's what I say, you get very, very . . . drunk." She scribbled a note to Hom, who paused some seconds before replying. Lalana eyed the note. "You parents come?"

"Lalana, we might talk about this some other time."

"You parents dead?"

Emmanuel rubbed his unshaven stubble. He adored this dimpled girl. "No, they are alive. I am not that old, you know."

"Good. Her brother her family. No father. No mother," said as she presented Hom an offering of red duck curry with lychee, then penned a note and pushed the pad. Hom studied and replied with quick scribbles.

"What parents like?"

"Who's asking?"

"Me and Hom."

Emmanuel dipped a piece of sashimi into a dish of soy. "Happy, I think. They love each other more than before." He marveled at the revelations that Lalana could extract. "They would like you."

"And Hom?"

He swallowed the tender fish and savored the flavors. "Yeah, they would, I think."

Lalana scratched the note and pushed the pad. Tears pooled in Hom's eyes. She stood and held her friend's hand. "We eat more now."

He watched them move over to food they had yet to taste, hands still held. Emmanuel took the pad and began to write. Ink painted with ease.

In the distance, the girls juggled mounds of food, then found the manageress of previous feasts. The trio soon huddled around well-known waitresses. Emmanuel kept writing, for he had much to say.

When they returned, Lalana offered some of her food to Emmanuel. He forked small mouth-sized bits onto his plate.

"You want to live Bangkok?" Lalana said.

"That's a good question, but I'm not actually sure. Perhaps for some of the year, around the cooler months."

"Yeah, it too hot here. You stay cold place?"

"Perhaps. I haven't decided." But guessed her meaning. "Lalana, I need to tell you something. I'll be going home for a few weeks."

"When you go?"

"On Wednesday."

"Where you go?"

"I need to clean up some things. Important things."

"You take Princess, take Hom?"

"No."

She stirred her food without purpose.

"Chosita knows about it. But I shouldn't be long." He breathed deeply. "Could you tell Hom? Please?"

He pushed the pad to Lalana, who wrote with care, covering a full page. Hom had continued to eat throughout the conversation, though she interrupted her dining as Lalana transcribed beyond the norm. Hom read the finished note and scratched a brief reply. Lalana glanced at the pad, then gazed at her friend.

"She say, 'Will you come back?'"

Emmanuel squeezed Hom's hand that rested softly on his thigh. "Of course I'll come back. It should take only a few weeks. She can stay here. Nothing will change. Nothing."

Lalana penned the message and pushed the pad to Hom, who grinned.

"I want you to do me a favor, Lalana. I want you to write in Thai this message I've written. Give it to Hom when I've left." He handed her the two pages of notes, and with it a five hundred baht note concealed within the sheets.

Lalana glanced at the scribbling, then nodded.

And at the feast's end, just before she ventured out through wet air, Lalana squeezed the baht note back into Emmanuel's hand.

"You give it to me . . . when come back," she said.

He watched her. The balcony doors thrown open to full, the curtains tied back, the room bathed in the light of the day and the hot wind and the horns that bellowed afar and up from the twisting river. He watched her. She walked out, bony flesh naked brown, onto the balcony. She turned to giggle at him, a broad beaming giggle, her hands over breasts and down, skipping a dance with grunted laughter, arms now floating high and revealing. He watched her. She scampered back inside the room and picked up the empty flute and scrunched her face in wanting; then yanked the bottle buried in ice, splashing the frost onto her naked hide, shrieking high with wide barbed teeth. He watched her. She poured the frothing lava that overflowed onto the carpet, and sucked the spill away that dribbled down, and poured again, and spilled some more, and took the bottle to her mouth that gushed the froth down cheeks and laughed and laughed. He watched her. She fell onto the bed and molded into his naked, her head settling on his shoulder, her hands drifting down, her palm softly lifting, stroking softly, sliding softly, and lifted her thigh over and touched him with her wet and softly.

The afternoon gust slowed inside their room; heaved and sighed its heat, down and over them. And after, in the quiet of this heat, as she slept, he watched her. Emmanuel saw her shallow breath rise and fall on his, her face calm amber, still, against his chest. He touched her sleeping arm, her sleeping hair.

And then, like her, deep inside this blissful warmth, he also slept.

SIX

My darling Hom, I need to go away for a short while to sort out some important business back home. It should take only a few weeks at the most. I have spoken to the hotel so they know you will be here. I have left some money in the room safe and you can charge any food to the room. If you need anything else the hotel staff will help you. When I come back I would like to look for a place for us. I want to learn sign language and Thai so we can speak easier. I have so many plans—too much to write here. But I had a dream last night. A wonderful dream with mountains and lakes and us. Darling I want to tell you that I have been more happy with you than any other time in my life. I want to tell you that I love you. See you very soon.

Lots of love

Emmanuel

Hom folded the much-read page, transcribed in neatly penciled Thai. Pink paper that smelled of roses; 'E loves H' within hearts drawn neatly in red felt pen around the text and sealed with ruddy lipstick imprints of three pouting lips.

"Don't you love the kisses?" Durudee said. "Did you tell her they're my lips? So kissable."

"Maybe he didn't want anyone else to read it," Lalana said.

"If he didn't, he would have given it to someone else to write."

The three girls lay prone on outstretched deck chairs, positioned so each touched their neighbor. Lalana lay in the middle in long shorts and a dripping T-shirt, Durudee with a matching outfit; Hom's pencil frame of oiled coffee flesh and white bikini in stark contrast. Overhead, umbrellas protected still-wet skin from the midday sun.

"I'm thirsty," Durudee said.

"You had a drink before we went in the pool."

"Ask Hom to get us another."

"Not yet. Did you see how much they are? I can buy dinner for that price."

"We can bring drinks next time."

"I don't think we're allowed to."

"Then ask Hom to get us one soon or I'll die! It's so hot." Durudee lifted the clinging shirt from her skin and whispered, "Would you ever wear a bikini like Hom's?"

"Of course not," Lalana said, without opening her eyes.

Durudee turned to scan the pool's edge. "We're the only Thai girls here, I think."

"What about those people behind us?"

"Japanese. No Thai mother wears a bikini like her. Not even your mother would."

Lalana lifted her head and peered at her friend. Eyes stabbed.

"Only joking. Anyway, Alak's sister said she wore a bikini to Krabi once."

"She's only eleven, and I don't believe anything she says."

"I might look good in a bikini. What do you think?"

"I think your mother would kill you."

"Only if she found out."

Lalana remained silent.

"Hom's skin is so dark from the sun. She looks like an African almost." Durudee again pulled at her stuck shirt—peeling it away to squeeze the cool onto wet skin. "It's so humid. My top will never dry. I can't go home with a wet shirt."

Lalana giggled. "You would look like a slutty American."

Hom sat up on the edge of her chair, adjusted her bikini that just covered her small breasts, and gestured to her friends for more drinks.

"See, Lalana. Yes—please, please."

Hom grinned. She handed the menu to Durudee, whose eyes danced over the offerings.

"Look. Cocktails, Lalana."

"They won't sell you cocktails."

"Oh... lime, orange, and melon... this one sounds delicious. Japanese slipper. What a pretty name."

Lalana lifted herself on bended elbows and snatched the menu away. Pointed to the orange juice. Hom waved to the waiter. By the time he arrived, Lalana had resumed her resting position.

Durudee took command. "Hom will have a Coke, Lalana an orange juice... and let me see," she said, pretending to study the menu. "I'll have a... I'll have a Japanese slipper."

The waiter kept a calm façade. "Are you sure you wouldn't like something else? It's such a hot day."

Durudee's face folded in feigned reflection. An awkward period of silence followed, before:

"She'll have an orange juice," Lalana said, still with eyes closed.

Durudee poked her tongue out at her friend—whom she loved.

He wrote he had a dream with mountains and lakes. It is too hot to stay in Bangkok all year he said that. I know he will buy us a house in my purple daisy place. School starts in two weeks. It's so hot!!

"Chosita, why don't you put a pretty cover on that light bulb?" Durudee said.

The old woman added more water into the shallow bath tray.

"I made one for Lalana. It made the whole room green, like sleeping in a forest."

"But it melted." Lalana shifted Princess from one hip to the other. "Mum said it might catch on fire."

Chosita added more hot water from the kettle and smiled.

"I think I'll make a red one for this room. Or yellow."

"Red will match the flames. Won't it, my little Princess." Lalana spooned lukewarm water into her palm and gently patted the naked baby's cheeks, limbs, and chest with soft sprinkles. "I would like a nice cool bath, too," she cooed.

"When is Hom arriving? We could go to the pool after."

"She might get in trouble with us being there all the time."

"Nonsense. Chosita, could we take Princess for a swim?"

Lalana lifted the baby into the shallow water. Limbs splashed.

"Maybe when you're older," Durudee said, "on your first birthday. Chosita, what is Princess's date of birth?"

The old woman shrugged as she caressed the baby's skin with a moist washcloth.

"Who's going to teach her Thai?" Durudee asked. "Emmanuel and Hom can't. Chosita, are you talking to Princess every day? I can bring a book from home that my niece used. Chosita, would you teach little Princess to read?"

"She's not even eight months old, yet," Lalana said.

"But you can never start too early. I saw it on TV. A baby in Japan or China could read before it could speak. Pointed to the words. It was amazing. I'll get you the book Chosita."

"The baby's parents were probably geniuses," Lalana said.

"Perhaps. Emmanuel doesn't seem too smart to me."

"Not too smart."

"The mother might have been smart, though," Durudee said. "Do you know anything about her?"

Lalana, supporting the baby's head with one palm, brought her slowly to the basin's depths. "He gets angry when you talk about anything like that. But I got mum to try and find out after he had a lot of her expensive wine."

Durudee flipped over on the mattress, lifting her chin on bended elbows.

"Said she was a teacher. Died when she had Princess. He said she was from a very wealthy family." Ladled more water onto the baby's flapping arms. "Must have been horrible."

"A teacher... see, Princess... you will be smart. Chosita, you must teach her to read. Promise!"

Yanisa nodded to her customer with a smile, pleasant as always. Pulled out the chair and glided her into position, lifted the cotton napkin gently to her thigh, poured iced water into her glass, gave comfort to her. While the sun had fallen hours before, respite from the day's heat had yet to arrive. Other patrons fanned themselves with menus, wiped sweat from their brows with cold towels, or simply endured. Soon she returned with the menu, its contents well known to the woman. Would she have the same meal, display the same lack of imagination? No disappointment found as she pointed to the well-tried—tom yum goong followed by sticky rice with custard and tea ice cream. She nodded and smiled. Then moved away.

Boats draped with fairy lights idled past, clad with passengers weary from the day's stretched heat. Hom eyed the drifting couples with linked arms, then glanced around to fellow diners—she the only one who sat alone. But knew this would be short-lived, and she could wait. Waiting was a gift learnt from dark times past, and this wait was so exquisite compared to others. She drank more of the iced water, though later she would consume a stronger brew before bedtime. She liked the bubbled wine with cork tied by metal string; the small bottle magically reappeared each day in the tiny bedside refrigerator, and afterward gave its reward with sleep so easily found.

Yanisa brought the steaming soup. Lifted the lid to reveal prawns floating in lime and lemon grass nose. And smiled at her customer, a smile echoed in return. Poured more chilled water into her glass and removed the wine flute, for the woman never drank wine, not alone. Nodded and moved to the neighboring table that gave compliments in rich tones of Americana; accepted with smiles, smiles that forced cheek muscles to pinch—and throughout stole glimpses at the dark-timbered skin nearby. No Thai boy likes dark skin. To flaunt such ignorance amused her. Then she moved to the tables and beyond. Away.

The soup was hot and sour, yet soothed cooked skin—soothed from the wet engulfing heat. The prawn was hot; pulled the head off that floated amongst jetsam of mushroom, its succulent flesh burning the inside folds of her lips. Licked dribbled savors with her hand, yet to learn napkin etiquette. And giggled to herself.

Yanisa took the empty bowl; surprised she hadn't consumed the prawn head as on some other occasions. Smiled. One returned as always. Poured more iced water. And away.

Hom reflected. One week had passed—he should be back soon. He had told Lalana only one week, or a bit more. But waiting was so easy here. She watched as the waitress brought the sweet food to the table, placed the dish down with care, removed the soupspoon and replaced it with a shiny new one, and filled the tall water glass to its top. The woman was a friend of Emmanuel's. She was kind, made her feel special, made her feel at home. It was nice to have a friend here. And she was pretty. Very pretty.

Baroque moldings of white and gold garnished the restaurant's walls. Zürich's finest. Outside, a light gray rain blanketed the city. The two men sat at the corner table, with its lone candle remaining unlit; crystal chandeliers glittered overhead, burgundy curtains draped. The waiter had interrupted the conversation, he knew, yet filled both glasses that bubbled to the brim before leaving the men to resume their whisperings.

"You told me not to tell you anything, Ronnie . . . tell you anything."

Ronnie stared at Arthur and remained unmoved.

"I only told you when you asked, Ronnie, . . . asked." He picked up his flute, gulping the champagne, and glanced around the room nervously before continuing. "We made a deal! We still have a deal, don't we, Ronnie? We're still friends, aren't we, Ronnie? Still friends?"

The snow-haired man sipped his wine, then placed the glass down gently, pushing it closer to his companion as if moving a chess piece. He took his napkin from his lap and patted his lips, then carefully folded it twice before placing it down on the table. He lifted his hand to catch the eye of the waiter, who moved on over. "We want the bill."

"Yes sir. Credit card or cash?"

"My friend here will pay in cash."

The waiter shifted along.

"Happy to pay, Ronnie . . . happy to pay." Arthur swept a glance in a wide curve across the room, before leaning over the table in a hush. "In fact, Ronnie, I've been thinking . . . let's increase your commission . . . increase it, Ronnie," and chewed into his lip.

Ronnie moved his chair out from the table. Then said, with his soft hypnotic drawl, "When I leave this room, I will leave alone. I do not want to hear from you, or see you, even from a fucking distance. As far as I'm concerned, you do not exist."

He stood and walked toward the revolving glass door, collected his coat from the tall mahogany rack, and pushed out into the gray rain.

And Arthur—with breath held beyond its limit—expelled stale air. His shoulders hunched in resignation.

The hotel's white dressing gown was stifling in the heat but kept her at ease. Durudee moved past the oiled bodies, through children ballooning at arms and hips with yellow plastic flotation devices; past waiters serving iced drinks to sweating trade. Then found her friends lounging on deck chairs closer to the river's edge than poolside, and untied the cord, allowing the gown to drop on the vacant chair.

She giggled nervously. Ventured some steps toward the pool, then halted. Frozen. Then quickened her pace almost to running and jumped within the cool, sinking below with breath held for as long as her lungs could take; found the surface, shoulders still submerged, and surreptitiously glanced at her poolside audience—who seemed surprisingly self-absorbed. She lifted her shoulders, then chest, tentatively out of the water. Then swiveled, with arms outstretched like an unwound top, glorying in the newfound freedom. She eyed her favorite waiter, muscular and handsome in white tight pants and shirt, who smiled at her. Yes—smiled. Then ducked shoulders under the water in brief escape. But only brief. Pushed off the wall and floated face down, kicking her legs to stay afloat. Felt the heat on legs, back, and buttocks. And gloried in newfound freedom.

After fifteen minutes of play, she lifted herself out of the pool, adjusted her bikini that barely covered her breasts, and crept up to reveal a crease of one buttock. And ventured back. This time more slowly, parading almost, slender hips rising with each step.

"It's so lovely in the pool."

Hom grinned, a thumb raised.

"I think it's not as hot as yesterday." Lifted her gown and wiped her face. "I might take a little nap." She rotated the large overhead umbrella, ensuring no sun would find exposed skin, and brought the deck chair to its flat position. Slumped prone. "Ah, that's so nice. Lalana, make sure you wake me if you get any drinks."

After a few minutes, she rolled over onto her back, stretched arms and legs out straight, then whispered. "Lalana. What do you think? Do I look good?"

"Yeah . . . you look good."

Durudee adjusted her top that had slipped an inch or more. "It's Hom's. We're the same size." She waved at the drinks waiter. "Don't tell any of the girls, though." She paused a moment. "I don't mind if you tell Alak, though. You know, how gorgeous I look in a bikini." She poked Lalana playfully in the ribs.

Lalana giggled. "I bet Alak's sister's bikini isn't as small as yours."

✿

> *Finished the first week of school. Teachers all good except Math (and maybe English). D hates all of her teachers but hasn't worked out whom she hates the most. Saw Princess after school. It's been 3 weeks since E left. Chosita and Hom said they haven't heard from him yet. Hom seems not too worried. Have a lot of homework tonight.*

Lalana sat down on the asphalt with its parade of shoe leather marching by, and wiped at a smudge of polish on her hand. "How's business Mr. Intalak?"

"Not bad . . . and you?"

"Not bad."

She scraped some black from under a fingernail, flicking the crud onto the pavement.

"How are your savings going little one?"

"Actually, Mr. Intalak, quite well."

"I'm jealous."

The vendor lowered the gas flame to simmer and scraped at the black from his wok. He poured water onto the hot metal that spouted a steamy haze into the air.

Soon, a pair of tattered sneakers, attached to gangly legs, presented themselves to the slouched girl. Lalana looked up to see a boy with a grin painted wide on his face.

"Alak. What are you doing here?"

The teen crouched low next to Lalana. "I'm helping out at my uncle's store, just a few blocks away." His head curved up and down in a wide arc, trying to take in the whole landscape with one giant scan. "This is such a cool place to work, Lalana. Man, a real cool place."

"Okay, I'll swap you then."

"Really?" Though he quickly shook his head. "No chance. I would be dead if my uncle knew I was here. Let alone my father."

"I bet I can guess why you want to work here, Alak Phanrit!" Lalana twisted her grimace at the boy.

He just grinned back. "Is that your mum over there?"

Lalana remained silent into the swarm.

"Does she own the bar?"

"No, just the manager."

"Man, I would love that job."

"Perhaps you could take over when mum retires. I could organize it for you."

"Really?"

"No, you idiot."

The boy sighed into the night, the neon bright in his face. "Is that Durudee over there?"

"Yep. Do you want me to call her over? She likes you, you know."

The boy turned a hangdog glance at Lalana. "Really . . . you're not joking?"

Lalana climbed from the ground, the boy trailing a shy rise, and waved at Durudee who sauntered over with dancing hips.

"Well, well, well, what have we here? You're a bit young for the Plaza, aren't you Alak?"

The boy peered at the tray of gum. "Can I have a pack?"

"Fruit or mint?"

"Fruit."

She handed a packet to the boy. "That'll be fifty baht."

"You can't be serious."

"Okay. Twenty."

He tossed the packet back into her tray. "I can buy it for five at my uncle's store. Anyway, I don't have any money."

"So, how do you plan to take us out without any money?" Durudee sneaked a wry smile at Lalana.

While the boy was a head taller than the girls, he stood with shoulders hunched, a slinking low, uncertain on how to respond.

Lalana rescued the fidgeting teen. "Why don't we take you out for dinner, and you can take us next time?"

"Sure!" He looked at his watch. "I'll run off and tell my uncle. I'll be back real soon." His gaze drifted to a young woman in a sailor-schoolgirl outfit that came out of the plaza's mouth. A cartooned fawn seductress.

"Excuse me, Alak," Durudee said, hands on hips. "If *we* are taking you out, the least you could do is not goggle-eye other girls."

The boy shifted his head down, then moved a slow retreat, with wayward glances, out of the walkway and into the bustling street.

Lalana walked over to the vendor's cart. "That's a lot of noodles, Mr. Intalak."

The spiral-whiskered man raised his gaze up to the girl, then resumed his silent scraping.

"What happens when they go cold?"

"They taste better."

Lalana lifted herself high on her toes, her head now hovering over the basket of rice noodles, then raised a broad smile at the man, flashing all her teeth. "I was saying to mum the other day . . . Mr. Intalak makes the best Sen Yai I've ever had. Even better than the Shangri-La Hotel."

The man stopped in mid scrape. "You have eaten at the Shangri-La?"

"All the time, Mr. Intalak. And I can honestly say their Sen Yai is nothing compared to yours."

"I can't really argue with that, since you've had more than any other customer." He added more water into the pan that puffed a cloud up into the gray-blue. "Not that you would be considered a real customer."

"You are right. I am more *family* than a customer, aren't I, Mr. Intalak?"

The vendor chuckled. "That's not really what I meant. Anyway little one, what can I get you tonight?"

"Well, I have sort of invited a friend to eat with us. And Durudee of course."

The man added some oil onto the cleaned wok that cackled on the heat. "Your friend will have to pay."

"But he has no money."

"At this rate, neither will I. Someone must pay."

"You wouldn't take money from *family*, would you, Mr. Intalak?"

He threw a small slice of beef onto the pan and adjusted the flame.

Lalana gave a loud sigh. "My school exams will be starting soon, so I won't see you as much anymore. Will you miss me Mr. Intalak?"

The man shifted his gaze back to the dimpled girl, twisting his long chin hairs into a winding gray string. "My profit margin is sure to improve."

Lalana tilted her head to study the man's face. "Why do you grow those whiskers of yours?"

"I think they make me look wise."

"Yes, I can see that." She unzipped her moneybag. "How much for Alak's dinner?"

"What do you have?"

Lalana displayed the scattered notes in her purse.

"One of those will do."

She turned around to spy a glance at Durudee who was sifting through the bar's outer skeleton, facing away from the cart. "Okay, but let's keep it a secret," and handed him the crushed note.

The trio of teens stood well into the path—an island within the torrent—twisted their noodles and wiped their greasy faces.

"These are the best," Alak said. "You get to work here and eat free food. What a dream job."

The girls beamed.

"So Alak, where will you be taking us out?" Durudee asked.

The boy sucked a long noodle into his mouth. "I have a few ideas."

They moved over to the vendor's cart.

"Thanks for the noodles Mr. Intalak," Lalana said.

The man nodded a long bow as the young schoolgirl woman drifted over to the cart. The teens watched Alak's eyes dance down and over.

"That smells good." The schoolgirl woman smiled. "Can I have a taste?"

"Sure." Alak twirled a noodle clumsily and raised his fork uneasily toward the woman's mouth.

"I don't think she needs to be fed, Alak!" Durudee said.

The boy tried to tack the fork, yet managed only to drop the noodle onto the asphalt.

Lalana giggled. "Here, try mine."

The schoolgirl tasted a small piece of the flavored noodle. "Nice, can I have three plates of these?"

"I'm just about to do a fresh batch if you can wait five minutes."

Lalana raised her brow. "I thought they tasted better cold Mr. Intalak?"

"We can take them up to you," Durudee said, "no need to wait."

The woman nodded her thanks and paid the vendor. "If you bring them up to the doorman at Kitty's, I'll let him know you're coming."

"Kitty's?" asked Alak.

"Don't worry. I'll show him," Durudee said.

The woman moved on, her cobalt pleated skirt offering a glimmer of cheek with each step—and away into the torrent. Durudee dragged her friends to a hushed corner of the lane.

"Good old Kitty's, hey, Durudee," Lalana said.

"We can each take a plate up."

"You know I'm not allowed up there, and if mum sees you, she'll cut you down before you reach the shrine."

Durudee scrunched her face up into a pondering grimace. "Okay, Lalana, you can be the decoy."

They stole up onto the dim gray stairs with bowls of noodles held out like steering-wheels.

"Did you bow at the shrine, Alak?" Durudee whispered.

The boy shook his head.

"That's bad luck for you. Remember next time."

When they mounted the top, neon of liquorice-allsorts shone a vivid greeting—a ponytail grin with skirt lifted up, the curves of yellow buttocks flashing high and round and plump. The open balcony shone back at the teens, a mirrored wall reflecting the candy lights and their wide-eyed faces, scrawny, out of place, lost on this platform of loitering harlots and their help; lost amongst the cerulean brushed eyes and painted on shorts, the thin wrapped chests and skirts curt or split open, the heavy farang and light-footed Thai, the cigarette leanings. The two teens stood uneasy here, with freshly-made noodles their flimsy passports.

At the entrance of Kitty's, cross-legged girls hunched forward on beer can stools. In the middle, a long crimson curtain dangled down to peek through.

"We are here to deliver the noodles," Durudee said.

The slouched girl eyed the pair, motioning her head to the entrance.

"Can't we give them to you out here?" the boy said.

"Who are they for?"

The teens shone a faltering frown.

"The Sailor-Moon girl," Alak said.

Durudee glared at the boy.

"Sailor-Moon. Don't know anyone named Sailor-Moon."

"Don't mind him, we'll find her." Durudee beckoned the boy to follow in kind.

And they entered through the velvet slit together.

The rainbow lights beamed bright into the carnal techno, red shirt waitresses held drinks up high, threading past girls on emerald platforms, long black stockings an inch above dancing knees, waif white skirts, panties black too, dancing against squirming silver poles. Durudee swallowed the scene in one large gulp, stood back and quiet, with a chili perfume rising up.

The boy saw only the girl—high on a lone pedestal—no skirt or stockings or black, just a writhing naked with hands down slippery silver shinings, bubbles frothing over glistening skin, wet and sliding, squirming legs up and down and open and loud. She smiled through to the teen, a fleeting beam that went deep and lingered well into the writhe—his breath of rushing pants, heaved when pulse raised up. The boy saw only this girl—stood too back and quiet—a silent open-mouthed vigil.

Durudee tugged at the boy's arm. "Hey, Sailor-Moon guy. Can you see her?"

The boy turned to her, then back and away. Durudee arched her neck up, squinting to find a focus into the shimmer. She took the bowl from the boy and slinked further into the bar, holding the plates above her head—snaked a ragged course through the hustle. After a few steps she felt a hand on her leg, behind and out of sight, a forced caress that swiftly rose between her thighs. She kicked back—a blind swipe that failed to connect—the tower of bowls a tottering quiver that manacled her arms up high. She wanted out now, but not back toward the hands, and moved forward, closer to the raised platform of dancing black.

Durudee looked up, with the bowls still raised, and made an offering to one of the stockings who snubbed it away with a shrug. Durudee felt a tight panic swell up, though didn't look back—in case the hands had eyes. And wanted away.

For a moment she stood still amongst the writhing heat, the lantern of food held aloft, and looked through the black dancing legs. She felt a tap on her shoulder, and twisted her neck to see the schoolgirl woman tendering a gentle smile. Durudee handed the bowls over, almost spilling the upper plate, and fled, with eyes fixed always at the floor, that speckled a laser light. She bumped this hurry through the dense huddle of heavy-set legs and back to the vermillion slit, dragging the boy, and through and out.

Outside, the loitering balcony sat a sullen quiet. The teens descended the stairs together, side-by-side, though without a word spoken, and scuttled down the pedestrian corridor against the tide. Lalana sat leaning on the bamboo railing at the edge of the bar. As the pair approached, she raised her eyes, tilting her head up and behind, to her mother who stood tall on the bar's raised platform.

"Durudee, I don't want to see you up there again."

The girl looked down at her feet. "Okay, Mrs. Songpow," and crouched next to Lalana; the boy slouching an uneasy stance some yards away, with shifting eyes.

And, as the calm settled slowly down, Lalana whispered to her friend, "So what was it like?"

To which Durudee replied, without intonation, like giving the answer to a math question.

"Terrible."

Yanisa brought the steaming rice to her customer. Dished a large mound onto the gold-lipped plate and opened the ceramic bowl of chicken and green curry. A sweet nose vapored. Spooned a small portion to the side of the rice and gently lifted two peppercorns away from the sauce; tender care that sent its comfort softly down—though, as it had in recent times, her customer's smile trailed off quickly, became lost in dark clouds that seemed to hover. And poured more wine into her glass. Then moved away.

Hom gulped at the flute, played with the chicken pieces with fork and spoon, and ate little. The friendly waitress poured more wine. She liked the pretty woman. Liked to order more dishes and space them out to extend time with her and the outside. Saw others come and go, mostly for one night or two, but soon replaced by others, usually in pairs or fours, some alone—but few. Sometimes she smiled at lone diners if they seemed nice, but knew she couldn't communicate with them, as they were rarely Thai. And the thought of writing hello to these transient strangers made her want to cry.

Yanisa brought the salad to her customer. Barbequed beef thinly sliced, nested in a bed of cucumber, onion, and tomato, all wet with sauce of lime, garlic, ginger, and chili. Spooned more rice, and smiled. Genuinely.

Hom unfolded the note. Worn creases left small holes in part of the paper. Read it again. He had important business to sort out. Important business makes time go fast; she knew that. But why hadn't he phoned? He could have left a message; the hotel could easily write her a message if he phoned. It would be a month tomorrow since he was gone, since she held his hand, fell asleep in his arms.

He is selfish.

SEVEN

The boy held the envelope into the light of the sky. This was the sixth that had come, so six hundred bucks in total—easy money. The post office was on his way home from school, to check the post-box took only a second—which was normally empty, and so he usually just continued on home. But today the box had the large envelope with the smaller inside. And the hundred dollars in cash.

He rotated the envelope so the sun hit its back. He could see the shadow of a thick card that snapped flat after he bent it from the outside. Made of plastic he thought. He shook the envelope but it didn't rattle or puff out with powder like his friend Ted had told him it would. 'They put anthrax in envelopes, you know. You're probably going to kill half of San Fran by the time you're finished.' Ted said that his brother had hacked into the CIA and he was sure it was anthrax. But he had told Ted that it was always addressed to the same place. 'That's so they can contain it when they need to,' Ted said. 'They'll pin it on you and they'll take you away like Winston Smith, and you'll come back to school with a lobotomy scar hidden in your scalp.' He had even shown him where the scar would be.

He shook the envelope again but it seemed like a normal letter, other than the plastic card. It would be hard to post it up on Van Ness today. He had to go shopping with his grandmother on Thursdays, so it would be touch and go getting back in time. He thought about posting it in the red box just out front, but the man had been very clear with his instructions, and he didn't want to risk losing the job. It was such easy money. So he licked the stamp and stuck it on and jogged on through the Dragon Gate and away—leaving Chinatown to itself for a while.

"I don't want to play by his rules anymore."

"This is no time to lose your nerve, Jillian," old gray Stephen said.

"It's not about losing her nerve, Steve, it's about getting back some control."

She looked at her father. She liked how he called old Stephen, Steve.

They all sat in the long room that shone bright from the clear pale outside. The Stephens on the hippo chair, her father on the Queen Anne, next to her on her mouse chair. She sat so still, it didn't make a squeak.

Old Stephen gulped at his port. "I understand that. God knows I like control more than most. But there is a time for action and a time to retreat. The most successful men know which is which . . . something you don't necessarily learn working in a post-office, Henry."

"Fuck you, Steve," her father said without raising his voice.

"Dad, you're not helping any," her Stephen said.

"This isn't the time to be shy of an opinion, son."

"Then fuck you, Steve," her father said again.

"Henry, please," her Stephen said.

She looked at her husband sitting forward on the hippo. Like he wanted to jump off. Or fall.

"Should we vote on it?" Old Gray said.

"This isn't a fucking board room, Steve."

She kept watching her Stephen lean on forward. Lost with his head in his hands. But she knew what he was going to say. They had talked it over before. So he said it, though he spoke with his head in his hands.

"Dad, I agree with Jill. We've got to tell the police."

They all sat quiet, lit up by the sun's rays through the high glass wall.

"It's their decision, Steve," her father said.

Old Gray took out his cigar cutter, a stainless steel guillotine, kept in the inside pocket of his jacket. He wasn't allowed to smoke inside. But she didn't much care. Not now.

"Those diamonds can be traced." Old Gray cut into the cigar butt. "I have every trader on the planet onside if we need. These big ones are easy to track."

"It's not about the diamonds, Dad," she said softly. She rarely called Old Gray 'Dad'. Maybe only once or twice when they first met. Not because of disrespect, really. He was just so unlike her father. It sounded false to say it.

She watched him put the cigar back in his pocket and sit forward like his son. She offered a little smile to the old man. And made a squeak in her chair. "I'll go and phone the police now."

There were too many Stephens and Josephines in this family, Jill thought. While it never could happen—old Josephine dead long before young Josephine was born—she could easily imagine the family at Thanksgiving: 'Stephen pass the plate to Stephen; Josephine could you feed Josephine.' Like an old vaudeville routine. What was it that caused this family to keep on without revision? Had it been so good they dared not risk a change?

The table was cluttered with the smell of pork chops and gravy. Big roasted potatoes as large as cue balls, brown crusted, cauliflower and peas and beans, with a carafe of claret that splashed as it passed around. Not really a celebration, but an attempt at least.

"Pass Steve the gravy, Stephen," her father said. She suppressed a smile.

Old Gray sprayed the saltshaker over his meat like confetti.

"Hattie, why don't you sit with us and eat?" young Stephen said.

"Go on, Hattie," said Old Gray.

"Go on," they all sung up.

But Hattie didn't sit.

They sat with the smell of pork chops and gravy and the taste of the claret. The big table was set for four, even though it could take ten, or twelve at a squeeze. Jill, the young matriarch, felt weightless and unreal, as she swigged her wine. Old Josephine was a teetotaler she had been told. Except for the taste of Christ's blood, she had never touched a drop. Not even when they said it would ease her pain at the end of her long struggle—a saga of some twenty years back.

"I like the red, Steve," her father said.

Old Gray grinned. "And your daughter likes it too, by the looks of it."

"She takes after her Dad," her Stephen said.

Jill saw Hattie smile at this, and followed her smile as she took the empty water jug away and kept on smiling into the kitchen. So Jill imagined.

"Pass the apple sauce to Henry, my dear," Old Gray said.

And she passed it across the heat of the table.

"Have you got an extra one of those fat cigars, Steve?" her father asked.

"I might just have."

"We could share some fresh air after dinner then?"

"Sounds like a plan, Henry," Old Gray said. "We'll leave our offspring to the table clearing for once."

She smiled at this with her Stephen. And saw Old Gray smile with her smile.

"I hope you don't take offence, Jillian," Old Gray said, "but you're quite a looker."

"Takes after her Dad on that as well," her father said. "I could've been a model too, you know."

"Perhaps not paid quite as much," her Stephen said.

"Perhaps," her father said. "But perhaps not."

"Give us a poem, Henry," said Old Gray. "But no bloody Ginsberg this time."

"Now? With all this good food yet to be eaten?"

"I'll swap a cigar for it."

She watched the gleam in her father's eyes—the lids lifting to show all of their blue. Josephine had their name, but his eyes. She watched these eyes as he stared into Old Gray.

> *"This is just to say Steve,*
> *I have eaten*
> *the plums*
> *that were in*
> *the icebox*
>
> *and which*
> *you were probably*
> *saving*
> *for breakfast*
>
> *Forgive me*
> *they were delicious*
> *so sweet*
> *and so cold."*

Her father kept his stare at Old Gray, his knife and fork held out front, with a chunk of chop skewered on his fork.

Old Gray grinned back, with his dentures flapping as they did on occasion. "Well, you better bloody replace them then."

And they all laughed over the food and the wine and she felt light and unreal.

Hattie came out of the kitchen and back to the table carrying the full water jug, the table now laden with all that was needed.

"A toast may be in order," her father said.

They raised up their heavy crystal goblets.

"To happy family times," he said lifting the red higher. She saw his eyes as he said this, spotted the instant when he realized his mistake—his lids falling to squash in the blue, his brow heavy and down.

And Jill—this young matriarch—sat with the smell of pork chops and gravy, through the silent toast, without even bothering to clink at their glasses.

They lay in bed with the light off.

"I took the speaker out of Josephine's room," she said. "The buzzing kept waking me up."

"You could have just disconnected the wire."

"I guess."

"But her room is right next door, and with her door open, any sound will be just as loud," he said. "And without the buzz."

"Do you think it's too cold in there, with the window up just an inch."

Her Stephen didn't answer.

"Hattie cooked a good meal tonight," she said. "The four of us haven't eaten like that for some time."

Stephen kept on quiet.

"She cooked your father's favorite," she said.

"Second favorite, behind roast chicken."

"Hattie has an uncanny ability to know when to treat your father," she said.

"Nothing uncanny about it. He's trained her at it for years."

"I guess."

"Your father and Dad settled down okay during dinner," he said. "Kept away from politics for once."

"They were making an effort, Stephen. For us. Dad respects your father you know. He understands the effort of building the company up and everything. With your mum gone since you were little, bringing you up alone and doing the company stuff, all by himself pretty well much."

He rolled over and faced her. She felt his warm arm dangle over her midsection.

"You know, Jill, I'd give anything to start again. Go back in time to our wedding day, with all our memories after wiped clean away, and start from scratch, without any diamond business, without a dollar to our names."

She felt him soften into her. But she didn't reply. It was her time to keep on quiet.

"You not reading Pepys tonight?" he asked.

"I finished it a few nights ago."

"How'd it end?"

"He went to the pub with his wife and a friend. And they got drunk."

"Really?"

"Really."

"And that was the last entry in his diary?"

"Yep."

"Nice," he said.

She rolled over facing the open door, keeping his arm around her. The little pilot light in the hallway painted the open rectangle a dark blue-gray.

"Yes," she said into the dim. "A perfect ending."

EIGHT

I stopped in after school with D again. She brought another reading book from her niece but Princess was asleep so we didn't stay long. Chosita looked worried. I saw more animals and another candle in the spirit house. We will spend Saturday with Princess and Hom. It's been 8 weeks since E left.

The fan purred, turning to eager faces dripping sweat, then moving away just as relief was found. The open balcony doors let in what feeble breeze there was, but also the baking rays. More squeals from irritable children echoed from the courtyard below. Heat stifled all.

Durudee turned the page and continued instruction. "I think I'd make a wonderful teacher. D-u-rud-eeee would make a wonderful teacher, wouldn't she, Princess?"

"But you don't like school," Lalana said.

"Doesn't mean I wouldn't be a good teacher. I just don't like to listen much, or do tests. Or homework. Say Durudee. Du-rud-eeee." The baby stared at the girl's animated face, then blinked as the fanned air kissed.

Lalana gestured to Hom with fingers to mouth. "I'm hungry. Mum has packed us all a nice lunch."

"It's too hot to eat yet."

The three girls sat cross-legged on the mattress, with Princess in the middle. A silent Hom stared through the scene. Lalana picked up the pad and scribbled a note of some length.

"So what do we think has happened to Emmanuel?" Lalana pushed the pad to Hom, who glanced at the note and shook her head with downcast eyes.

"He might be hurt," Durudee said. "Or worse."

Lalana scribbled her statement and pushed the pad to Hom, and throughout their banter continued this action, as was their custom.

"Possibly. It would explain why he couldn't contact anyone. But he'd have to be very hurt—or worse—not to have phoned. But how many people get that badly hurt?"

"Alak's grandfather got cancer, stayed in hospital for two months before he died."

"But he could have phoned at the beginning. He didn't just die overnight." Lalana paused. "Emmanuel was a bit thin, though he didn't eat much."

"Not like you, hey."

"We are talking serious, Durudee!"

Durudee fell silent, pulled at the worn mattress cover. "Do you think he'll come back?" Pushed the pad to Hom.

Both girls eyed their friend, who shook her head, with tears welling.

Lalana grabbed the pad. "Why would he write that letter if he wasn't going to come back?"

"You'd have to be evil to do such a thing. But he didn't seem evil to me."

"Maybe he thought he was going to come back, but something stopped him."

"Like what?"

"Maybe his wife isn't dead."

"Maybe she hurts the baby. Maybe he doesn't want her to look after Princess. Maybe she's crazy. A psycho."

"But what about Princess? He must come back for Princess eventually." Lalana pushed the pad to Hom who nodded and smiled. This conclusion she had also reached.

"Okay then, let's eat." Lalana crawled over to the basket and brought it close to the girls. "Let's see. Strained apple and custard for Princess. Lovely. Warm noodles with vegetables." She dug further into the basket. "Oh, and mum's special sticky rice and mango dessert. All for me and

Hom." She dug further to bring up a small jar to display. "And since Durudee is not hungry, she can share this lovely strained tomato and sheep's brains with little Princess."

Chosita came through the side door, holding a bag of groceries. She nodded to the girls but continued toward the spirit house at the opposite corner of the room. From her bag, she removed a small ceramic banana, not larger than her thumb, and crouched to place the offering amongst the others nested in the enclosure. She took a match, struck its flame aquiver, and lit the crimson candle at the rear of the teak interior. Then closed her eyes.

And, seated cross-legged on the mattress nearby, the girls looked on in silence.

"This must be the most beautiful restaurant in the world," Lalana said.

They sat on the outside veranda of Salathip, Hom's reserved table that hovered over the river now replaced with a larger to seat four.

"Aunty, have you ever eaten in a more beautiful place than this?" Durudee said.

Chosita's toothless grin radiated as she stroked the gold-lipped serving dish and glanced around to scan her fellow diners before straightening invisible creases in her skirt.

"That's a pretty top, Aunty. Isn't it Lalana? I like the little blue beads."

The old woman smiled; had taken some time to choose the outfit— her sister's wardrobe extending the choice.

"Did you see how gorgeous those dancers were ... better than the girls at the Plaza," Durudee said. "We should never have stopped those dancing lessons, Lalana. I bet these girls make a fortune here." She twisted her neck, bringing bended arms into a frozen pose, fingers akimbo, mimicking the just-retired dancers. "What do you say, Aunty, do you think they'd let me join their group?"

The table lit with giggles.

This was Hom's reward for them, with all three yet to be paid since Emmanuel had gone. Lalana had dressed for the occasion, her lilac rouge softly applied, with matching painted eyes. Durudee, too, wore cheeks of washed pink, and smirking cherry lips.

"It was so nice for your sister to baby-sit tonight, Aunty," Lalana said. "What a treat this is, and we haven't even eaten yet."

Yanisa moved over to the table. "Can I get you ladies something to drink?"

Hom passed the wine menu to Chosita. The old woman shook her head.

"Go on, Aunty, have a Japanese slipper," Durudee said. "They're great here."

"Go on, Aunty," Lalana said.

Chosita bashfully submitted, her mood also rising with the table's zeal.

"And for yourselves, ladies?"

"Lemonade please?"

"Me too."

Yanisa lifted her hand onto the shoulder of Hom, who shook her head, pointing to the water glass. "And for dinner, Miss Hom has selected the seafood banquet. This is Salathip's specialty."

"Seafood banquet!" Lalana gave a wide-eyed gleam in Durudee's direction.

The table approved the menu with open-mouthed nods, Yanisa confirming each of the individual's taste for chili, though she should have known that Thais rarely requested their spices be diluted.

"I am happy to see Miss Hom eating with her friends tonight."

Lalana grinned. "We are her best friends."

"With Emmanuel," Durudee said.

Yanisa began to refill the water glasses. "You all know Mr. Emmanuel?"

"Yes. He pays us to look after his baby."

Yanisa glanced at Hom, her inquisitive stare noticed by Lalana.

"Hom is not the mother though," Lalana said.

Yanisa smiled. "Mr. Emmanuel has been away a long time. He will be back soon?"

Lalana looked at the others. "We hope so."

"You are not sure?"

"Well, we haven't exactly heard from him lately."

Yanisa peered over the shoulders of the women, her eyes aimed at one of the Oriental's boats that moved slowly across the river's expanse. She lifted the empty water jug from the table. "Perhaps I might see whether he has contacted the hotel. If you wish, that is?"

Lalana scribbled the message onto her pad, and pushed it toward Hom, who eagerly replied with staccato nods.

"And if not, perhaps I can find a contact address or phone number for him. Again, only if you wish?"

"Please do!" Lalana said, not bothering to document the request in writing.

"Very well. I will bring your first course out soon. Please enjoy your meal and don't hesitate to let me know if you need anything."

The sister waitress glided to the table, balancing the drink tray with one hand.

Durudee screeched. "Look, Lalana, a Japanese slipper!" And clapped her hands.

It was the nights she hated, the mix of dark and silence leaving her vulnerable to the strange. In old times, she and her brother usually took turns staying awake, to guard what little they had. And, if the heat allowed, they often slept during the day, though only if vitals had been snatched before. So, while she was now protected, the door locked but not chained, the *Do Not Disturb* button flashing, she found it difficult to escape these night terrors. Alone.

She moved to the bathroom and showered, lathered her skin with sweet soap, scrubbed to remove nonexistent grime. After soaking, she dried herself and applied the perfumed balm—daily replaced, like the bubbled wine. Naked, she walked to the bed, peeled the sheets back on her side, and carefully placed the card on his pillow. Then took the wine and drank straight from the bottle. That frothed its sleeping medicine.

She moved to the bathroom and scrubbed her teeth, scrubbed her tongue until she gagged. Rinsed and smelt her breath. While on this night she was content, on many others she had to repeat the chore one or two times more. She now staggered, full of wine breath, back to bed—on her side—his side empty. But waiting. And then, completing the ritual, she repositioned the inscribed card more centrally on his pillow: *Welcome home, my darling.*

> D has a boyfriend. Yes, it's Alak. They were caught holding hands after school. She said she was going to tell me as soon as she got home but I don't believe her. He's okay, I guess. I came first in my Math test, a higher mark than B (the super genius) again! He was so annoyed. Mr. L said I could become a lawyer if I work hard. He said that to B as well but I don't think to anyone else. Mrs. M wasn't at school again today. There is a rumor she is very sick. Going to die sick. The replacement teacher isn't as good as her. Today is exactly 3 months since E left. I wish I had kept the 500 baht.

The boy leant against one leg of the pine desk, the timbered floor hard against his rear.

"You're so my best friend," she said. But not to him.

The boy watched the two girls frolic on the small bed, had watched them for some time, occasionally taking part in the banter himself. More often, a cloak of confused, alienation settled comfortably over his shoulders.

Durudee rested her head on Lalana's lap. "The best friend in the world!"

Lalana smiled and briefly stole a glance at the boy, who squirmed against the hard floor, then returned her gaze back to Durudee.

"My mum was so horrible to Alak," Durudee said. "Wouldn't let us alone in my room for one second . . . kept coming in pretending to clean . . . always looking at her watch and asking Alak what time he was going? My poor baby." She glanced at the boy who slumped below them on the floor.

He feigned a smile.

"I told her to stop being so horrible. She just stormed out, and said she would get dinner ready . . . when he left! My poor, poor baby."

Lalana slowly curled Durudee's hair into another plait.

"Oh, and did I tell you? Alak played with Princess the other day. He was very good with her, weren't you baby?"

The boy started to scratch up a reply, but failed to produce a meaningful sound before Durudee's dialogue continued. "He played with her for fifteen minutes. That is, until her nappy needed changing." She frowned up at Lalana, and whispered, "He lost marks for that."

Both girls held their giggles, as the boy followed their eyes in silence. Lalana arched her back, then lifted her friend's head gently from her lap. "I might give you some time to yourselves then."

"Okay," the boy forced out with the high pitch of unused cords.

Durudee turned quickly in the boy's direction. "No! That would be too rude, wouldn't it, Alak?"

The boy's gaze lowered. Confused, alienation engulfed.

"Well, you're welcome here anytime," Lalana said.

"It's such a good alibi. I spend half my time over here anyway, so mum doesn't suspect anything. 'Just make sure you finish your homework,' she says, 'and don't get Lalana to do it for you.' As if I would!"

The two girls broke into a playful performance of laughter and false squeals, as the soft hum of a long-tail boat drifted up from the klong below.

"And I'm certain your mother wouldn't tell my mum about Alak, since she absolutely adores me."

"Yeah, we knew your mother wouldn't mind." The boy straightened his back from his slumped position, resting higher against the leg of the desk. He had finally found some entry into their world, though he suspected such entry would only be brief.

"What do you mean by that?" Lalana said.

Durudee turned to the boy with a blank expression that offered no guidance. Alak shifted uneasily, unclear of the best response. His aim was to remain within their world, but not to offend. At least, not too much.

"Well, you know, we wouldn't expect your mother to bother about us being together."

"Because?" Lalana said.

"Because she sees a lot worse at the Plaza."

"Don't be a dick!" Durudee yelped, and rose up on the bed.

The boy's skin flushed, respiration quickened. He was out of his depth and had no idea where to go.

"Apologize!" Durudee said.

The boy remained with his back upright against the desk; shoulders yet to slump into submission. But he didn't respond.

"Apologize to Lalana *now*, Alak."

Lalana took a pillow and positioned it to cushion her back against the wall. Durudee continued to stare at the boy, yet he remained silent. The sticky air suffocated all.

"I think you better go." Durudee swallowed the lump that swelled in her throat.

Alak stood, and rubbed his aching hip. He wanted to say so much, yet had no idea where to begin. He stooped to lift his bag from the floor, draped it over one shoulder, and then moved slowly through the door and down the stairs—without replying.

Durudee lay back down on the bed, again using Lalana's thigh as a pillow, but faced away from her, and stared toward the space recently occupied by the boy. "So that didn't last long. Three weeks, yesterday."

Lalana lifted the unfinished plait from her friend's resting head, and slowly twisted the strands back into some order.

"He wasn't a good kisser anyway," Durudee said softly, "I kept hitting my teeth against his."

"You probably just need more practice, since he's your first boyfriend."

"Probably, but he wasn't the first boy I've kissed you know."

"What? Who else have you kissed?"

"Guess."

"Mr. Intalak?"

"Gross!"

"Then tell me! Anyway, why haven't I known about this before?"

"It was only once. Or was it twice?" She closed her eyes, with lips pouting into mock kisses. "If you must know everything, it was with Jao."

"Jao? Your cousin Jao?"

"Maybe."

"He's two years younger than you! And your cousin!"

"So, he was good to practice with. Better to make mistakes with him and not a real boyfriend. And besides, if he told anyone, he knew I would kill him."

"You are so crazy!"

"But adorable." Durudee pouted back into kisses. She paused a bit. "Why are boys such idiots?"

"Boys and men."

"They can't all be bad? My dad's okay, and uncle Chai, and . . ." Durudee frowned, "I'm sure there's more."

"I think they need to get to a certain age before coming good. That's what mum says."

"What age does she say?"

"She didn't, but older than my dad was. And obviously older than Emmanuel."

"So let's say thirty ... thirty-five for safety." She gazed up at Lalana. "Let's make a deal. No dating boys, that is *serious* dating, like your father, Emmanuel or Alak, unless they are at least thirty-five."

Lalana resumed coiling her friend's hair, as the sound of slow but deliberate footsteps timbered from the stairs below, and soon up to the bedroom's entrance. Durudee twisted her head eagerly, the plait unraveling for the second time in as many minutes.

"Oh, it's you, mum," Lalana said.

"Are you staying for dinner, Durudee?" the woman asked, dressed for her evening's toil. In her hand she had a small vase of long-stem flowers. White petals with yellow eyes.

"No, thank you, I better be going." Durudee lifted herself from the bed, slipped on her thongs, and, with schoolbag in hand, dragged her feet to the doorway, before turning. "I'll miss him though. Miss him a lot." And left.

Lalana's mother placed the vase of flowers on the small writing desk, carefully rearranging the stems to create the largest bloom. "Wasn't it nice of Alak to bring us these daisies, Lalana? I thought they would look good in your room."

Lalana sat on the edge of the bed and studied the flowers.

Her mother, having completed the arrangement, slowly ventured to the bedroom door. "Dinner will be in fifteen minutes."

Lalana lifted herself from the edge of the bed and sat at her desk. Studied the flowers. They are pretty, she mused, as she rotated one of the stems—its white petal face twirling like a miniature umbrella. She glanced briefly at the door to confirm she was alone, then swiftly grasped the vase in one hand, bringing the full bunch to her nose. And savored the perfume expectantly.

"Mum, can I ask you something?"

"Of course."

"Promise you won't get angry."

The woman twisted away from the bouquet of flowers and eyed her daughter. "No I don't."

Lalana scrunched her face at her mother. "I'll only ask if you promise not to get angry."

"What makes you think I'll get angry?"

The girl shifted her gaze away, eyeing the daisies. "Well you shouldn't. But you might."

"That's a risk you'll have to take."

Lalana grimaced, before, in tentative tones, addressed her question instead to the vase. "How come you wear that short skirt at work all the time?" She stole a speedy glance at her mother, who displayed no signs of trouble—as best she could tell.

The woman began rearranging the stalks again, brushing her fingers across the milky petals. "Why do you think I do?"

Lalana paused in feigned contemplation, since she had already considered the question many times before. "To make yourself sexy, I guess."

The woman beamed at her daughter who mirrored with a grin. "For who?"

"For the customers at the bar."

The woman lifted one of the daisies from the bunch, this time addressing the flower. "Wrong."

Lalana sprung upright on the bed—all inhibitions now quickly dissolving. "A secret admirer? Mr. Intalak and you are always smiling at each other, and he gives us free noodles. Is it because he's madly in love with you?"

The woman laughed.

"Well who then? Not Arthit the barman? Mum, he's half your age."

"He is not!" She moved over to her daughter, tugging at her ponytail.

"Oh my. Arthit. Doesn't he have a girlfriend though?"

"No silly. I don't do it for the Arthit, Mr. Intalak or the customers." She placed the twirling daisy back into the vase and sat down next to her daughter, wrapping an arm around her shoulder. "You asked the same question about Aunty Wattana at her fortieth birthday."

"Mum, Aunty Wattana's outfit was embarrassing."

She squeezed at the girl's shoulder. "She thought she was a movie star that evening." And grinned. "And I helped her choose that outfit you know."

"That'd be right." She giggled, and laid her head on her mother's shoulder. "So, you think you're a movie star when you wear this skirt?"

"Something like that."

"But you aren't saying the girls at the Plaza are not dressing sexy for the boys?"

"Why don't you ask them yourself?"

"The ladyboys too?"

"Especially the ladyboys."

With both hands, Lalana pulled at her mother's cheeks, twisting her shoulders around so they now faced each other, pushing into her cheeks that pouted her mother's lips. And kissed her. Then, with a wide-eyed beam, Lalana declared with a shrill, "I've got to phone Durudee!"

The single timber desks within the classroom were evenly spaced, leaving a small walking corridor that separated any teen angst that might intermittently bloom. Blue and white uniforms feigned attentive glances toward their teacher as the day neared to a close.

"Meet up after?" Durudee whispered.

Lalana nodded.

"Your place or mine?"

Lalana shrugged.

"Yours then. Mum's doing a cleanup job at home for her school reunion friends, who *may* visit on the weekend. She's sure to ask me to help."

"Durudee, is my lesson of no interest to you?" The history teacher's eyes stabbed. The blue and white uniforms twisted to gaze at her target.

"Yes, Mrs. Narmsra."

"Yes, it is of no interest to you?"

"No, it is very interesting, Mrs. Narmsra. In fact, I was just organizing to form a study group with Lalana after school. A history study group."

The blue and white uniforms giggled.

"A history study group? Interesting. And who will be attending?"

"Well, so far we have only two. But it's still early days, Mrs. Narmsra."

The woman screwed on her whiteboard pen-cap and placed it on the table. Cocking her neck she stared into a vacant space over her students' heads. Silence ached.

"Are you okay, Mrs. Narmsra?" Durudee said.

The woman's head nodded in a shallow staccato motion, extending the silence before peering back towards the girl. "Yes, Durudee, thank you for asking. I was in another world for a moment, wading through the long and rich history of Thailand."

Durudee glanced at Lalana with raised eyebrows.

"As you know the Kingdom of Ayutthaya was a fascinating period in our history. Wouldn't you agree, Durudee?"

"Fascinating, Mrs. Narmsra."

Muted giggles from the surrounding uniforms spluttered.

"I'm so glad you agree, since that will be the topic for your study group to present to the whole class. Tomorrow."

The uniforms erupted in laughter. Durudee waited for the cacophony to settle. "That's very nice of you, Mrs. Narmsra, but we are a bit too small a group for that yet."

"Nonsense. I have complete confidence in your ability. I would like your study group to give a ten minute presentation on what aspects of the Kingdom of Ayutthaya are important to modern Thailand." The teacher clasped her hands together, her broad grin shining through the girls' despair. "I am so looking forward to tomorrow. You know students, being a teacher is a wonderful life."

A siren trumpeted the day's end, the blue and white uniforms rising from the chairs. Lalana frowned at Durudee, the two teens yet to ascend from their desks. Smirking grimaces prodded from students who drifted past.

Durudee sighed. "Sorry about that." She stood slowly, as if carrying an invisible load on her shoulders. "I'll meet you outside."

Lalana lifted her bag to the desktop and began to stack her books neatly inside. A boy's voice from behind interrupted the task.

"That was a bit tough." Alak stood with his school bag draped over one shoulder, nervously fidgeting with the strap.

"Yeah. Durudee can sometimes be too smart for her own good." Lalana stared at the boy with interest. He was actually quite good looking. "Would you like to be in our history group?"

"Perhaps. When there is no class talk to give. Anyway, I don't think Durudee would want me around."

"I could talk to her. Don't worry, she still likes you."

The boy shifted his bag to the opposite shoulder, lowering his gaze to the floor. "Did you like the flowers I bought you?"

"The daisies? For mum?"

"Actually, I bought them for you, to say thanks for letting us hang out at your place."

Lalana's pulse raced, yet she managed to keep a calm façade. Her first flowers from a boy.

"Durudee thought it was weird to give you flowers, so I gave them to your mother."

"That was nice of you."

"Durudee said you liked daisies. I had to go to a few places to find them. Did you know they're much cheaper than other flowers? The roses were ten times as much."

"Well, I think they're much prettier than roses."

"Me too."

"A boy who likes flowers. You're a funny one, Alak Phanrit."

"Funny good, or funny strange?"

Lalana stood and lifted her bag to one shoulder, mirroring the boy's stance. The two stood alone in the empty classroom.

She grinned. "I haven't made up my mind yet."

"Let's play truth or dare!"

The four teens sat in Lalana's bedroom. The youngest, Alak's sister, the game's advocate.

"Sirikit, keep quiet," Alak said.

"Are you too scared to play?"

"Like I really want to play 'truth or dare' with my kid sister."

"It might be fun," Durudee said. "Anyway, I'm sick of studying."

Lalana grimaced. "Fun like a tooth-ache."

"I'll go first," Sirikit said. "Dare!"

Durudee giggled. "Only your sister would ask for a dare first."

"Dare, dare, dare!"

"Okay then. Take off all your clothes and run outside and jump in the klong."

"Okay."

"Don't be an idiot, Sirikit!" Alak said.

"You don't think I'll do it, do you?"

"That's the problem, we all know you will."

The young girl started to remove her blue skirt as laughter erupted.

Durudee beamed. "Take it easy, I was only joking. Anyway, you're the youngest, so you go last." She scanned the room with a mischievous grin, returning her gaze back to Alak who sat on the floor with his back resting against one leg of the pine desk. "Boys first I think."

"Forget it. If you want to play so much, you start."

Durudee sat upright on the edge of the bed. "Okay then. Truth."

"Do you love my brother?" Sirikit shrieked.

Lalana giggled.

"Sirikit shut up!" Alak said.

"She has to answer, or it's a dare!"

"I can answer for her," Lalana said. "She only loves herself."

"Sirikit," Alak said, "why don't you go and find Lalana's sister. Isn't she in your class?"

"No . . . and yes." She poked her tongue out at the boy. "Durudee, you must answer, or I'm the one who gets to ask you a dare."

Lalana beamed. "This is much more fun than I thought."

"It'll be your turn soon." Durudee turned to face the boy. "Of course I love you, baby."

Lalana eyed the boy with a warm smile. "I told you."

Alak's face blushed vermillion.

"Very romantic . . . kissy kissy," his sister purred.

"Sirikit, if you don't behave you won't get a turn," Durudee said. "And I know you can't wait to strip off that skirt of yours and have a nice swim in the klong."

The girl stood and lifted the knee-length skirt up displaying her white briefs, her hips swinging to a silent tune.

"She reminds me of you at eleven, Durudee," Lalana said.

Alak aimed a fiery-eyed stare at his sister. "I hope you're enjoying yourself, Sirikit, since this is the last time you will be coming here."

"Lalana Songpow, I believe it's your turn," Durudee said. "Truth or dare?"

Lalana moved to the edge of the bed. "Truth."

"Now, let me see," Durudee said. "What don't I know about you, that would be nice and juicy?" She rubbed at her cheek, studying her friend's grimace. "Nice . . . and . . . juicy."

"Who did you kiss last?" bellowed the still standing Sirikit.

"No. I already know the answer to that one. A . . . very . . . short . . . answer."

Lalana giggled. "Yes. I don't have any younger cousins like you."

Durudee glared at her friend before stealing a glance at Alak, who had lifted himself higher on the floor; displaying greater eagerness than she had wanted. She turned again to Lalana. "Pretend you are sixteen. Emmanuel returns from wherever he is, says he doesn't love Hom anymore, and wants to buy you a shoe store in the mountains somewhere in Europe . . . if you marry him. Will you marry him? Yes . . . or . . . no."

She laughed. "No."

"You must not lie, or you will be cursed forever."

"No, I wouldn't. You have to be seventeen to marry in Thailand."

Durudee raised her brow with a nod.

"What a waste of a question," Sirikit said.

"Don't worry, we can ask it again next round."

"I might go for a dare next. I feel like a swim in the klong." Lalana grinned. "Alak, it's your turn. Truth or dare?"

The boy glanced meaningfully at his sister, then said "Truth."

Lalana took her time, the boy's anguish rising with the extended silence.

"Come on," Sirikit said. "I can give you a great question. Ask him if he's ever sucked a dick?"

The boy dived from his slumped position to strike at his sister's legs, the girl just managing to dodge the assault.

"It's not your turn to ask though, it's mine." Lalana twisted her gaze to Durudee, then back to the boy who fumed below. "So Alak Phanrit, who do you love most in the world?"

The boy shifted on the hard floor. Considered the question carefully. "Well not, Sirikit."

The older teens laughed as the girl responded with her skirt-lifting dance, this time facing away from the audience, pulling her briefs up to expose the cheeks of her buttocks. "But that is not an answer. Who do you love love love!" she sang up, and dropped her skirt back to a knee-length respite, though now with hands on her hips.

The boy held his gaze down toward his feet. "Durudee."

"Another wasted question!" the young girl screeched. "You lot are hopeless at this game. My turn." Hips dancing. "Dare!"

The older girls huddled in a whispering conference.

"Isn't it my turn to ask?" Alak said.

"No, you're too boring," Sirikit said in mid dance.

After some minor disagreements, the two girls responded together. "Sirikit, kiss your brother on the lips."

Alak's eyes pierced at the girls who rolled with laughter on the bed. "Very funny."

"No way, he will hit me."

"No he won't... otherwise he'll have to answer any question that *you* give him," Durudee said.

The girl squinted at her brother. "Promise you won't hit me." She looked at his silent grimace that offered some hope of avoiding a confrontation. "Promise!"

"Promise," the older girls sung up.

"I've always thought it would be interesting to find out what girls get up to when they hang around together." He shrugged, shaking his head. "It's a bit of a letdown, really."

Sirikit turned to the girls seeking guidance, and, with nodding encouragement, moved tentatively over to her brother.

"Kissy kissy," the teens sang.

The young girl bent her frame down to eye level with her brother, closed her eyes, and approached with puckered lips. Then, just inches from contact, the boy swung his arm violently, smacking the girl on the one calf laid bare by a lowered sock.

Screams from all resounded, the girl lashing out with kicks that were easily controlled by the boy's long reach.

"Alak, you promised!" Durudee said.

The boy lifted himself quickly to stand above the others, then stooped down to shoulder his schoolbag. "No I didn't, and it's time to go. But that *was* fun."

Sirikit marched with heavy steps down the rickety stairs, examining the hand-shaped welt that had swelled on her calf. Durudee had followed the girl soon after, leaving Lalana and Alak alone.

"I don't know why you girls play this game," he whispered. "No one, ever, tells the truth." He moved to the doors entrance, then turned. "I know I didn't."

Yanisa brought the larb gai to her; chicken pieces cooled over green and red onions, sliced green peppers and mint leaves, fish sauce and lemon juice. She spooned the steaming rice on her plate, a dollop of the salad. Touched her arm. Then off.

Hom ate a mouthful of the spicy mix. A nice choice. Her friend chose dinner now, brought some surprise in the evening. Broke the usual. She drank steadily from her wine glass, its contents chosen by randomly pointing at the menu, so she tried more flavors. But she liked the whites best; the reds seemed harsh and puckered her mouth. Yet both eased her into the evening—like the vapors of old.

She had drunk too much. She pushed the plate of larb gai away only half-eaten, bringing the wine glass in its place. And gulped more down.

Her friend came over, her pretty friend who touched her shoulder gently and left her hand resting. Then handed her a neatly penned note. She read it twice, alcohol confusing its meaning only at the start. After her meal, she would go to the hotel manager. Her friend would come with her, the note said. She nodded to the woman, who seemed tenderly concerned. Was it news of Emmanuel? Any news would be better than none.

They walked with arms linked through the path of palms lit by a soft orange, past the open bar with lovers huddled—like her and Emmanuel before—and into the hotel proper. A chilly air. They mounted the stairs, crossed the marble expanse, and entered the office—a bright white clutter—together.

The manager stood tall and shook her hand. He seemed nice. They had smiled at each other before, smiled when the girls came to visit. He was kind. He handed her a page of typed notes.

No need to read twice. She was told in gentle verse she would have to leave. The room account had not been paid for some time. She looked at the money owed, not fully grasping the sum. Was the amount real? Could someone have such money? She was asked if she knew where he was? She shook her head. Her pretty friend held her hand. He was sorry, he wrote, he knew it was not her doing. She would not have to pay.

Hom took out the folded paper sealed with faded lipstick, and handed it to Yanisa, who read the letter. Tears slowly welled from Hom's eyes, then suddenly flooded into weeping moans. Yanisa held her friend close, kissed her forehead and cheeks, tried to share the burden through a bridge of warm touch.

And throughout, the manager remained seated, sharing too the suffering, with eyes that fell down to the floor.

It was after midnight. The taxi driver slowed the vehicle to stop near resting tuk-tuks in the tired street below the Shangri-La. Waved at his daughter. The man quickly alighted from the car and helped the girl with her luggage; three garbage bags with clothes folded neatly within. Both girls entered the taxi's rear, held hands, sighed almost together.

"Father, this is Hom," Yanisa said.

He turned and smiled at the pretty girl with swollen eyes.

"She will direct you, father. She cannot speak and doesn't know the street name. But it's not far, she says."

They drifted slowly through the quiet. Hom leaned forward in her seat, pointing with staccato murmurs and nods, the taxi venturing tentatively at her signal. After five minutes, she signaled a building with animated grunts; the car now parked in a vacant space only fifty feet from the entrance. They left the taxi together, the man helping her again with the luggage.

"I will go with her, father. I shouldn't be long."

He took some money from his wallet and handed it to the girl. Hom smiled at the man but shook her head.

"She is all right for money at the moment, father."

The man frowned, then watched the girls move to the door of the concrete block, and disappear within.

They climbed the stairs, lugging the clothes inches from the steps. On reaching the first floor, Hom veered right and turned the key, opening the blue door. The room was barely lit, with stray light entering the open window from the fluorescent street below. She could see the sleeping figure of her brother on the single bed at the room's farthest corner. She turned and embraced her friend, who kissed her sweetly on the cheek. As Hom closed the door, Yanisa moved down the stairs to her father waiting below.

Hom paused to study the room in the dim light. Before long, she flicked the light switch that flooded a yellow glow. The once-sleeping man lifted himself quickly from the bed, disoriented by the brilliant light, and focused on his sister standing with bags at her feet, and saw the sorrow in her eyes that would surely soon find them both. They communicated with fingers to palms, agitated expressions on both faces. Within minutes the discourse was over. The man stood and moved over to the bags and flattened them as best he could into a mound of soft, undulating knolls. Then he nested his body on the plastic.

Hom switched the light off and moved over to the bed. She did not sleep.

Both sat before him silently on the bed, staring down at their feet, glancing up on occasion. The sapphire man scanned the room. All surfaces were clean, both toilet and kitchen. Unusual for a surprise inspection. He rubbed at his cheek and reflected. Six months of rent had been paid in advance. That time had now crawled to its end.

"I need rent money." He took out some stray baht notes to indicate his need.

Hom scribbled a note and handed him the pad. *How much?*

The sapphire man penned the options; sums listed monthly or six-monthly depending on their needs. Handed the pad to the pretty girl, who studied and passed it to her brother. The mute eyes met, then glanced without direction—the stare of the vulnerable. The sapphire man had seen these eyes too often; small balls that looked through all objects in their path, gazing out and beyond, never finding an end. He took the pad and scratched a note. *I come on Monday for the money.* Then he left.

Today saw Princess and Hom. Chosita is using her own money to look after P. I have given my saved money to look after H. Haven't told Durudee or mum. Haven't told anyone.

"Dudee... Dudee... Dudee... Yes, Durudeeee."

The two girls yelped in unison.

"She *said* Durudee. Clever Princess."

"After hearing the name a million times, what do you expect?" Lalana picked up the baby, who stood with unsteady legs against her trunk. "Say La-lan-aaa, my little sweet one. Lalanaaa."

The late afternoon breeze drifted through the open balcony doors, December bringing cool respite to Bangkok's skin.

"You're so smart, aren't you, Princess?" Durudee cooed.

The baby swayed, with soft limbs wanting.

"She will walk soon. Come on Princess, take a step for Lalana." She loosened her tender grip from the baby's wrist, though staggered legs promised more than they could give.

"I haven't seen Hom lately," Durudee said. "She should take more interest in little Princess."

"More interest than finding food?"

Durudee picked at the floorboards. "He's dead... I'm sure of it."

The girls sat quiet for a bit.

"If he is dead, what will we do about Princess?" Durudee said. "Chosita is too old to be her mother. Hom can't . . ." She paused.

". . . look after her," Lalana followed. "No. Hom can't look after her."

"There is always Phayathai babies' home, I suppose."

"How can you say that," Lalana said softly.

"I don't want it to happen. We are her aunties. We taught her to talk." Durudee chewed at her nails; the pulps of some fingers were already smarting from too much attention. "I don't want it to happen. You know that."

She managed to pull the shoe from his foot, dodging the swinging limb that struck out.

"What the fuck are you doing, you brat?"

"Need shoes clean." She peered up at him.

"No I fucking don't. Piss off."

She held her breath and started to polish.

"Give me my fucking shoe back."

Continued to polish.

The man gulped at his beer and belched. "Clean away then, but I'm not giving you any fucking money."

Lalana had worked the asphalt for two hours now, yet to snag a customer. So she continued to polish away—never lifting her gaze from the scuffed leather—through a fine mist of tears.

Dear diary,

I have a big plan. Bigger than anything before! You are the first to hear it. Are you ready—well here it is. I am going to ask mum if we can adopt Princess!! Chosita can help look after her during the day and I can pick her up after school. It will be so much better being a sister than an aunty. How cool is that! I wish you could talk and tell me what you think.

NINE

The room rolled and tossed him on the bed. Emmanuel hung his head down and choked into the bucket—a bitter straw liquid spewing out that caught his breath. It felt like his red face was swollen and might explode. And he spewed again.

They had moved him up from the bottom deck a day ago. It was supposed to help, though now he could hear the sea as well as feel it—see the spray splashing against the porthole—a constant reminder that made it worse.

He had tried to stay on deck—the salt-spray spitting at his face, cold and clean compared to the warm bile air that stifled below. But he was scared up there when the ship rolled—when the base of the waves sunk down three boats in depth or more, and threatened to swallow them whole. He saw himself flying off into the sea, his hands tight-fisted at the railings, his feet slipping against the timber. Everything wet, with the taste of salt. So he preferred to stay below in the warm bile air. And he spewed again.

This was the only way back. He had come this way before. He couldn't fly, so this was the only way. He looked up from his bunk at the porthole—a bit of blue behind tears of salt, which found time to crust when the swell had gone flat. The medic had come a while ago and gave him an injection that made him drowsy, so Emmanuel lay on his back, pale, his mouth caked like the glass, and tried to sleep.

And thought of her before he did.

TEN

Waves kicked within the laundry tub, leaving the timber floor slippery underfoot. Arthur waded in the music delivered by both earpieces of his iPod, floating in the operatic splendor of Lakmé's *The Flower Duet*, programmed to repeat until the chore was done. These angels soothed and calmed him. Anaesthetized. Splashes licked his shirt, as both hands submerged in the half-filled tub went to task. Cries from squabbling children in the nearby courtyard were drowned out by the sopranos' sweet music. Water sprayed and cooled.

His thoughts drifted back to childhood, fleeting images painted with a faded brilliance. The worn timber cart was patched with nails that stuck out and scratched, and pulled with a rope by screaming children. The loose wheel, he remembered, came off when the speed reached its threshold. It sat two, he remembered well. But only one when it was his turn. He remembered the protests when it was his turn. Sometimes they wouldn't play or pushed him off or blamed his bulk when the wheel came off. Blamed him.

He liked to play alone. It was easier that way. He remembered a menagerie of plastic soldiers collected over time from boxes of cereal— he had often been scolded when he opened more than one to add to his collection—with spears, muskets, helmets with pointed tops, or wrapped to protect faces without eyes. Roman, Mongol, Indians with bows and arrows, British standing tall with expansive chests above tapered waists. And the Indians always won.

A splash poked his eyes and broke the spell, yet allowed better-formed images to invade.

You want some food fat man? Stick a pin in and watch him burst. Ronnie's girls had also laughed at him, like girls had done since he could remember. Some hid their mirth, but most flaunted it. When, in sticky adolescence, he tried on a few occasions to steal their affection, he was only trodden on. And, as an adult, when cash bought affection, he saw the revulsion in their eyes. They were the filth, not him. They were the dogs, not him. So he found solace in giving them the shit they deserved. Found solace as they wiped foul excrement from their skin. His excrement.

Oh, how the music calmed him.

Sweat dripped from his forehead, stung his eyes, yet he continued the task, with shirt soaked and stuck to tight skin. As a child, he thought he came from another planet, he was so different from the others. He hid from the games he couldn't perform, shrank from the boys that mocked him. Taunts of the penguin, the beach ball, the greedy grub. These were Ronnie's words, and he was a friend. Even when adorned in suit and tie, he noticed the gaping mouths as he paraded. But he'd only ever had one true friend in his life. Not like the others, and few enough of them, who were entertained rather than wanting. Emmanuel had hugged him at the dance party—only Emmanuel—was genuinely pleased to see him in his smart attire, always offered words of encouragement, never made him feel awkward, never made him feel strange.

He loved Emmanuel.

The splashes ceased. The chore was done. The infant's swollen face, now washed of any color, gazed up at him from beneath the tub's shallows. Sunken and naked. With bits of ginger hair torn away, some in chunks still held together by wound elastics.

He rinsed his hands in the tub to wash away these ginger hairs. But they kept on sticking. He dunked them down again. But they kept on.

As the infant floated up to the surface.

Arthur's shoulders slumped; submitted to exhaustion. Closed his eyes.

And the angels sang.

The little refuse of a street traced its gentle incline down to the Chao Phraya River's edge; bikes swerved on the slender tarmac, pockmarked with divots and junk that spilled down from the cramped footpath. Only bikes or tuk-tuks came down this way—the dead-end path too narrow for fatter vehicles. And so he too came down.

The sack lay heavy over his shoulders, the child's twisted limbs coiled haphazardly within. Arthur stopped to swat the sweat that had collected on his brow—the never-ending ooze his labor's companion. Around him, the small street's slanted eyes seemed to poke in his sides, straight through flab to ribs, and deeper. A child skipped by, his mother in hand, both slowed to look, a seller of fruit arced his gaze at him—they surely knew, he saw they knew—and lugged his bulky load further along, as the quiet street screamed at him this knowledge.

He stopped and heaved a sweaty sigh, dropped the sack down carefully to his feet, saw the infant's form molded by the bag's sculptured relief, the little head that bulged like a melon, an elbow that pushed the canvas out, or was it a hand?

He lifted the sack over his shoulder, first the right, which now ached, then involuntarily to the left, and dragged his feet, step-by-step, closer to the river's edge. The hessian soon pinched at his skin, so he swung it over to the opposite side, yet now found little relief. I will have to, he thought, I will have to, and swung the sack from his smarting shoulder, catching it with one arm—and then the other.

And nursed her in his arms.

❀

A hessian sack full of straw doesn't sink. It floats on a pond in early spring to keep the Blanket Weed away. Bacteria break down the straw—a slow rotting chew—and use up the nitrogen to keep down the algae that otherwise would choke the pond, and all in it, if it were left to itself.

The hessian sack floated down the Chao Phraya River. But not to keep the Blanket Weed away.

❀

It was late afternoon, and Bangkok's clammy air brooded. The bearded man quickened his pace, jostling through street stalls, though never glancing at their keepers, and moved somewhat breathlessly up to the Shangri-La's entrance and through.

"Sa-wat-dii kha," a silk-clad woman said with a smile.

He nodded, but made no eye contact as he moved quickly to the registration desk, and addressed the female attendant. "I'm trying to contact a young woman who was staying at your hotel one year ago. She was a deaf girl by the name of Hom. I wonder whether she has left any forwarding address."

The attendant stared at the man, then replied tentatively, "Yes, sir. I remember her. However, it is hotel policy not to give the contact details of our guests."

"Yes, I understand. But you should realize I have information that would be of great benefit to her."

"Our manager has left for the day. I could ask him to contact you tomorrow."

"That would be helpful. But I'll be leaving Bangkok tomorrow, so it might be easier for me to contact him."

"I will leave him a message that you called, sir."

He nodded and moved to leave before turning back. "Do you know how long ago she left the hotel?"

"I am not exactly sure, sir. Around eight months ago, I would guess."

He thanked the woman and walked quickly to the entrance and out. At the road below he motioned to a tuk-tuk driver. "I'll show you where to go," and handed him five hundred baht. "I would like you to be my driver for a while. Is that okay?"

"You the boss."

He shouted directions over the bustling street life as they moved through the afternoon traffic, idle travel that seemed to be slower than walking. The perfume of diesel nauseated him, the wet air choked. Everything moved in slow motion.

The tuk-tuk driver turned and pointed to the man's head. "You should wear hat. Thailand sun too strong."

The man scratched at his bald scalp, as the tuk-tuk lurched further into the rabble.

As they approached the destination, he instructed the driver to find the nearest parking space and alighted from the vehicle. "Could you wait? If I'm not back in fifteen minutes, you can leave."

"I'll be here, boss. No worry." He grinned wide, a gold filling shining in his mouth.

The bearded man walked to the entrance of the building and moved up the stairs, turned to his right and approached the blue door and knocked. From within, he heard shuffling steps, and soon the door opened, revealing a potbellied man in shorts and white singlet.

"Hello. Do you speak English?"

The man wiped at his eyes and nodded. "Little, some."

"Thank you." He took a deep breath. "I am looking for people. They were living here last year. They were deaf."

The man frowned.

"Deaf. Could not speak." He made hand gestures in an attempt to translate.

"No one here. Just me."

"Do you know them?"

"No. No one here."

The bearded man tilted his body to gain a better glimpse within the small apartment. The room was cluttered with stacked boxes, but no other signs of life. A writing desk with a tray full of papers sat at the open window. He couldn't see a bed.

"No one here," the singlet man said. And slammed the door closed.

He sighed high into the ashen corridor. Stale air suffocated. With no further purpose on offer, he moved away, and down the stairs to the waiting tuk-tuk; the driver slumped in the semi-enclosed rear of the vehicle, his limbs squeezed to find space within its cramped casing.

The driver unfolded onto the saddle perched above the motor. "Where to, boss?"

He looked at his watch; it was nearly six o'clock. "The Plaza please."

"Plaza not open yet, boss. What you looking for? I help you."

"Please. Just go to the Plaza."

"You want girl? I show you place good."

The bearded man stabbed a glare deep into the driver, who nodded, and jerked the tuk-tuk back into the stream of traffic. He rubbed at his tender scalp that blistered tiny bubbles from the sun.

The journey seemed to take hours, but after thirty minutes they arrived. He lifted himself off the seat as dusk settled over the plaza, breathed in heavily, as if drawing the scene into his lungs, and scanned the surrounds. The bamboo bar was only scantly occupied; hunched shoulders skewered on stools, or bent over the long timber slab; and gazed at the barman, who seemed to look through him. He ordered a drink and found a chair overlooking the pedestrian traffic, and sat, watching the slow flow of trade.

As seven o'clock approached, he turned and saw her seated at the bar; cigarette glowing from painted lips, legs crossed, revealing glimpses of upper thighs and cotton that crept higher. She glanced briefly at him but, like the barman, also stared past. He felt invisible. Detached. But not for long.

He beckoned to the girl who stood some twenty feet away on the pedestrian corridor. She nodded and danced up, bringing her wares to the bench.

"What flavor you like?" the girl said.

"What do you have?"

"Fruit or mint." She sorted through the packs, suggesting more could be offered. Then, with manufactured surprise, shook her head and declared, "Today just fruit or mint."

"How much?"

"Fifty baht."

"I'll take two packets of mint, Durudee."

The girl fixed her gaze into his eyes. Then returned the packets to her container. "Why you shave head?" she said firmly.

"Do you like it?"

"No."

"Then I'll be sure to grow it back again."

Durudee glanced around and started to move away.

"Where are you going?" Emmanuel said.

"Got to work."

"But you haven't taken my money yet."

She hesitated before handing him the packets of gum.

Emmanuel gave her the baht. "Is Lalana coming tonight?"

"Where you been?"

He shifted in his chair. "I had to stay away much longer than I thought."

Durudee continued to glance around.

"Are you looking for Lalana?" he said.

"No. She not come."

"Do you know where Hom is?"

"No. Lalana does. But she home."

He glanced around to the bar. "What's her address? Could you write it down for me?"

Durudee fiddled into her tray, rearranging the box of gum without purpose. "Where you been? Why you not phone? Why you not write?"

"Durudee, just trust me. Can you write Lalana's address for me?" He clawed at his beard through to skin that chafed a layer of sweat.

Durudee bit her lip. "You ask her mother."

Emmanuel again twisted to see the manageress talking to the barman. He turned to face the teenager and took out notes from his pocket and quickly counted to one thousand baht. Handed it to the girl.

"Please, Durudee. Could you write down Lalana's address for me?"

The girl kicked at vacant air with the Plaza's trade thickening around her. Emmanuel leaned over the edge of the bar and saw the tuk-tuk driver slumped in the back seat.

"Please, Durudee."

The girl folded the notes into her moneybag and slowly lifted her head to meet his gaze.

"You ask her mother." And she turned to glide quickly away, swimming with the pedestrian traffic beyond the shrine and into the center of the plaza.

Emmanuel gulped at air that seemed not to nourish. Sweat crept from his forehead into his eyes. He rubbed his red scalp, aggravating the bubbled ooze, then moved quickly through the bar and away to the nearby tuk-tuk.

The driver flowed back into the front seat. "You okay, boss, you don't look well?"

"Can you take me to the river where the small boats are? Near the Grand Palace."

"Lots of traffic. Long time take."

Emmanuel handed him more baht. "Please, as quick as you can."

"Sure thing. I know fast way."

The tuk-tuk exploded into its staccato rhythm that continued until the journey's end. Despite protests, Emmanuel rid the driver from any further contract, and moved down the narrow street to the river. Vendors had long since quit their day, leaving littered carts wrapped in colored plastic at each flank of the road. He approached the small ferry terminal, but glanced beyond its entrance proper to the long-tail boats bobbing on the river's swell. Emmanuel thought he recognized the rainbow-colored boat used in past excursions, yet, like all of the boats, it slowly raised and slumped without its owner. He squeezed through the terminal gate and approached some boatmen huddled at the pontoon's edge.

"Do you speak English?"

The men shook their heads or stared blankly. Emmanuel rubbed his beard, gulping at sticky air.

One man jumped quickly to his feet and produced a worn map of the Chao Phraya, with its main branches and highlighted tourist routes.

Emmanuel studied the map. He thought he roughly knew the location of Lalana's klong house, and pointed to the area on the map. The boatman nodded and jumped onto the closest boat, then scampered from boat to boat until reaching his own. Started the engine with a cough and splutter, and guided it to the pier. The boatman extended his hand and directed Emmanuel clumsily to the center of the boat. Then churned it away into the swell.

As they darted across the river, Emmanuel closed his eyes. A wave of nausea clawed at his insides, diesel fumes no longer calming as of old. Nothing calmed. A charcoaled barge laden with cargo drifted nearby, shirtless men lay resting on its surface. Some smoked. Some chatted to their neighbors. Some slept. He glanced at the boatman, who nestled easily into the river's life. This boatman was just like them, just like the others they had left huddled at the ferry terminal, like the tuk-tuk driver and the bar attendant, like the woken man in shorts and singlet and the Shangri-La silk-clad women. And just like Durudee selling her mint-flavored gum. They all hovered around him, hovered without worries sitting heavy, not burdened with cares that suffocated and tore. They all hovered close, but without connection.

The long-boat needled slowly into the black-fingered klongs, Emmanuel scanning to find a familiar bearing. He thought he would be able to recognize the fence of potted plants that marked the boundary of Lalana's house and the canal, yet he had never been at night, and the small dimly lit klong houses seemed to purposely hide away into the black. Occasional laughter from the timber boxes whispered over the purring of the engine. But mainly they travelled in silence.

They drifted further into the night. After an hour of aimless wandering, his despair sat heavy. He wasn't certain he had seen any landmark of old and became worried they had moved far beyond the area he had wanted to explore. He felt an overwhelming tiredness fall down. And so, after waving to the boatman to return back to the ferry terminal, he slept.

He woke to a gentle hand on his shoulder, the boatman nodding to indicate their return. Emmanuel felt a sharp pain in his neck and slowly twisted his head to stretch taut muscles. Yet sleep had nourished. The boatman helped him to his feet and steadied the vessel as Emmanuel climbed onto the pier. Then took a large wad of baht from his pocket and handed it to the boatman, who beamed a nodded thanks.

Emmanuel moved up the narrow street to the main road facing the Grand Palace and smiled. The grinning tuk-tuk driver moved into the driver's seat as Emmanuel slumped in the open rear.

"Where to, boss?"

"If you get me near the Shangri-La Hotel, I can show you where."

It was nearly ten o'clock as the tuk-tuk hiccupped onto the road. Bangkok's traffic had now settled into a less hampered flow. Soon they reached Silom Road and moved up to its junction with Rama IV. Emmanuel gestured to move slowly east on the expansive road, the tuk-tuk hugging close to the pavement, allowing the streaming traffic to pass. He motioned to the driver to stop, and alighted directly outside the supermarket. A light rain sprinkled down, not enough to clean. He handed the driver some cash and moved up the stairs to the store.

"I'll wait here, boss."

Emmanuel opened the door and entered the supermarket. With the exception of the attendant, the store was empty.

"Could you help me? I'm looking for a deaf Thai girl who may come into your store. She is thin, eighteen, about this height." He held an outstretched hand to shoulder level.

The bleary eyed attendant nodded.

"You have seen her?"

"Sometime girl like that come."

"When was the last time?"

"Yesterday, or two days. Not sure."

Emmanuel purchased a bottle of Coke, left the supermarket, and began moving east. As he approached the bodies that hugged concrete walls to shelter from the increasing rain, he slowed, studied their faces, and moved on when failing to recognize. He followed the path onto each side street, many faintly lit and devoid of life, until he reached their end. Then returned back to the main road and continued the process. A methodical dragging wander, until weariness became an open sore.

He entered a tiny bar and sat at the window with a view that squinted through the traffic of the wide Rama IV—to the supermarket lit bright on the opposite side of the road. The waitress approached him with a menu in hand, and he ordered a coffee and packet of crisps, for he never drank alcohol. Not now. He stole a quick peek at the bar's few guests, dim forms within a smoky haze. A young Thai woman shone her smile through the dim, a warm beam within the turbid air, yet he moved his gaze back to the window and through to the supermarket beyond.

Over an hour he sat, sipping at the bitter black liquid in his cup, his gaze fixed on the market's steps that sat still and empty into the now-cleansing rain. He glanced at his watch that showed a need to move on, paid the bill, and ventured back into the dank outside.

The rain fell down without rest, soaked his skin, cooled his tender scalp. Slowly he moved into the dense jungle of street life, with the neon glowing like a bowl of fruit into the blue-black night. He turned onto a small side street then stopped. Some thirty feet away, a girl of slight build rested her back against a wall that found shelter from the rain. He moved some steps closer. His pulse raced. The girl glanced at Emmanuel, but turned to her companion, who handed her the food.

Emmanuel stopped, a wave of nausea bloated deep from within. He hunched over, resting both hands on his knees, and struggled to find his breath. The rain fell harder, streaming water down his beard. The gushing rain hid tears that welled, then flowed. The rain now in sheets; Hom's "I love Bangkok" T-shirt stuck to her chest as she continued to take the food from her brother. Emmanuel clutched at his scalp in pain. He had never felt such despair.

He moved some steps closer—then stopped, his mouth ajar yet silent, and gazed further into the girl, who put her plate down on the cardboard square, wiped her mouth with her hand, then looked up at him—this strange gray fountain sculpture. And saw it was him.

And from behind, a crowd had suddenly ballooned, a froth of twisting heads lit up by a red and blue pulse, and the emerald and gold of neon that shone high and down. Emmanuel turned to see the colored spectacle. As he focused on the scene, the dead weight of fatigue hung heavy. Then, as if descending from the heavens, a peculiar wave of relief dissolved all other emotions.

His burden removed.

They hadn't moved for some time. A cigarette nearby slowly burned without being consumed, like a timepiece measuring the minutes by the increasing length of ash. Tears ached and flowed from both mother and daughter. Yet she, the elder, could survive, had learned the skills. But how could her daughter bear this pain? What had Lalana done to deserve such grief, grief that throbbed and clawed?

She held her tight, rhythmically cradling the girl. Her daughter was smart and loving, she was so proud to be her mother. Since her father had left, Lalana had become an adult, only hidden beneath a child's skin. Unmarked. Lalana was also proud of her, even though she had been teased by fellow school friends about her mother with the short skirt and heavy makeup. But her daughter understood. Always held her arm when school functions brought them together, introduced her to all of her teachers with her head held high. Proud.

Lalana's sobs retreated, but soon returned almost heavier than before. Grief swallowed her whole. An hour had passed. No words spoken. When her father had left, they had talked for hours, never ignoring their plight, made plans and drew strength from them. But now she could find no words to comfort, no plans that would ease her daughter's pain.

At the foot of the bed, Lalana's leather-bound diary was opened to the current day's page, only half-finished before sorrow interrupted. She would never complete the entry.

Two Years Later

ONE

Journalism's first obligation is to the truth.

The woman walked up the stairs, her mop of tangerine-stained hair sprawled down to her shoulders. This was her second visit to Telegraph Hill. She loved how the foliage was thick and green and was a part of the houses—budding out as if the cottages were themselves vast trunks of trees. Hidden away. This wasn't her town but she loved how it settled so easy in its skin. A much bigger easy than the town that held claim to the phrase.

But she hated this part of her job.

She stopped and rested against a fire hydrant that pierced though the timber boardwalk, its helmet and valves pale blue. She thought it would be nice to walk up from Chinatown but she wasn't as fit as she'd like, so she stopped every so often and imagined living in one of the cottages that sprouted with green.

She had tried to visit the boy in Chinatown before she came. She had planned to take him out for dim sum. Make it clear he was not to blame. She would put this in print. He was seventeen and old enough to be interviewed alone, but she wanted to see them through the boy's eyes. See how he saw them. She needed more eyes than her own.

Chinatown was much larger than she had imagined. They say it's smaller than the one in New York, but it didn't seem so to her. Maybe because it was hot. All bustling in the heat. She had knocked on his door soon after school was out. The safest time she had thought. Timing was all in her field—pick your spot, pick your time. His mother was home and answered the door. She was hoping her English was poor—a confused Cantonese discourse with a few straggling pleasantries thrown up in English. She was hoping she wasn't home at all. But she was and her English was fine. So she never even sighted the boy, let alone shared dim sum with him. She might try again, but she didn't like her chances.

This was her second visit up on the Hill. She loved how the stairway was in timber and creaked like the trees if a wind blew up. Or so she imagined. She saw herself sitting and writing in a loft in the mauve cottage she had passed some minutes before. A pot of brewed coffee. A view out at the trees.

But she hated this part of her job.

She got to the top of the stairs and walked along the slate path and stopped with the cottage up front. Two stories, or three when you counted the loft. She looked at the windows on the second level and tried to guess which was the one. She took out her camera and took some pictures, kneeling on the slate to get the angle right—took a close-up of each of the three windows, their timber shutters closed on the inside, that could peek out but not in. She guessed which was the room. And she looked how high it was from the ground and what it would take. And she took some more pictures, with her great mop of tangerine-stained hair brash against the green surrounds.

The woman went up to the door and pressed the bell and heard it ring inside and the steps that came. The same gray-haired maid—dressed in black like her skin; not a uniform as such, and different from yesterday.

The maid looked into her eyes. "Don't you take no for an answer?"

"Sometimes."

"Then I suggest you take it now."

"I've come a long way."

"Then you best be getting an early start back."

She opened her handbag and flicked her fingers inside. "I didn't get a chance to explain yesterday." She paused. "I'm sorry, I don't know your name."

The maid just stared back.

Journalism's first obligation was to the truth. But she hated this part of her job.

"Would you tell Mrs. Abbot that I'm not from a newspaper. I'm a writer. I write long pieces. I can give her a copy of some. I have them with me."

"Then I will give them to her, but you are not coming in."

She took out a recent *Vanity Fair* article on Hemingway's friendship with Scott Fitzgerald and handed it to the maid. "If you don't mind, I'll wait here while you give it to her."

"I do mind, but I doubt that much matters." The maid closed the door and went away.

She stood on the porch and looked back into the garden. A Japanese Maple Waterfall hung a light lime along one edge of the path. She imagined sitting on the porch in a white wicker chair and reading Natsume.

The door opened after a minute.

"You can come in," the maid said. "You don't stay long though, okay?"

She knew this was the maid's instruction, not her employer's. But she nodded anyway.

She followed down the hallway and through to a long open sitting room and saw her standing there. *God she is beautiful.* She had seen many models before, and always marveled at their glamour, the perfect symmetry of their face, and something else she couldn't explain. "Mrs. Abbot, I really appreciate this time."

"Jill." The woman looked over to the maid with a face all blue eyes and lashes. "Hattie, could you bring us some tea."

She didn't look at the maid but felt the chill of her fury in the quiet. And she sat down and looked out at the Bay Bridge, silver across the harbor.

"You have a magnificent view, Jill." But somehow she preferred the garden out back and the wicker chair that wasn't there.

"Hemingway is my father's favorite novelist," Jill said.

She smiled a little at this woman who sat lower down in an old recliner.

"And I have read your article before," Jill said.

Bull's-eye. "I hope you liked it."

"Yes. The story of big egos is something I've got to know a bit about over the years."

"I've seen your work too, some remarkable images."

"Remarkable. Is that really the word for them?"

She gazed at the perfect symmetry of her face full of eyes. She was about to reply but didn't get a chance.

"My father always said that beauty is more remarkable when described in poetry." Her face with all eyes looked out into the harbor. "'I am as lovely as a dream in stone,' he used to tell me as a child."

She was intelligent as well. If you didn't know her story you would think she was blessed. "Your father writes good poetry."

Jill's eyes lit up. "Actually, that was Baudelaire. We never knew at the time what was his and what were others. And in some cases I still don't know."

The maid brought in the tea on a wide metal tray. Some fruitcake. And some lemon and milk.

"Hattie, would you like to stay and sit a while?"

The maid looked at Jill and shook her head. She put down the tray and went back out of the room.

"I thought you might want to talk to Hattie as well."

"I would love to, but I don't think she approves of me."

Jill smiled. "No, I think you are right."

She looked down at the woman who sat back on her chair and rocked a few times. She tried to imagine her old and knitting in the chair, but this face of hers seemed unable to age. Journalism's first obligation is to the truth. But she didn't like this part of her job because no good would come of it. Not to these people at least. Hattie knew this and probably so did Jill. The questions she had to ask were cold. But there was no other way.

She watched the woman shift her gaze from the harbor and back at her—this face all blue eyes and lashes.

"So, what would you like to know?"

She sat forward on her chair. And thought it unlikely she would get to finish her tea. "I would like to understand the delay . . . the reasons for the delay that is . . . in telling the police."

She would like to spend some time with this woman, but knew it was unlikely. Her questions were too cold—but there was no other way.

TWO

It started to bloom. At first an outline of mauve that etched its sting, clawing up and around. A slow scratching bud that sung out a mechanical purr as it went. Up and around her back.

Lalana lay face down, her head turned away from the churning pen and the rubber-gloved man. And she held her friend's hand.

"You could stop now if you want," Durudee said.

The rubber-gloved man stung a glance at the girl who sat on the other side of the bed. Alak stood back a bit but wanted to be closer.

"You could easily stop now, you still have time." Durudee looked around at Alak but the boy stood quiet into the purr. "Don't look at me like that," she said to the rubber-gloved man.

He turned his head back down and kept on with the churning pen that slowly crept its course.

"Have you told your mother yet? Promise me I don't have to be there when you do."

"I'll be there if you like," Alak said.

"Well, I would suggest you take a bigger bunch of flowers with you this time, Alak Phanrit," Durudee said. "Like from a whole garden."

Lalana stole a slight smile into the hurt.

"What's the legal age to get tattoos, Mister?" Durudee said.

"Haven't you got somewhere else to go?"

"Unfortunately for you . . . no."

"Sixteen."

"And have you checked her birth certificate?"

The rubber-gloved man kept on with his mechanical purr. He thought himself a dentist with an artist's brush. And loved to work on such a clean canvas.

"These needles are new I hope?"

"I only use dirty needles with someone like you."

"Alak, are you going to let him talk to me like this?"

Lalana saw the boy's anguish through the purr. Even though her eyes were closed.

"You two a couple then?"

"Not that it's any business of yours," Durudee said, "but no we are not."

"You available then?"

"Lalana, you know it'll be impossible to remove this without scarring."

"I take that as a yes then."

Durudee turned to face the man. "Where are we going on our first date? Perhaps a visit to the prison you have probably spent some years in . . . or plan to?"

The man smiled, wiping the skin as it inched up higher.

In time the mauve flushed bright on its amber canvas. And the yellow. The colors destined to become more vivid through the ooze that would crust over the next few days. That would blossom up and around her back. Etched deep in her skin. Branded almost.

And she liked the pain.

"This might sting a bit more, Lalana," he said.

"That's okay."

"I have to fill in the color . . . it hurts more."

"That's okay."

"You could come back another time."

"No, it's all right. Really."

He looked down at her face that now turned to his side. "You haven't flinched a bit. You're a tough one, aren't you?"

She smiled her dimples up at him.

"I've been thinking," Durudee said. "How much is it to get a little teddy bear on my hip?"

"You promise to visit me in prison, and I'll do it for free."

"Weekends only."

"And Valentine's day."

"You're a brute. Is that a picture of your mother on your arm?"

"You like her?"

"Not really."

"It's my sister."

"She visits you in prison?"

"Only on weekends."

The late afternoon continued to purr. As time went on, it blossomed loud on her back. Mauve and yellow over coffee with milk. A flourish of bee-stung spring. And throughout, Lalana panted through the bloom—holding her friend's hand—as the ache followed the color that curled up and around.

And she liked the ache.

In the classroom, rows of blue and white uniforms squirmed, as if the teens had pointed buttocks that kept them tipping on their chairs. Some of the white shirts were decorated with messages scribbled in pen; parting words that shone with excitement, yet reached out with fingers that strained to clutch at vestiges from these safe days. Days soon to be lost.

Ratana Narmsra entered the room with a pace slower than usual. Before two steps were taken, the blue and white uniforms erupted in screams. Some of the uniforms stood, some drummed on their desktops, some wiped tears—both boys and girls. Ratana Narmsra, in her twenty years of teaching, had never tired of this day.

She lifted her hands to soften the shrieks. "My favorite history class!"

The cacophony erupted with more force. She always started her speech this way—these students deserved such pampering.

"My dears, you are making me feel like a queen."

The pounding of drummed desks escalated.

"Class, please sit . . . for we have much to talk about."

The blue and white uniforms fell in their chairs. Silence enveloped, though some of the pointed buttocks continued to squirm.

"My final year students, on this day, your very last day of school, I plan to move away from the study of history and focus on the future. And, as this day is not about me, I will hand the class over to your capable hands, with my role reduced to a humble moderator."

Scattered desks drummed their approval.

"So, in this short time we have left together, I wish to find out, from each and every one of you, what plans you have for the future." She scanned her students' faces carefully, meeting eye contact with warmth that each teen felt was meant for them alone. "Do not despair if you believe your dreams seem not to be as exciting as others, for they are your dreams . . . the most important in the world."

She sat on her desk, carefully scanning the faces again, until she was sure all had met her gaze.

"Hansa, let us start with you. What are your plans?"

The girl stood, twisting to glance at the uniforms. "I plan, if my grades are okay, to study hospitality."

"Excellent! I will have a five star hotel to stay whenever I like." Laughter resonated.

The beaming girl sat quickly down, and, when seated, curved her shoulders back, high and proud.

"And what of my special history study group. Alak, what can we expect of you my dear?"

The boy stood sheepishly and lifted one hand that scratched against a spike of gelled hair. "My uncle has a small store. A mini-market. He wants me to learn the business and help. I might do some accountancy or business studies. Something like that."

"I can see you as an owner of many stores in the future my dear. Many stores! And my darling Durudee. I am most interested to hear your plans."

The teen rose to the sound of spluttered giggles—though bearing warmth, not ridicule. She turned to gaze at the uniforms in mock annoyance.

"Well, I have many plans."

"I am sure. Your dreams have always managed to sparkle from those bright eyes of yours."

Durudee grinned. "Yes, my eyes are one of my best features." Laughter spilled as she pouted her lips at two of the boys seated nearby—they, like the other uniforms, were entranced by the theatre before them. "Anyway, I plan to take a bit of a rest. I'm exhausted from all the recent study."

"A well deserved rest, I'm sure."

"And when I'm well rested, I plan to try and become . . ." she twisted around again to glance at the uniforms, "a teacher."

The desks drummed, hoots bellowed. Ratana Narmsra lifted her arms to soften the din. "I am speechless, Durudee . . . and thrilled. Another recruit to the most wonderful profession I know. And what subject do you wish to teach?"

The girl shifted her gaze to her desktop. "As a matter of fact, if I was able to get the marks—which as you know might be hard—I thought history would be fun."

The uniforms erupted into a frenzy that Ratana Narmsra did not attempt to quell. Durudee lifted her gaze to the eyes of her teacher, who nodded with a beaming grin. The teen's face, flushed with crimson, mirrored her smile.

As the clamor settled, Durudee continued. "And, of course, I will be married by twenty-five and have three babies."

Laughter again erupted.

"I am sure you will . . . but not all at once I hope." She shifted her gaze to the hunched shoulders of the girl sitting adjacent. "And what of you, Lalana? What dreams have blossomed from such a talented girl?"

Ratana Narmsra focused on the slouching girl. She had watched the dark clouds hover over her for some time. Clouds that seemed to suck any joy from the teen into their sodden gray mass, ready to pour down. But it had yet to rain.

They had met recently—the school principal, Ratana, and Lalana's mother. A nice woman and a bona fide mother, though the harshness of Bangkok had left their scars. The recent meeting had been their second. The first was over a year ago, and, in retrospect, should have been earlier. Her grades were down then, the usual first or second place relegated to average. And Lalana was not average. But school meetings of such importance usually needed something tangible to start off, and the scribbled numbers of grades on a report card, though a poor depiction of a child's journey at school, was usually that something.

"The whole school knows of the tragic death of the baby girl, Mrs. Songpow," the principal had said.

"Ms not Mrs.," Lalana's mother had replied. Ratana had smiled at this, though the principal's face displayed his discomfort. Mr. Wiriyapong's face often displayed uneasiness—particularly when meeting with Ratana Narmsra. Such a double assault may have been too much for him.

Ratana had taken charge. "I am worried about Lalana, Ms Songpow."

"I am worried too," she said softly.

"Has she seen a doctor?"

"Twice. Soon after it happened. He wanted to put her on tablets, but my daughter didn't want to. My daughter is strong willed, Mrs. Narmsra."

"Yes, this is one of her charms. But such a strong will at an early age may also lead her on a winding path."

"Perhaps the tablets would be a good idea," Mr. Wiriyapong said.

"Perhaps," Ratana said. Perhaps not, she had thought.

"We also have an excellent school counselor," he said.

Excellent might be stretching the truth a bit.

"She is away at the moment, otherwise I would have asked her to join us."

And so plans were made for tablets and counselors. Her grades improved somewhat, but the dark clouds persisted. Hence the second meeting of recent times—a more complicated meeting.

"As you know we have a strict dress code in the school," Mr. Wiriyapong said. "And tattoos are strictly forbidden."

"I'm not happy about it either," Lalana's mother said.

"I must say, it's usually the boys that get the tattoos," he said.

Ratana followed. "We are becoming a more progressive society."

His brow rose up. "Tattoos are progressive?"

She kept on quiet, since she knew the discussion wasn't helping.

"Tattoos in men are often a sign of defiance . . . the young warrior," he said.

"I know about men," Lalana's mother said.

"But in teenage girls, especially someone like Lalana, it worries me."

Ratana had seen the tattoos. They had taken her breath away.

"Your daughter has told me that she spends much of her holidays at the Plaza, Mrs. Songpow." Not the best words the school counselor could have opened with, Ratana thought.

"Ms not Mrs."

The counselor shifted her gaze to the principal. He always sat comfortably around the conflict of others, Ratana observed.

"Ms . . . I apologize. But is it true, Ms Songpow?"

"Yes. She earns money by shining shoes."

"The Plaza is not, in my opinion, the perfect place for a child to spend her time."

Ratana focused on the mother's eyes—surprised such strong words had brought no change in the woman's expression. She must have pondered on this many times.

"Perhaps you are right. But I am with her all of the time, she is amongst friends, she has learnt the value of money." Her eyes drilled into the principal. "And she learns some things that school cannot teach."

The lengthy pondering confirmed.

"But she is soon to become an adult, and the Plaza will have served its purpose."

"I am still worried about Lalana, Ms Songpow," Ratana said.

"And so am I."

The meeting delved into doctors and tablets, school grades and sadness—the importance of the school's support, soon to end. Finally, plans were made of sorts—as best as could be expected, Ratana begrudgingly agreed.

The blue and white uniforms had now turned toward Lalana, who remained silent.

"I have always found the blossoming of dreams in the most talented to take the longest time," Ratana said.

"Yeah, my dreams came to me in a second," chimed in Durudee, attempting to lighten the mood. Laughter heartened, yet uneasily.

"Talent can bring a rapid blossoming as well, of course."

Lalana lifted herself from her chair, and nodded with resolve. Her wide eyes brightened. "I've always had plans, Mrs. Narmsra. My problem is how to get them."

Ratana was buoyed by the girl's strong will. She could almost see the dark clouds dispersing. "With our dreams, we usually focus on the endpoint my dear... the glitter... however, the journey to those dreams is sometimes the greatest gift of all. But share with us your plans even though the path is yet to be found."

Lalana straightened her shoulders, her prior slouched position transformed.

"My dream is simple. It is to leave Bangkok."

Durudee laughed. "You guys alone again. Why don't you get a hotel room?"

The two had nested on a bench in one of the few shaded corners of the playground. Blue and white uniforms scurried past, occasionally slowing to shout farewell messages, nothing philosophical or weighty, but nevertheless with great zeal.

"You know you love each other," Durudee said, "and since I love you both, and we have broken up more than a year ago, Alak Phanrit, you have my blessing to set off together."

The pair grinned at their friend.

"Anyway, Deng just asked me out on a date. I let him carry my bag for a week, so the least I could do was give him the pleasure of taking me out for a meal." She moved her head in the direction of a boy shouldering two bags in the middle of the swarming playground. A scarecrow in a field of crows. "Look at him, so strong and handsome." She lowered her voice. "But maybe a bit *too* athletic. I'm leaning towards the more intellectual type these days."

Durudee turned to wave at the boy some fifty feet away. "I must be off, Lalana. Let's all meet at your mum's bar tonight at seven. She always promised me a free drink after I finished school. So tonight I collect." And moved away to the boy in waiting.

The two sat on the bench, a comfortable distance apart.

"Mum won't give her a drink, you know," Lalana said. "Not until she's eighteen. But it'll be fun to watch how she wriggles out of it, since she promised it a thousand times."

"I like your mum," Alak said.

"She likes you too. She says you're still the last man to give her flowers."

Man? He didn't feel like a man. He scanned the horde of darting students. This really would end today.

Alak turned to face Lalana. "How are you feeling?"

The girl moved closer and gently placed her head on his shoulder. His pulse raced—but not hers.

"Tired," she whispered.

He tilted his head to increase the contact. Not forceful, but with a gentle touch. "Have you seen that counselor lately?"

"Yeah. She's okay. And it makes mum happy that I've kept seeing her, even though she doesn't have any of the answers I need."

"Can I help?"

She lifted her head, giving the boy a kiss on the cheek. And, this quiet time, on an aluminum bench overlying the sweating asphalt, Alak Phanrit would remember for the rest of his life.

"You're such a nice boy, Alak."

He kicked at some gravel that nested at his feet. "But you don't love me . . . do you?"

Lalana sighed and moved her head back onto his shoulder.

"That's okay, I guess." The boy retrieved the stones back into kicking range with his shoe. "Tell me though, tell me the truth."

Lalana lifted her head and peered at the frowning boy.

"Is it because I got caught with my cousin?"

Lalana giggled. "What makes you say that?"

"Durudee said you couldn't be with anyone who did that."

Lalana laughed, and kissed the boy firmly on his lips.

"Durudee says lot of things . . . most of which are crazy."

They walked down the narrow street just before the sun went down. They knew it was the place because of a newspaper clipping Durudee had found. Chosita had come many times before, in the early days once a week or more. But they hadn't—and they thought it was about time they did.

The fruit seller was shutting down his cart and watched them walking past. The strip of road threw up shades of sepia and gray—from the wet asphalt, down to the river in front, and the sky that spread a gentle rain into the dusk; this vista as seen from an old silver gelatin box-camera.

Durudee held on to the soft underside of Lalana's arm, clutching a bunch of flowers, all color in the gray. The narrow street was no more than two hundred feet in length, and so they soon made the slow incline down to the river's edge.

Lalana looked into the water and understood why he had chosen the place. The long-boat pontoon was worn and used less than the ferry terminal just up the way. And it fell down sharply and out of sight of the road further up where they came.

The fine rain slanted into the river. Durudee took the flowers from Lalana, knelt down on the pontoon, and placed them in the water.

And they both sat on the step together, and watched them float down with the river's swell, breaking up into little strands of color into the wash.

THREE

Arthur lay within the meadow of green, green that was meant to soften and soothe, as best it could. Tannhäuser's repentant pilgrims hovered around him, sang of their remorse, repentance bringing salvation. Two of the pilgrims shuffled with purpose nearby—with gentleness, he thought—and he saw their crowded faces further afield. Not far, but beyond touch, layered as in a theatre, with gaze meeting his, their chorus that slowly surged, that sweetly calmed. He looked at his arms that tried to raise, but were unable, and looked at the folds of loose skin that draped like curtains. He liked this slender body, so light it almost floated, and pondered what would be different if he had possessed this slight frame of old?

Arthur closed his eyes as restless violins sounded from heaven, their crescendo pushing his soul, bringing tears that welled from relief not found before—nor again. An insect from the meadow pierced his skin, and soon another, but managed only brief distraction from the pilgrims' crescendo, who sang as one, without fear of hell or death:

Hallelujah! Hallelujah!

Forevermore.

The pilgrims' faces began to fade, the emerald meadow bruising to a softened olive, then gray. And soon darkness.

Behind the window glass, Jill and Stephen Abbot sat close together—though not quite touching. He was dressed smart—a well cut navy-blue suit that hung with sharp lines, the white of his shirt and the red of his tie, like the lapel pin—a small worn flag of the United States, neatly fastened at the level of his heart. This his grandfather's who served in the Great War, handed down to Stephen's father, Old Gray, who served in Korea, and then to Stephen, who didn't serve at all. He had learned to count with this pin, and his father before him, up to forty-eight since Alaska and Hawaii were yet to tally when the pin was made. He meant to teach his children to count the same way. This was the family tradition. But he wasn't sure he could.

Jill knew the story of the pin—of this family who moved out from Oklahoma before it was named, well before the Dust Bowl hit hard, to start a new trade out west—the story of this great San Franciscan family of forty-eight counters. There had been too many Stephens and Josephines in this family. So, unlike her husband, she knew no child of hers would learn to count from the little worn pin. She would take care of this herself.

The others were all gone now. They left like they were leaving a cinema, some straight up and out, others like waiting for the credits to end, or perhaps to see an unexpected scene play out just before the screen goes black. Strangers some, others they knew—some well, some just a bit. The orange haired woman stayed the longest—busily scratching notes down on her pad—though they wanted to avoid her the most. But that wasn't why they stayed on. It was right they were last. Perhaps not for the best—for the soul that is—but right.

There had been too many Stephens and Josephines in this family.

Old Gray Stephen had stayed away. She was surprised at this. But he blamed himself. She didn't much care, but he blamed himself. Old Gray was old now, that turning old, stooped and wizened of spirit. Hunched and muttering. But she didn't much care.

She looked at the walls and thought the green an odd choice of color. White would be more suitable. Not hospital white. An off-white, bone or sandstone. Yes, sandstone. A color not alive or dead—not dark like soil but still of the earth.

Her father had stayed away as well.

She saw her Stephen sit up, expanding his chest to full extent, sniffing the air as it entered his lungs. But Jill sunk lower, and dropped her gaze to the iPod cords dangling from the bed, the ear-pieces just hovering above the floor's surface.

Stephen motioned a slight rise off his chair then dropped back down. Like something tied him there. She saw this from the corner of her eye—her gaze still at the green. They didn't have much of a journey back home. That was a relief. Forty minutes or a bit less—the highway an easy run, particularly at this time. She might drive, she thought. She would give him a rest. But what would they talk about? She could listen to the radio. Not the news of course. Jesus, not talkback. Music. Not pop either. Classical better. Music the color of sandstone.

She started to cry.

And Stephen held her hand.

There had been too many Stephens and Josephines in this family.

Now

(Part 2)

ONE

Emmanuel swallowed the last of his apple juice, washing away any remnant of hollandaise sauce, and lay on his side. Beside him, his pillow of duck feather down molded perfectly into his trunk and limbs. When he rolled into a new position, it followed him without effort, as was his want. He caressed the pillow's cotton casing tenderly, kissed its hem, and found its lips or cheeks or forehead with ease. He felt the warm soft down that stole its heat, and soon whispered thoughts without sound.

"Everything will be all right, my darling; you know that, don't you? You're so strong and beautiful, so very beautiful. And what wonderful times we had, what laughs. Hey, do you remember?" He squeezed the pillow's flesh gently. "But rest in my arms awhile."

The pillow's face now drifted into a new guise, an adolescent with dimpled cheeks and ponytail of ink, and, still warm from his warmth, it turned with him to face the opposite side. "Oh, you're awake now. How peacefully you've slept. What places are we to explore today, what adventures have you planned?" He prodded the pillow playfully, then held it tight. "Oh, how I loved the breakfast of fruit on the canal that time . . . what an early start we had . . ."

"Oh, it's you," he said.

The tangerine-haired woman stood tall at the doorway.

"Hello, Emmanuel. How you feeling?" Facile question number one. She must do better than that. She glanced down at the empty tray at the foot of the bed, surprised he had eaten. "I came early. They told me you'd just finished breakfast. I won't stay long. I promise."

Emmanuel nodded.

She entered the room and dragged the lone chair to within a few feet of his knees—he seated on the edge of the bed—and placed a digital recorder on her lap.

"How's your writing going?" he said.

"Not that well, I'm afraid."

"Can I help?" He threw up a faint smirk.

And he could smile. Another surprising achievement.

Emmanuel lent back on the bed, supporting himself with bracing arms. "Have you come up with a title yet?"

The woman studied his face—withdrawn cheeks and depressed eye sockets—and reflected on the slow shedding of flesh that perhaps best symbolized his last twelve months of life. Yet today he had eaten all his breakfast. How very strange. And managed to trap his wandering gaze with hers. "I was wondering whether you can suggest one?" She needed to challenge him.

Emmanuel lowered his eyes to the digital recorder on the woman's lap, focused on its heartbeat of pulsing red light. He remained silent for a while, she unable to sense the tone of his muses.

"Not really, but I'll think it over."

The woman took out a small note pad from the pocket of her jeans. "Let me read the opening sentences to you," and flicked through the pages until she came to the one required—although she knew the prose by heart. "Emmanuel Stephen Soutard is a shoe salesman from Sydney, Australia. He is a likeable man, in his mid-thirties, of gentle disposition, with no rough edges. He is a man I feel fortunate to have met."

Emmanuel smiled. "I like the start." He stretched out his legs and briefly brushed against the woman's calf, then retracted both limbs into their bended position.

Always the gentleman. Even now.

"Go on, I like to be read to."

"Unfortunately, so far, that's all I've got."

He shifted his knees again, this time avoiding any physical contact, and again focused on the rhythm of the recorder's throb.

"Tell me more about your old job," she said.

Emmanuel squinted, the lines of his forehead folding into view. "Why on earth do you want to know about that . . . and today?"

"Did you like it?"

"No. Selling shoes for ten years, the only job I had since leaving school, became very boring." He shifted forward, closer to the woman, his knees interlocked with hers, the tiny room hugging them gently together. "But tell me, what do you need from me . . . right at this moment?"

She was really missing something, and she had little time to find it.

The woman again stole into Emmanuel's eyes, and reached out to place one hand on his knee. He sat still, neither shirking her touch, nor slinking for more.

"This whole thing doesn't make sense to me Emmanuel. It doesn't sit right." And left her docile hand in place. "Most importantly, I need to know why?"

Emmanuel brought both hands to his face, rubbing his closed eyes, and then squeezed at his mane of chocolate-colored hair. And shrugged.

"I don't see how it really matters . . . why? Do you?"

Ronnie James was seated when the strangers entered the small, windowless room. The cream walls were uncluttered with the exception of a timbered crucifix facing an officious framed sign stating only three visitors were allowed at any one time. A woman shuffled slowly, assisted by her husband, who held her other arm firmly, easing her carefully into the chair. She patted her permed hair while acknowledging Ronnie with a brief stare that soon moved, directionless, to the floor. The man moved his chair closer to his wife, and gave a more definite greeting with a nod and strained grimace.

After an awkward period, Ronnie broke the silence. "I can see the family resemblance."

The older man nodded.

"Would you be Emmanuel's parents?"

The man again nodded, his wife motionless, with her gaze remaining fixed to the yellow linoleum.

"I'm Ronnie. A friend of Emmanuel's."

"Donald Soutard. This is my wife, Sharon."

"Pleased to meet you, yes. Pleased to meet you."

"He's just having a shower. He shouldn't be long."

"There's no rush, Donald. No rush for me."

"Nor for us." His eyes now downcast like his wife.

"You live in Australia?"

The older man confirmed with a nod.

"Nice. I'm from Blackpool. I'd love to take some of that warm weather of yours home. Even in the summer, we only get a few weeks of good, hot sunshine."

"We've got plenty of sun to give, that's for sure. It was hot before—"

"Where do you know my son from?" the woman said, her gaze still fixed at her feet.

"We met on travels, Sharon. We're old travelling companions."

The woman nodded without lifting her head.

"We became good friends and had some wonderful times. Really, some wonderful times."

"He was a good child," she said hesitantly, almost to herself. "A bit naughty when he was very small. Easily distracted. That's what his report cards used to say. All through his schooling. Easily distracted."

The man held his wife's hand.

"He never really liked schoolwork." She lifted her gaze at last to Ronnie's. "But he was a very good sportsman, wasn't he, Donald? Soccer, swimming, snooker. We bought him a snooker table when he was fourteen. Only a small one. But he practiced as soon as he got home, weekends, often for hours on end. Played for the Workers Club. He was Bankstown junior sportsman of the year for soccer, you know. A goalkeeper. For the YMCA."

The pace of the monologue slowly increased, the recent expressionless mask seemingly torn from her face. Distant memories crystallized into barely connected themes. "He loved his dogs. Except for Wolf, who bit him. I don't think he has any memory of it now. He was only tiny then, but was scared of any dog for years after. Remember, Donald? We bought him a Labrador soon after he was bitten. You might have seen the small scar on his upper lip. But he was scared of her. Even though she was as gentle as a lamb. But he was easily distracted at school. Easily distracted."

She lifted her head to face Ronnie. "Once, he and two of his friends were expelled from primary school. Just for a day. They wrote in a library book. You know, dirty pictures. Like most boys. When we went up to the principal, he asked me if I knew why he was expelled. I told him I knew. You know what he said? Do you remember, Donald? He said that none of the other boys told their parents the truth. He was the only one." She smiled, turning to her husband, who had heard all this before. The man let the talk run its course, though it grated at his innards. "I must say, I asked Emmanuel about it when he just woke up in the morning, still with his head on the pillow. I think that helped. But just the same, he was the only one to tell the truth. He won an atlas for soccer. A really expensive one. I still have that at home. Leather bound and—"

"I remember using it for my projects." Emmanuel stood at the doorway.

All lifted their gaze to the frail man who leaned against the open door.

"Emmanuel, my boy." Ronnie stood quickly and embraced his friend, while the older couple looked on with blank expressions. The woman's mask now tightly fitted; her lips and brow painted with a horizontal stroke of the brush.

"Let me look at you." Ronnie couldn't look into his friend's eyes; rather he shifted his gaze to Emmanuel's skeletal frame.

Emmanuel moved slowly to his mother and gently placed his hand on her shoulder. "Do you mind if I have a few moments with Ronnie alone?"

"Of course, son, take all the time you want. I'll take your mother to the toilet."

"No need to go. I'll talk with Ronnie in my room."

"Do you need to go to the toot, girl?"

"No, Donald. Let's stay here and wait."

"You can make some coffee or tea outside, Mum."

"No, thanks. We'll wait here."

Emmanuel led his friend to the room next door, with identical cream-colored walls and banana flooring. A small window allowed banded light of the late afternoon sun to enter, but was set too high to let in visible evidence of any life beyond. Emmanuel sat on the single bed that lay in one corner, occupying just a quarter of the room's surface. Ronnie lifted a timber stool and moved it closer to his friend.

"I'm so happy to see you, Ronnie."

"Me too, my boy." Ronnie faltered, straining to meet his gaze. "So, how do you feel?"

Emmanuel scratched at his shaven cheek. "Actually, I'm not too bad. I sometimes feel relieved. Though I'm terribly tired, Ronnie. Tired of everything. I sleep sometimes twenty hours a day. It's nice and quiet here. Peaceful, in a strange way."

Ronnie nodded, though he didn't understand. "Your parents are nice."

"They're stronger than I thought they'd be. But they shouldn't have to see this, Ronnie. Parents should never have to see this."

Ronnie nodded. This he understood.

"Have you been back to Bangkok much, Ronnie?"

"Sure, my boy. You know me, I can't keep away."

"The Plaza is still your favorite?"

"On and off. I get a bit bored of the same place, all the time."

"I never noticed you bored there."

Both eased comfortably into a grin.

"We had some laughs, my boy. Some real giggles." Then, shaking his head as if trying to solve a puzzle, "That fucking Penguin . . ."

Emmanuel smiled and met his companion's gaze. "You were too hard on him, Ronnie."

For the second time, Ronnie couldn't understand the words of his friend. He moved his eyes aimlessly away, clawing at his scalp. Then, after what seemed an eternity, "Oh, I ran into that young schoolgirl friend of yours last time I was there."

Emmanuel sat upright. His pulse quickened. "Lalana?"

"Not sure of her name. Skinny girl. She used to try and sell me bloody gum all the time."

"Durudee."

"Could be. I don't think she remembered me. She was picking up glasses in the bamboo bar at the Plaza."

"How was she?"

"I had a bit of a chat. My sweet talk didn't seem to attract her much. I'm getting well and truly past it, my boy." He sighed. "She had these big braces on her teeth. Picking up glasses with big bloody braces and still wasn't interested in me. I'm well and truly fucking past it."

Emmanuel smiled, comforted by Ronnie's anecdote delivered with his soothing English drawl.

"She would be finished school by now, I suppose," Emmanuel said.

"She didn't have a school uniform on. Not like some of the girls in the Plaza."

"Was the manageress still the same? Lalana's mother."

"I think so. I reckon she'd be a real ball-breaker."

"She certainly would find good reason to bust your balls, Ronnie."

They both smiled, now settling into the easy banter of old.

"Probably would do me good. I'm thinking I might settle down, getting too bloody old for it all."

"Have you found someone?"

"No." He lied. The thought of any exchange of newfound love seemed crass to him—at this late hour. Indeed, before this meeting, as he took a light breakfast in his hotel, Ronnie had worked out exactly on what basis he would lie to his friend. The principle seemed simple—anything that he thought would cause grief, he would spare Emmanuel. And, since weaving deception into the truth came naturally to Ronnie, Emmanuel took his words at face value. As he always had.

"So you never saw Lalana?"

"No."

"She probably has her own tour company by now."

Ronnie nodded.

"You know what I had for breakfast, Ronnie? Eggs Benedict. They really made an effort."

Ronnie shifted on his stool.

Emmanuel sighed, and then, "You didn't see Hom by any chance?"

"No, my boy."

"Durudee never mentioned her, I suppose."

"No."

"You know what, she could easily pick up glasses. That would give her some spending money. Perhaps you could suggest that, Ronnie. When will you be there next?"

"I'll be flying there as soon as I leave here. I'll be sure to suggest it. I'm sure being deaf would be an advantage, working at that bar. Some of the trade there is really rough these days. These young guys have no fucking class."

"You gave her some money soon after . . ."

"Yes, my boy. Don't you worry. I'll keep an eye on her."

"Let's get mum and dad in here."

Ronnie returned with two chairs for Emmanuel's cramped room.

They all sat close, Emmanuel at first seated, then, as weariness overpowered, lying on his side. But close. For over an hour, the four whispered memories, gave comfort—or attempted—held hands, sometimes brief, sometimes refusing to let go. A blanket of intimacy covered them. Until in a brief lull.

"What was this about?" his mother said. "Why, Emmanuel?"

"Quiet, girl," the older man said softly. Words to calm, not command.

"No, Donald. He's never told us. We have a right. I have a right."

All looked to the floor except the woman, the mother, whose eyes pierced, pleaded, fixed on her son. Emmanuel continued to stare at the clean linoleum without sound. Silence ached and twisted hard.

"Never mind, son," she said. Then repeated the phrase, in the same way she did when he was a child—after a spilt drink, or soiled pants, or less.

She clutched at distant memories.

He was a happy child. Never helped around the house, but neither did any of the men. His friends were nice, just a few were trouble, but only minor squabbles—at least, that's what she'd thought. He was kind to her, of a sort, as kind as any of the men. He was kind to his animals, cuddled the dogs when he felt safe. She should have made him save better—this was her fault. She let him spend the money as soon as it was earned, not like the younger brother who treasured his savings. She should have made him work harder at school, she knew that. Yet he was so easily distracted.

But was this a reason?

At ten minutes before six o'clock the man stood at the doorway. He looked like a penguin, too, Emmanuel thought, with a white-banded collar the only relief from his black clothes. Emmanuel lifted his gaze to the high-set window. Streams of light reflected fine dust sparkling. He lifted his hand into the beams and moved his fingers playfully, but felt no warmth, watching the veins of thick blue cords collapse and fill.

The woman reached to touch the sleeve of her son's shirt, pulled it toward her, at first tentatively, then with increasing force. The older man, father, grimaced with feeble attempts to remove her hand from their son. Their flesh.

No parents should ever see this.

Ronnie tried to find escape from the grief, turning his head up and high to the ceiling, to the little barred window, to the slice of light that seemed to scream down instead of the woman's howling. But the tiny room held the grief too tight. And he could not escape.

No parents should witness the death of their child.

But, as the law was currently penned, any man or woman convicted of abduction and murder of a child, whether with remorse or in cold blood, will, too, have their last breath stolen.

TWO

Journalism's first obligation is to the truth.

She carefully placed the Polaroids on the table. She had scanned them of course—on the first day she was given them—at a cheap photo lab in North Beach that had kept open late. She had downloaded them on her laptop on the same evening and sent the jpegs to her second email address. And then she had lingered awake, excited, into the night.

She sat in the cool with the high glass doors shut and Chao Phraya twisting its course in view. She moved the photographs around on the table in the order she would see them in print. One whole page of six colored Polaroids, in chronological order, all on the title page. She would demand it. In a journalist's life you are rarely given such a gift, and to this day she wasn't sure why. Perhaps it was because of Jill's father and his love of Hemingway. But she didn't think so.

Jill had brought them out in a box when she first saw them. A black lacquered trinket that sung an oriental tune when the lid was up. She thought she knew the tune but wasn't sure.

"What are these?" she had said.

"You asked why we delayed telling the police . . . and this is part of the answer," Jill said.

She opened the singing box and picked up the first Polaroid. God Almighty, the baby had her eyes. The baby's face was up and she wasn't smiling but she wasn't upset. She just looked up—like a baby mug shot. Above her ginger head was a newspaper—sharp in focus—San Francisco Chronicle in large old English font, and the lead story title easily read. The camera must have been good quality—they could afford it of course. She took up another from the box. The baby's head was at a slightly different angle to the first, with her big blue eyes wide and alive, and the Chronicle lying above with a different cover story. She took up another, shuffling the photos like cards.

"We saw Josephine healthy in these photos." Jill lent back in her recliner but didn't rock. "We saw her alive and growing and close by." She sat up tilting forward on her chair. "Can you see how she is getting older over time?"

She could see it and she nodded.

"I never read the Chronicle anymore," Jill said. "Whenever we received one of these I used to race down to the library—they keep the last month of them in the reading room—so I could make the match." She looked out to the harbor. "To know that Josephine was well on that day."

She kept the box in her lap and listened to Jill.

"You see how the bottom of the photo is cut clean without the white border? We never thought about it, but the police showed us. It was the date stamp. They weren't clever enough to change the settings . . . you can switch the date stamp off you know. Maybe they were just lazy, so they just cut it away, so we didn't see the delay in the date of the photo and the newspaper cover." She rocked back a bit in her chair. "But we weren't as clever as them because we never noticed it. We saw they were posted in town so we never thought about it. I think we wanted to believe she was close to us. I used to keep the front door unlocked and her window open . . . so they could bring her back . . . you know, for an easy access, without scaring them off." She raised a sigh. "We keep everything locked now."

She kept still with the box in her lap but closed the lid to stop it singing. "You can't blame yourself, Jill."

"Can't I?"

"She was looked after. I know this. She was cared for . . ." She paused because anymore would be futile.

"Did you look at the back of the photos?" Jill said.

She opened the box that sang up again, picked up one of the Polaroids and turned it over, and read the typed label that was fixed to the back.

You tell cops and she is dead.

She turned the others over and they all said the same. And she understood their delay. And their guilt.

She looked out at the heat of the Chao Phraya, then back to the arranged photographs on the table. Baby Josephine stared up at her, each time with her head tilted in a slightly different way—but her doll's eyes always looked straight at the camera—and so now at her. They'd been clever to take them that way.

Journalism's first obligation is to the truth. But she knew she wouldn't use these Polaroids. It wouldn't do anyone any good.

Wet air left moisture that clung to her armpits and groin. The tangerine-haired woman climbed the few steps to the open platform of the bamboo bar and squinted—her myopia a constant enemy—and tried to focus on the faces that were poorly lit by soft aquamarine neon. She glanced at her watch that confirmed she was slightly early, squeezed between patrons through an ether of stale beer, and sat at the bar.

"You writer lady?" A woman sat cross-legged on the next stool, her short skirt riding high on a swinging fishnet-stockinged limb.

"Ms Songpow?"

The fishnet woman nodded.

"Thank you so much for meeting me." She shook the woman's hand.

"What you drink?"

"A Scotch and Coke would be great. No ice."

The fishnet woman nodded and gave instructions to the barman. "We very busy . . . not talk long."

"Of course. Do you mind if I tape our conversation? I have an awful memory."

Affirmed with a shrug.

"Because it's a bit noisy, we might sit closer. If that's okay?"

"What you like."

She took out a small digital recorder from her handbag, placed it on the bar, and moved her stool closer to the woman, their faces now only a foot from each other—so close, she could almost taste the burnt tobacco that seeped from the fishnet's lips.

"As I told you on the phone, I'm doing a freelance piece on the abduction of baby Josephine Abbot. In fact, I've been working on this story, on and off, for more than three years now. I'm afraid it's consumed too much of my life."

"Not as much as baby's life."

So she had pain to offload—just like the others.

"I understand this must be hard to talk about, and I know you haven't given any interviews before—"

"You interview killers?"

She took her glass and quaffed half its contents. "Yes I have."

"What you learn?"

So, this was why she had agreed to this.

She turned and studied the bar; the fake bamboo of molded plastic, the timber bench with its sprinkled dandruff of pealed lacquer and soggy coasters. Then faced back to the woman.

"Most of the hard facts are on public record, Ms Songpow. The baby was kidnapped by Emmanuel Soutard and Arthur Murray from the Abbots' home in San Francisco. Taken to Thailand soon after—"

"They rich?"

"The Abbots? Yes, very. They're diamond merchants. Old money. And Josephine was their only child."

"How they know them?"

"They didn't. But kidnapping is not a difficult crime to commit, Ms Songpow. At least, not at the start."

"Yeah, not hard." The woman lifted her arm to acknowledge the street vendor who had begun to set up his cart in the nearby walkway.

Without shifting her gaze from the spiral-whiskered man, she said, "Why take so long to catch them?"

"They were clever . . . at least in some ways."

She pondered the events, though they in themselves had never really interested her. While Emmanuel's interviews had run for countless hours, she had only documented the crime over a period no longer than an hour. Probably a bit sloppy. But it was the men that kept her curiosity.

As a good journalist could, she relayed the events to the woman.

"It easy to get baby out of America?"

"It's a big coastline, Ms Songpow, too big to police properly. Illegal immigrants enter the West Coast all the time. Getting out is even easier." She paused to gulp more drink, and, raising her voice slightly higher to register above the boisterous clamor, "I don't know how they talked the boy in San Fran into mailing the letters, but he wasn't aware of the crime."

"Emmanuel talk to kids like adult. He knew how to get what he need."

"Yes, that's something I would like to know more about."

"Why he away from Thailand so long, before he get caught?"

The reporter gulped the remainder of her glass. This was going to be more difficult than she imagined. "They got greedy, and asked for more than the original agreement. The Abbots contacted the police, and Emmanuel nearly got caught picking up the diamonds in San Fran. He was on the run for over a year, before he was captured back in Bangkok . . . thanks to you."

"I not stop fat pig killing baby."

The fishnet woman lowered her gaze, losing eye contact for the first time. There was more vulnerability here than one would guess. She checked that the digital recorder was still in operation—for she knew this would be her only chance.

"You interview pig?"

"Arthur, yes, a few times."

"Why he do it? Why he drown baby in tub?"

The reporter reflected through the bars humming din. Perhaps, as much as anyone, she should know. But she didn't.

"I'm not sure, Ms Songpow. Maybe just to remove the final evidence of the crime."

"Perhaps he just evil pig?"

"Did you know him?"

"No. Just saw him around . . . not talk to. You want another drink?"

The tangerine woman pondered. This interview was like the others, her investigation yet to scratch the surface of the killers' psyche.

"But Arthur was sorry for what he did," she said.

"How you know?"

"Partly because of what he said to me on the day of his execution. But mostly because of the way he died." The barman handed her a refilled glass. "Will you join me?"

"Don't drink with customer. How he die?"

"It is hard to put in words, Ms Songpow, even though it will be my task soon. But it was written on his face. And his manner was almost . . . gentle." She moved closer to the woman. Could smell her strawberry lipstick. "You might not know, but they let him listen to music as he was executed. I was allowed to take his iPod home after. Such music. The most beautiful I've ever heard." She sipped her Scotch. "It was from an opera by Wagner. I don't know if you know opera much, Ms Songpow?"

"No opera in Bangkok."

"I must admit, I didn't know it either. Tannhäuser. I went to see it after Arthur was executed."

The barman moved over to the woman, but was immediately dismissed with a faint sideways stirring of the fishnet's head. "Keep talk."

"At the end of the opera, Tannhäuser, a knight of the king, asks for forgiveness of God for the sins he has done." She placed her empty glass onto the timber bench. "This was the part of the opera that Arthur played to himself when he died, Ms Songpow."

She lifted herself higher on the stool and arched her neck, gazing at the bamboo ceiling, the blend of Scotch and wet air having briefly sent her on a journey away from the task at hand. "This is strong Scotch."

"Only for special customer."

The fishnet woman brought the yet lit cigarette to her mouth, drawing her back to face level, with her eyes, lips, and tongue. "Who else there . . . when he execute?"

"Lots of media people, baby Josephine's parents—the Abbots—but nobody from his family. Or any friends."

The woman nodded, then shifted her gaze to the barman who hovered close by, and delivered some task in local dialect. Soon he returned with a bottle of white wine and two glasses. And poured both large.

"You interview Emmanuel?"

"Many times, over about a year."

"You must be good at job if you see them many time."

"Perhaps. I only interviewed Arthur a few times, and he only agreed because Emmanuel asked him to."

"But Emmanuel like to talk."

She studied the fishnet woman's face—lips of claret, cheeks flushed with makeup. And insight.

"Yes. Emmanuel liked to talk." Or maybe listen was more accurate. She placed her glass on the bench. "I think he wanted people, particularly his family, to know the whole truth about what had happened. Not just the hard facts seen on TV."

"Thai paper say he not know pig kill baby. He not want to hurt baby."

"That's what he said in the trial . . . and to me."

"You think true?"

"I don't know." She sipped her wine. "But he was sorry . . . very sorry. He lost so much weight over the period I interviewed him, hardly ate at all. In fact both men didn't."

"But they still execute him?"

"Yes, Ms Songpow. You see . . . he had planned it all. Every detail."

She swigged her wine, settling comfortably in the engorged bar washed with blue light.

"Yes, every detail . . . at least up until the time he was nearly caught. And in California, if you plan a kidnapping of a child, and that child is murdered, you will be executed. No matter what the circumstance."

For the second time the fishnet woman's gaze lowered. She took the lighter from the bar and lit her cigarette.

"He never marry . . . never have kid. He trick us good."

"Did you know him well?"

Cigarette glowed from vermillion lips. "We busy. Finish now."

She felt her stomach sink low. She had to keep the embers blazing.

"I understand, Ms Songpow. Perhaps we could talk at a quieter time. Maybe over lunch tomorrow."

"Busy tomorrow."

"Yes, of course." She lifted her handbag onto the bench. "How much do I owe you?"

"My shout."

"That's very kind of you." She staggered off the stool, the fishnet woman remaining unmoved, though continuing to swing her leg in a slow pendulum motion. She took the recorder from the bench—but kept it running. "I would really like to talk to your daughter. I wonder whether you could give me her contact details."

The woman glared at her guest. Eyes pierced—yet she didn't reply.

"Perhaps just a phone number, Ms Songpow. I'll write it in my note book." She fumbled through her purse, her actions slowed by the alcohol. In time, she clutched the book in hand, and lifted her gaze back toward her host.

The fishnet woman sucked deeply. Cigarette's cinders blushed. "You talk to daughter . . . I kill you."

Lalana crept under her bed and put the box in the safe place, catching her hair in the springs like usual. She had two boxes now and no mousetraps. The magazine photograph was still there, split by a worn folding tear down the middle, separating the lake and the mountains from the spring field.

She heard heavy footsteps come up the stairs and stop outside her room. And she stayed under the bed until they went away.

It was early afternoon when she woke; the sweltering heat her alarm clock. The electric fan had kept her cool until the hot of the house slowly rose up to her room and had nowhere else to go.

It was Saturday. Lalana took out her earplugs, let the stir of the bright outside enter her bedroom, and thought about her day. She needed to take a long-boat to the floating market and have a look at the space again. This would be her third time and the manager was getting annoyed, but she didn't mind. The space was larger than she wanted, but the position good—easy access in and out, from the water and the road. The manager said it was a prime spot and he couldn't keep it much longer. But she wanted the rent to drop a little further, so she would meet him again, long after the market was closed, and give it another try.

She liked riding out to the fruit market in the long-boat, the air fresh and clean on her face.

The heavy footsteps came up again and she turned over and pretended to sleep. They had fought too much of late.

Later, she took a long shower; let the water cool over her skin. Her sister banged on the door, thinking it was her brother inside and not her. The heavy footsteps hollered at her to stop banging and wait her turn. And she heard her sister shout that she was sorry and move down the stairs.

The water felt clean, like the rushing air of the klong, so she stayed there a while longer.

They were sitting at the kitchen table when she came down, her hair still wet. Her brother and sister looked up at her in their strange way. With scared eyes. She looked back and smiled and they returned smiles of sorts. Scared smiles. Lalana sat down with them and spoke about their weekend plans—her sister's homework and her brother's soccer game. They were in third place, needed to win. The sentences strung together in dot points—like a conversation from a shopping list.

When the heavy footsteps came in, the conversation stopped. Lalana looked at her mother who stared back, not scared at all. Her mother went out with her heavy feet and came back with a bowl of noodles that she kept warm for her. Lalana smiled, but she didn't smile back.

They had fought too much of late.

Lalana ate by herself, since they had already eaten a while back. But they stayed at the table and watched her eat. She liked them staying and thought they liked to stay as well, even though they had somewhere else to go. Her mother came in and out, never staying long or saying much. But she knew she liked to stay too.

Her mother's eyes weren't scared. They looked like they should—worried and angry, sometimes more of one than the other, but mostly in equal portions.

The fights were unavoidable, of course. They could flare up at any time, a drawn out stare as good a reason as any. But her mother kept niggling at her. Kept on about it. And they had said some hateful things, things that made them both ashamed, especially the ones with an inkling of truth.

But she didn't know what to say to make her understand. So she had threatened to leave home more than once.

But never would.

They both knew that, she and her mother. But the brother and sister didn't.

Perhaps that's why they both sat and watched her eat, and stayed with her, until she left with the boatman in the late afternoon. With her brother's soccer game starting without him.

Was she really lucky . . . luckier than before?

She carefully peeled the plastic film off the container, hurting a finger with some of the hot juice. The chicken and soy and rice was still her favorite—though she liked the beef and chili, as well.

She used to have to share this food . . . before.

She wiped the metal spoon with the hem of her top until it shone. Then stirred the meat and sauce with gluggy rice, and relished the flavors.

It was raining but she was dry . . . She was never dry before.

The room was only small. Two single mattresses on the floor, and a table with one chair, all squeezed into the tiny space. And nothing else. They shared the kitchen and toilet with the others in the building, some not as lucky as her—the old, especially those without family, at least nearby.

She had more friends . . . many more than before.

She scanned the room cluttered with the silent people, all slumped against stark brown walls. Friends—of sorts. And her brother. The people mostly came when it rained, and sometimes stayed at night even though it was against the rules. Though her brother always stayed of course.

She was never really hungry now . . . not like before.

She watched the eyes that smelled her food. Eyes that could linger when they needed. Sometimes she might share her rice, sometimes vegetables, though usually only with her brother. For even though there was always money for food, there was only just enough, and she had promised herself she would never beg again—though never, she knew, was perhaps a dream more than truth.

Her hands were clean . . . and they were never clean before.

They shared the shower with the others in the building. She kept her soap and things alike in a bag on the table. Sometimes she showered twice a day, even though the rules said only once. But anyway, by night the water usually had lost its steam, and so no one really cared. The old habit of scrubbing skin was hard to stop.

Her pants were clean . . . and they were never clean before.

She focused on the mound of neatly stacked clothes that sat on the table. Some were folded in plastic bags, though one her brother now used as a cushion. She usually washed her clothes each day, in a deep sink, two floors down. Washed her brother's clothes as well—sometimes even her friends'—for this work she could easily spare.

Her brother still had his anger . . . though not as much as before.

She watched his rushing hands and fingers that shouted at his girlfriend. His girl sat facing him, with loud hands as well. And watched as he wiped his red eyes before shouting even louder. This time with tighter fists. The girlfriend is okay, but she never liked it when she stayed at night. The rules of the building said only two could stay at night, and she didn't like to break them. In any case, they always fought when he was away from the tin can too long—and the can was never allowed in the room. This was her rule.

But she had a special friend now . . . whom she never had before.

She waved at the young woman, with pretty dimples, who appeared at the open door. Lalana waved back and stepped inside, but faltered at the first hurdle of stray legs. Most of the eyes moved quickly from Lalana to the floor, some motioned to leave, some did. Her brother quickly lifted himself off the mattress and took Lalana's hand in greeting. With both hands. But the dimpled woman was really her friend—not his.

They left the room of stray legs together, standing alone in the dimly lit hallway, painted brown like all the walls. Lalana handed her an envelope—for weekly food, but no more, the rent having already been paid well ahead. They chatted with fingers to palms—her friend now clever in talking with hands—and she watched her take, from her bag, a folded page torn from a newspaper. And took it from her.

She read the title. She sat down in the hall under the one light bulb. And Lalana sat down next to her.

She looked at the photograph of the pretty blonde woman, hair long and straight without a curl. Parted in the center. Big blue eyes she saw, even though the photograph was in black and white. There were leaves around her hair from a tree or bush behind. She wasn't really smiling. It was a fancy photograph. Like an advertisement for lipstick or hair-wash. Maybe it was once. Her name was Jill, the paper said.

Lalana leaned her head on her shoulder, and kept it there as she read, under the yellow frosted light from the bulb above.

She looked at the other photograph. Two men shaking hands. They were smiling. One with white hair, older and shorter. His name was Stephen it said. They faced the camera but were shaking hands. The younger man wasn't smiling as much. He was larger than the other man. Not really fat though. His hair dark and short and cut around his ears and he wasn't smiling as much. He faced more toward the older man but turned his head straight at the camera. His name was Stephen too.

She read some more. About the ladder they put up to the window of her bedroom. In the daytime. Not at night as she had imagined. Jill was downstairs at the time, it said. Stephen was at work. They forced the window open without breaking it. The alarm was never on in the day, it said. It was easy, it said. She was four months old. Her name wasn't Princess. It was Josephine. And they didn't have a picture of her.

Lalana lifted her head, opened the bag again, and gave her another page. "Are you okay?" Lalana's hands asked. She nodded. And Lalana gently placed her head back on her shoulder.

She looked at the photograph. His beard was off. His head not shaven. His hair was long and not cut for some time. He was very thin. He looked sick. His name was the same even though he looked different. She read, but she didn't want to. He was dead like the other. They had killed him and he was dead. She looked at the date at the top of the page. It was old this newspaper. He was dead two months ago. She read more but she didn't want to. The page was brighter now under the yellow light. His face brighter too, as her heart raced. She read what they said about him. He did sell shoes. He did live in Australia. His parents did live back there. He did not have a wife.

She thought this was all she wanted to know. So she stopped reading.

They sat together in the brown hall yellowed from the frosted bulb. And she handed the pages back to her friend.

"You can keep them," Lalana's hands said.

She didn't know what she wanted. And so she gave them back.

"I must go now . . . if you are okay?"

She said she was okay, and gave Lalana a kiss on the cheek.

Lalana put her head back on her shoulder. And they stayed there in the quiet for a while.

She wanted to look at the photograph again. But she didn't.

After the quiet, her friend's hands said she had to go. "I'll come back soon. Just a few days. No more." Lalana kissed her lightly on the cheek, and stood and went down the hall.

When her friend had descended the stairs—and out of sight—she returned to the room and slumped on the mattress. Her brother had now settled into a softer form, his girlfriend resting her head on his lap. The straggling legs smiled, their eyes no longer injured. She took up the plastic tray, spooning the thick cold rice into her mouth.

She was really lucky . . . luckier than before.

"I like that one. Look at those legs."

"Not my type. I like a bit of meat on them." Saliva leaked down his bulb of a chin. Sallow stubble, not of nature, painted from the blue light down.

"You're crazy. The skinny ones are best. Look at that babe."

"I'm telling you, a bit of meat on those bones makes a better fuck."

"Well, I'll take your word for it, since nobody I know has fucked more Thai pussy than you, Ricky boy."

The podium rotated. Slowly. The girls branded with easily identified numbers danced to the techno music; white G-strings and bikini tops hid nipples, pudenda. But only just.

"Look at that juicy piglet."

"You're a fucking animal, Ricky."

"Takes one to know one." He swigged his beer. Animated testosterone belched a fine stale spray into the unnatural light.

"I wonder what the rest of the world is doing? Fucking losers."

"Just think, we were at work only two days ago."

"I'm so fucking horny."

"Then do something about it, you dickhead." Guffaws spluttered into his swig of ale. "I'm taking that chubby one. Taking her for the whole fucking night."

He waved at the girl, who met his gaze and returned the smile.

She knew his type. But relented.

"I like the purple flowers, baby," he hollered over the techno. "You got any other tattoos that are hidden away, that you'd like to show Ricky?"

She waved her finger at the man—sliding around the silver pole to keep his gaze trapped in hers—then lifted one leg just enough to bring his eyes down.

"What's your name, honey?" he asked.

The podium drifted on—the girl moving past the black hugging walls—dark souls of walls that soaked all light. She would make him wait for another rotation. Perhaps two. Yet, in a short while, always too short to flee, it returned back to the customer—beaming a frothing spittle.

"Princess. My name's Princess."

And so it was, on the stage's second journey home, she swiveled, and meeting his lustful eyes with pretended warmth, floated to its edge. The precipice. Then, while carefully sliding from the revolving stage, she breathed in the sticky air, and through a haze of sweat and cigarette smoke, came upon the scent of daisies.

Epilogue

She looked out through the tinted windows as the street life hovered by. Her working day was now folding to a close and, as the car moved along Silom Road, she slowly ticked off in her mind the few remaining chores to be done. Half an hour at the most. Maybe less.

"I'll only be a short while, Mr. Intalak," she said to the driver.

The old chauffeur lifted his gaze in the rear-view mirror and smiled as the car slowed to a halt. She was tired of late, more so as she neared her fortieth birthday. She collected her bag and papers and swung her legs out of the door, now held open by the man, who twisted his gray chin hairs into a spiral, as was his habit.

"Looks like we'll get home before dark tonight, Mr. Intalak."

"I'll believe that when I see it, Ms Lalana."

She poked him playfully in one rib and moved briskly up the steps of the office building that sat high in Bangkok's skyline.

Just outside the entrance a boy sat on a tall stool, swinging one leg aimlessly. "Hey Mrs., let me make those fancy shoes of yours look brand new."

Lalana twisted her head towards the boy, studied his face. "I'm sorry, I've some bad news for you . . . they're made of suede."

"What are you talking about bad news? I have a suede cleaner here in my kit." The boy jumped off his stool and took her in hand, motioning her to the stool.

She grinned. "Let me have a look at this cleaner of yours then."

He fumbled through his bag and produced a small bottle and a pencil eraser. The label on the bottle confirmed the boy's claim. A suede cleaner—who would have believed it?

"This special liquid does the job for a complete clean," he said. "It's very hard to get. *Very* hard. The eraser is an old trick to get rid of small stains and dirt, but only if they're tiny. For more damage you need the liquid. You've got to have the liquid!"

He took one shoe gently from her foot. "Nice quality, Mrs. Very classy. And good they're not high-heels. More comfortable for you. What we call in the trade, sensible shoes."

The boy examined the surface carefully, using the eraser to soften some of the scuffs. "I would recommend the complete works for these babies. A careful clean job, then a follow-up liquid scrub. Anything less would be a real shame." He looked up at her with wide eyes. "A real shame."

Lalana peered into the boy's eyes, whose gaze quickly averted back to the examined shoe. He was no older than twelve, maybe yet to start high school.

The boy glanced up at her, this time with a raised brow. "Let me do one shoe to demonstrate Mrs. . . . with a free foot massage."

"A complementary foot massage, hey?" A nice touch.

He sat cross-legged on the polished cement and cradled her shoeless foot in his lap. With the pulps of his thumbs he kneaded into her arch and up to her forefoot. "Wat Pho trained, Mrs., as you can surely tell."

"I didn't know Wat Pho took such young students."

"There are very few my age, that is true. But surely you can tell the hands of a true Wat Pho student? Surely, Mrs.?"

"Surely." She smiled. "I haven't seen you around here before."

"No, I've been moving down Silom Road, one block every week, 3.30 to 6.30, then I'm done."

"How's business?"

"Tough. Real tough. You're my first customer today."

She studied the boy who had commenced detailing the leather with his pencil eraser, all the while keeping her shoeless foot nested in his lap. "And what are you saving for?"

The boy shook his head. "That's a sad story, Mrs. Real sad."

She nodded, keeping her gaze fixed on the boy's face. After a second's lull he stole a glance at her, before quickly retreating back to the shoe. Lalana kept silent.

"But if you really want to know, Mrs., it's for my Aunt Chariya. She needs an ear operation. Not on one . . . but both."

"Really?"

"Yep. She's as deaf as a mule."

"I'm very sorry to hear that." She sat higher on the stool, easing some of her weight off the boy's lap. "Yes, I'm very sorry. But tell me, I didn't know mules are deaf?"

The boy continued the shoe cleaning without a flinch. "They can be Mrs. . . . and she surely is."

The boy took out a dry cotton towel and massaged some of the bottled liquid into the suede—its coat frothing into a lather. Lalana looked down at Mr. Intalak who rested with a grin against the shiny vehicle; the long black limousine that sat as a mountain around which flowed a stream of tuk-tuks. The boy twisted to see the chauffeur nodding his head slowly, while grinning up at the seated woman.

"Is that your limo, Mrs.?"

"Yes."

"Nice. And is that your driver?"

"I don't own him, but he works for me."

"Nice deal. What do you do for work to get such a flashy car?"

"I sell fruit."

"What kind of fruit?"

"You name it, and I sell it."

"Nice. You must sell as much as Songpow markets to drive in that baby."

Lalana smiled. "You're probably right."

The boy looked down at the gray-haired driver who kept on beaming up at them. "He's seems a happy guy. What are his shoes like? Standing outside all day has to get them dirty. I'll do his next. A bulk discount. A real sweet deal for both of you."

She glanced at her watch, realizing that a black sky would again drape her home before she could return. Ahead, the traffic of Silom had started to choke. "What's your name then?"

"Kavi."

"Hi Kavi, I'm Lalana."

The boy took out a cleaner rag, dabbing the moist leather dry. He then took the other shoe in hand, now resting both her feet in his lap. She watched his straw thin fingers go to work.

"Look at the difference, and wait until it dries. It'll look brand new."

He lifted her other foot and started massaging, this time keeping his gaze fixed on her face—the fine lines of her forehead now dissolved by resting eyes.

"You saving for anything other than your aunt's ear operation?"

"Well . . . if it all goes well . . ."

"Which I'm sure it will . . ."

"I might try and go to exchange-school in Africa."

"Africa?"

"Tanzania. Just for a month." The boy lifted her foot back into his lap, his face now animated. "We have a boy from Tanzania staying at our school right now. You should hear the stories he tells!" He beamed, forgetting the task at hand. "He lives in a tiny village of no more than a hundred people—in mud huts. There's a chief, and he goes to school more than two hours walk away." He picked up the yet-attended shoe and began to preen it with the eraser. "There are elephants and giraffes and lions all around the village. Lions! Just with a fence of sticks to keep them out. Just sticks. Can you believe it?"

"And you want to go there?"

"You bet. But just for a month." He started to blot the suede with the cleaning liquid. "I asked him, when we were playing at lunch, about the lions. You know . . . do they ever attack? He said not a lot. But Annan, he's my best friend, kept asking, what happens when they do?" The boy stopped buffing the shoe and left his resting hands settle gently on her toes. "You know what he said? This is mad I tell you. He said . . . that sometimes . . . someone in the village . . . gets eaten . . . eaten!"

The boy looked up to the bruising heavens with a grimace that climbed high. Lalana too looked high, through a furrow of light that sneaked between the clouds, and further on—deeper into the void. She raised a heavy sigh, and moved her gaze across to the chauffeur and over to the traffic that coughed and spluttered and pushed ahead with seemingly little care. All around her, the neon lights of dusk's slumber brightened.

Suddenly, a small girl with a bobbing ponytail skipped up the steps towards them, managing to hurdle the odd step or two. Lalana's drifting muses now focused on the climbing child.

"Mum . . . mum," the climbing girl chirped.

"Hello there. What a nice surprise."

"Aunty Durudee thought we'd steal you away from work."

Lalana looked down the steps to the roadside and the spindly figure of Durudee laughing with Mr. Intalak, and soon waved up at her with beaming painted lips.

"Hello, what's *your* name?" the girl said.

The boy introduced himself and resumed detailing the foaming shoe, since the girl, while at least three years his junior, hovered a weighty presence.

"What a good job you're doing. How much does it cost?"

"Show me your shoes," he said.

The girl brought both her feet together for inspection, lifting herself up on her toes.

"Now *they* could do with a good polish. Hey, Mrs.?"

Lalana silently waded within the scene before her.

"Yes, mum. They are looking pretty wrecked."

"A triple deal. Gets you twenty percent off with no questions asked."

"Twenty percent off. Sounds a good deal to me, mum."

"Yes, mum. A real good deal!" The voice came from some yards away. Durudee moved towards the trio swinging her hips to a melody that only she could hear. Landing at the huddled group she placed her hands on her hips and shone a wide grin down at Lalana. "Now . . . what . . . have . . . we . . . here?"

Lalana poked her tongue out at her friend, while her daughter imitated Durudee, lifting her hands to her hips, twisting to and fro.

"I want to do Aunty Durudee's shoes. Can I, Kavi?"

The boy sucked into the air, expanding his chest. "I'll tell you what. You can watch me do the first one and then I'll let you do the second."

"And can I stay with you a while and do some other shoes. Can I, mum?"

The boy swung his gaze up to Lalana.

"Yes, Mrs. . . . can she stay?"

ACKNOWLEDGEMENTS

For all those who helped.

ABOUT THE AUTHOR

PTG Man lives in Sydney, Australia. He is the author of two other novels, *Of Love and Guilt* (2014) and *A Very Human Place* (2016).

www.ingramcontent.com/pod-product-compliance
Lightning Source LLC
Chambersburg PA
CBHW022100090426
42743CB00008B/663